A GUIDE TO SMALL FIRMS
ASSISTANCE IN EUROPE

KW-267-734

EUROPEAN ASSOCIATION
FOR NATIONAL
PRODUCTIVITY CENTRES

EUROPEAN FOUNDATION
FOR MANAGEMENT
DEVELOPMENT

A Guide to Small Firms Assistance in Europe

Edited and coordinated by
GAY HASKINS with
ALLAN GIBB and
TONY HUBERT
with contributors from 17 countries

Gower

© European Foundation for Management Development, 1986

All rights reserved. No part of this publication may be
reproduced, stored in a retrieval system, or transmitted
in any form or by any means, electronic, mechanical, photo-
copying, recording or otherwise without the prior permis-
sion of Gower Publishing Company Limited.

Published by

Gower Publishing Company Limited,
Gower House,
Croft Road,
Aldershot,
Hants GU11 3HR
England

Gower Publishing Company,
Old Post Road,
Brookfield,
Vermont 05036
U.S.A.

British Library Cataloguing in Publication Data

A Guide to small firms assistance in Europe.
   1. Small business---Europe---Societies, etc.
   I. Haskins, Gay II. Gibb, Allan III. Hubert,
   Tony IV. European Association for National
   Productivity Centres V. European Foundation for
   Management Development
   338.6'42   HD2346.E9

   ISBN 0-566-05082-X

PLYMOUTH POLYTECHNIC
LIBRARY

Accn. No.	179706
Class No.	338.642 GUI
Contl. No.	0566050824

Printed and bound in Great Britain by Dotesios(Printers)Limited,
Bradford-on-Avon,Wiltshire

Contents

Acknowledgements

This book is the result of a two-year project directed and coordinated jointly through the European Association of National Productivity Centres (EANPC) and the European Foundation for Management Development (EFMD).

Our sincere thanks are due to the various individuals and organizations across Europe which have provided the country materials contained herein. Without their hard work, dedication and continuing involvement, a European-wide project of this nature would not have been possible. They include :

Austria : The Hernstein Institut für Unternehmensführung, Vienna

Belgium : Paula PAHLAWAN, EANPC in cooperation with Tony HUBERT, EANPC & Dirk DESCHOOLMEESTER, Rijksuniversiteit Gent

Denmark : Per RONNAU, Jutland Technological Institute in cooperation with Bjarne HAASTRUP and Jane WICKMAN, Handvaerksradet

Federal Republic of Germany : Dieter IBIELSKI, RKW Reinland/Pfalz, Mainz, with assistance from Detlef HUNSDIEK, Institut für Mittelstands-forschung, Bonn, for the start-up materials

Finland : Reijo MAUNULA, Finnish Employers' Management Development Institute, Oitmaki

France : Christophe DUPONT, Institut de Préparation aux Affaires (IPA), Lille

Greece : Emmanuel D. XANTHAKIS, Advisor, Ministry of National Economy

Iceland : The Technological Institute of Iceland

Ireland : Allan GIBB, Durham University Business School, U. K. in cooperation with Chris PARK, Irish Management Institute & William GLYNN, University College, Dublin

Italy : Giuseppe RUSSO, Chamber of Commerce, Milan in cooperation with Roberto ARTIOLI, Agenzia Industriale Italiana (AII) & ASSEFOR, Maddelena BASILE (AII) & Mr. Vladimir LODYGENSKI, ASSEFIN

Norway : Tor VANGEN, Norwegian Productivity Institute, Oslo

Portugal : Antonio LOPES PAULO and Luis PALMA FERIA, IAPMEI,
          Lisbon

Spain : Montse OLLE in cooperation with Robert TORNABELL,
        and Manuel LUNEVID, ESADE, Barcelona

Sweden : Magnus HULT, University of Vaxjo

Switzerland : Hans PLEITNER and Magrit HABERSAAT, Swiss
              Research Institute, St. Gallen

The Netherlands : Allan GIBB, Durham University Business School,
                  U. K., in cooperation with Pieter GROENEVELD,
                  Contactgroep van Werkgevers in de Metaalindustrie NV

United Kingdom : Allan GIBB, Durham University Business School

In addition, financial support was gratefully received from :

- The European Economic Community (EEC)
- La Fondation Nationale pour l'Enseignement de la Gestion des
  Entreprises (FNEGE)
- National Westminster Bank PLC
- The Swedish Management Group
- The U. K. Foundation for Management Education
- The U. K. Small Business Research Trust

This support was, however, by no means sufficient to cover all
costs. A great deal of time and energy was given freely by the
members of the project team and their organizations, by the
European Small Business Seminar Steering Committee and by
numerous other organizations and individuals across Europe who
supplied and reviewed the materials that were gathered.

But our thanks are due above all to the editors of this book :
Gay HASKINS and Allan GIBB and all those who gave them the
administrative back-up. For the book would never have been
completed without Gay's flair, enthusiasm and tenacity to extract
the last elements of information from the most clamlike sources
and Allan's ability to conceptualize (often on wearisome flights
to and from our meetings) and bring an academic's orderly and
constructive criticism to bear in such a way that this book is
of very real relevance.

We thank them all.

Tony HUBERT   Sybren TIJMSTRA
Secretary General   Director General
European Association of   European Foundation for
National Productivity Centres   Management Development

Introduction

A Guide to the Guide

Gay Haskins

*The Economist
and formerly of
EFMD*

INTRODUCTION: A GUIDE TO THE GUIDE

OBJECTIVES

It is now more than two years since we sat with Bjarne Hastrup, then Director of the Danish Council for Crafts, Trade and Small Industry and discussed the idea of a "European Small Business Project". Perhaps not surprisingly, our ideas were grandiose. We hoped, at that time, not only to be able **to assimulate data on the assistance available to small firms in the various countries of Europe** but also to be able **to compare the different approaches and to identify gaps in the service provision.**

For reasons discussed by Allan Gibb in Part I of this book, we were not fully able to meet our objectives. Nonetheless, the Guidebook does, we feel, throw some light on the services available to small firms in each country of Western Europe, particularly at the national level, and should provide a starting point for those wishing to delve more deeply into European small business policies and service provision.

CONTENT REVIEW

In brief, the Guide provides the following information and analyses:

*PART I: REVIEWING THE SERVICES - COMPARATIVE ANALYSIS AND THE SCOPE FOR TRANSFER OF IDEAS, examines the limitations of the study and their impact on efforts at comparison; national policies for small enterprise development; major sources and types of support for small businesses in the various countries of Europe; and the potential for transfer of programmes and approaches.

*PART II: COUNTRY OVERVIEWS, gives, for each Western European country:
- a one page **country statement** on: the definition of small and medium-sized enterprises (SMEs): employment in SMEs and, where available, their contribution to value-added; the policy orientation of the national government; and, the small firm assistance system (concentrating mainly on agencies/ organisations which are national or regional in coverage).

- A series of **tables,** each with seven columns and entitled "Small Firm Assistance in (e.g., Austria): General". These give:
  *in Column 1, the **names, addresses** and **telephone numbers** of the organisations providing services to small firms **in the language of the country in question.** Telephone numbers give first the country code, then the city code and finally the number.
  *In Column 2, the **name** of the organisation in **English,** the **type** of organisation it is (public, private), its **size** (number of staff, budget) and whether it is specialist SME or not;

3

*In Columns 3,4,5, brief descriptions of the "software"
services provided, i.e., Information/Advice; Counsel-
ling/Consulting; and Training and Education;
*In Columns 6,7, brief descriptions of the "hardware"
services provided, subdivided into Finance and Other,
the latter includes services such as the provision of
premises and shared facilities.

In these tables, the organisations are listed in approxi-
mately the following order:
  * **National/regional government** or government supported
    organisations
  * **Banks** and other organisations providing financial sup-
    port
  * **Private or semi-private organisations** engaged in the
    provision of software support, e.g., chambers of com-
    merce and professional associations
  * **Other organisations** such as research institutes

The above ordering should not be seen as a reflection of the
organisation's comparative importance but rather as an edi-
torial decision aimed at facilitating use of the guide. It
should also be noted that, for reasons of length, local support is not generally shown in the tables except on a group
basis, e.g. "Savings Banks", "Small Business Clubs". This
should not, however, lead the reader to underestimate the
value of these vital sources of assistance. As reemphasised
in the following section, local support (from family,
friends, priests, accountants, bank managers, lawyers and
consultants) is - and will remain - the most frequently used
source of small firm support.

It will also be seen that the length of the tables varies
from one country to another. This again should not be mis-
construed: a lengthy listing of services is not necessarily
an indication of the magnitude of support. Rather, the organisation of service delivery differs between countries
and, in addition, some contributors were more selective in
their choice of organisations than others. Despite our edi-
torial efforts, it has not been possible to draw up truly
parallel materials.

*PART III: ASSISTANCE IN KEY AREAS, shows the services
available to small firms in each Western Europe country in
three areas considered by contributors as of special current
importance:
  - **Exports**
  - **Start-ups**
  - **Technological Innovation and R&D**

In this section, the tables are designed in a similar manner
to those in Part II except that the names of the organisations are given only in English if they have already appear-
ed in the Part II tables. If not shown in Part II, the
names, addresses and telephone numbers are given in this
section.

EMPHASIS

It will be noted throughout that the emphasis is on the provision of what we have termed **'software services'** (information, counselling and training) rather than on **"hardware
support"** (finance, taxation, premises, etc.). This re-
flects both the special interests of the two coordinating
bodies, the European Association for National Productivity
Centres (EANPC) and the European Foundation for Management
Development (EFMD) and the strength of the Project Team members. In particular, the vital area of **taxation** is ex-
cluded from the tables. Following a preliminary review,
this was found to be so complex as to warrant a publication
of its own and beyond the scope, time and abilities of the
project team. (For information on this area, the reader
might refer to the 1983 report, **The European Climate for
Small Business: a ten country study**, available from Economist Publications Ltd.)

ERRATA

Despite our editoral efforts, there will inevitably be omis-
sions or errors in the data presented. Apologies are offered in advance for these errata and for the absence of French
accents, German umlauts and the like which, despite present-
day communications are still unavailable on an English key-
board.

Of equal importance is the fact that, by the time of publishing, several of the tables will be out of date. This is
unavoidable: the final touches to most of the material were
made at the end of 1984. It is, however, hoped that the
possibility will exist to update the information regularly,
even if only on a three to five year basis. Readers are
therefore encouraged to forward information on new policies
and services and/or errors in the existing data to : A.C.
Hubert, Secretary General, EANPC, Rue de la Concorde 60,
1050 Brussels, Belgium.

Part I

Reviewing the Services — Comparative Analysis and the Scope for Transfer of Ideas

Allan Gibb

*Durham University
Business School, UK*

THE SCOPE AND LIMITATIONS OF THE STUDY

One of the original purposes of this work was to facilitate
the transfer of knowledge and learning from European experiments and innovations in the field of small firms' support.
At the same time, it aimed to identify possible gaps in the
provision of services and the scope for European efforts in
closing them.

It became clear from the early data gathering and analysis
that there are enormous difficulties in meeting these objectives. While great care was taken in the preparation of the
country tables and the attempt was made to collate information in a standard form, there are inevitably many ambiguit-
ies. These include:
* "standard" provision: inevitably, different cut-off
  points have been used for the inclusion of institutions
  in different countries. It is impossible to list
  every institution that provides support for small
  business. The data therefore concentrates on the "standard" provision generally available nationally. Where
  there is less standardisation and wider local variabil-
  ity in a country it may appear that fewer services are
  provided than elsewhere, but this may not be the case.
* "specialist" institutions: whereas an attempt has been
  made to include only institutions or forms of assistance
  that are "special" to small firms, enormous difficulties
  arose in this respect. The principle problem is that in
  "small-firm economies" such as Denmark and Switzerland,
  virtually all "general" institutions will exist largely
  for the support of small firms. There will be few, if
  any, specialist institutions for small firms.

  Moreover, a plethora of specialised institutions for
  small firms' development does not necessarily indicate
  that the small firm is particularly well catered for in
  the economy. Indeed, it might well indicate exactly the
  opposite - that there has been a need to create specialist institutions because of the neglect of the support
  of small business in the existing institutional framework.
* scale: it is not always possible to judge the scale of
  operations of the institutions and provisions named.
  Thus, a large number of institutions may in fact collec-
  tively mean less support than one institution with a
  comprehensive network.
* public vs private support: there is inevitably a bias
  towards public, rather than private provision of support. This is because private support is more "embed-
  ded" into the normal business support system whereas
  public provision tends to be set up for a "special purpose." This may give a misleading picture of the

balance of support between the private and public sector. For example, in most economies, by far the major providers of financial support for the small firms sector are the private banks through their ordinary commercial operations. Yet it is frequently only special schemes which are given substantial mention, lending under which may be but a small fraction of the total.

* **informal support:** the provision described generally ignores the enormous amount of support given by friend, family, professional advisers and business colleagues, particularly on the "software" side. This may far outweigh, in effectiveness and volume, that of the official agencies.
* **the local level:** the inability to take into account local differentiation may mean that some of the most important provisions are left out: for it is locally that most small firms will look for support and indeed receive it.

The reader should bear in mind these limitations when using the tables and particularly in reading the comments below. It is for this reason that addresses and telephone numbers have been provided for all the institutions named so that the book can be used as a means to conduct a more detailed inquiry into those aspects of support that seem to be of interest.

It must also be appreciated that the information contained in the tables makes no comment upon the **need** to which support is directed. Here, there are a number of difficulties. Needs vary from one economy to another and indeed within each economy, from one region to another. Even within a local area, needs will vary with local circumstance and, for any small business, different needs arise at differents stages of development.

It can be argued, nevertheless, that implicit in the "supply" side, as demonstrated by the support services available is some official recognition of the needs which the supply is designed to meet. For example, specialist support schemes for innovation, business startups, exports and business development reflect an official identification of needs in areas deemed to require special attention. The point that supply must relate to needs is important. It cannot be assumed that, because one country has a substantial amount of support to meet the needs of a particular sector (for example, the start-up firm), there is a "gap" in other countries. It may be that in other areas, or other cultures, there is no need for such support or that needs are met adequately within the "informal" or "existing" structure. This makes it even more difficult to spot "gaps" from "supply side" analysis alone.

A FRAMEWORK FOR ANALYSIS

This analysis concentrates upon the "supply side" of the equation and upon institutions and the types of assistance provided. Recognition is also given to policies which shape this institutional support. The commentary below, therefore, is concentrated under the three headings identified in Diagram 1. A simple analysis follows of measures deemed to be of particular interest and of possible areas of transfer of ideas.

POLICIES FOR SMALL ENTERPRISE DEVELOPMENT

These might be described as the official guidelines laid down for the development of specific forms of assistance or institutional capability. They may be set out explicitly as a formal statement (officially documented) separately in respect of small business. Alternately, they may be explicitly stated, but as part of an overall industrial and corporate strategy. Or finally, they may have to be "inferred" from piecemeal statements or documentation justifying specific measures of support.

In very few European countries is there a clear and unequivocal statement of small firms' policy. Various West German governments have, for a number of years, produced separate coherent policy guidelines for small business development. Belgium is one of the few countries to have a national ministry, the Ministry of the Middle Classes, dedicated to the small business and self-employed. The creation of such a ministry emphasizes a certain basic philosophy of policy in support of this sector. And in Portugal, since 1974, there has been an updated policy statement for small and medium industry development.

The lack of a comprehensive policy statement does not mean that there is no coherence in the official structure of support for small business development. In a number of countries, for example, Austria, Switzerland and the Scandinavian countries where small firms contribute a major part of total economic activity, such coherence is virtually a tradition. This is typically complemented by a traditional institutional capability, as for example, the Chambers of Commerce and Chambers of Handicrafts in Germany and Austria, the Associations and Cantons in Switzerland, and the Technological Institutes in Denmark and Norway. Alongside this tradition (and indeed shaping it are) a number of key factors as shown in Diagram 2.

Of prime importance seems to be the **industrial power base** as reflected in the relative strength of the large and small firms' sectors in the economy and the way in which this influences the organisation of trade and other associations. It is arguably the case that an industrial structure dominated by small firms will create a very different work culture and power base in the economy. Thus the organisation and strength of the artisanat and chambers of handwork and commerce in certain countries, based often upon statutory membership, gives a strong power base to the smaller business.

DIAGRAM 1
THE FRAMEWORK FOR ANALYSIS

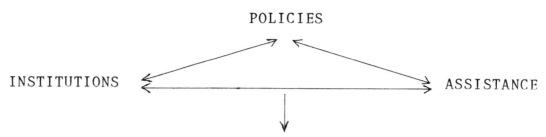

POLICIES

INSTITUTIONS   ASSISTANCE

INFERRED NEEDS
(eg: start-ups, business development,
exports, technology)

DIAGRAM 2
KEY INFLUENCE ON SUPPORT STRUCTURE FOR
SMALL ENTERPRISE DEVELOPMENT

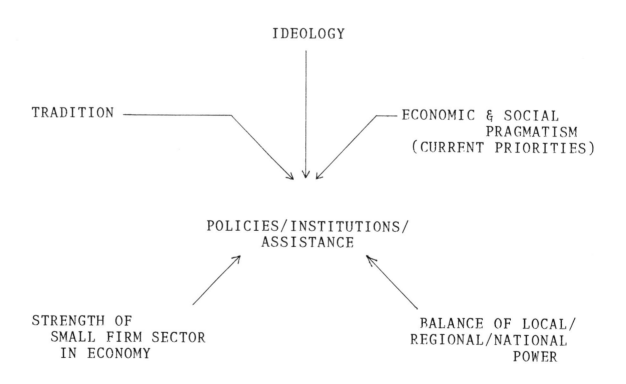

IDEOLOGY

TRADITION   ECONOMIC & SOCIAL
PRAGMATISM
(CURRENT PRIORITIES)

POLICIES/INSTITUTIONS/
ASSISTANCE

STRENGTH OF
SMALL FIRM SECTOR
IN ECONOMY

BALANCE OF LOCAL/
REGIONAL/NATIONAL
POWER

In turn, the strength of many of these small firm associations in the field of vocational training helps to condition the work culture.

The division of political power between central, regional, and local government is also of importance. Where local authorities or provincial governments are traditionally strong as in Austria, the Federal Republic of Germany and Switzerland or where areas of the country have been given considerable autonomy in economic and social development as in Belgium, Spain and Northern Ireland, Scotland and Wales in the United Kingdom, there is greater potential for local innovative measures to support industry indigenous to their area. In many European countries now, for example, Finland, Italy, Norway, Sweden and increasingly France **regional development funds or agencies** are providing a main thrust of small firm support. Federal forms of government or the breakdown of economic power and its devolution to regions means that policies can diverge substantially between different areas of the country. For example, policies in respect of small business vary greatly between different Lander in the Federal Republic of Germany, often more so than they do between some countries. And strong **local government** may lead to even further differentiation.

At a national level, however, the **current economic and social rationale** for small firms policy plays a major role in shaping the nature of the service provision. Substantial commitment to small firms' development, as a means to employment creation (as in the United Kingdom), leads to different support measures than a policy substantially based on preserving the strength of the middle classes and encouraging greater competition - the traditional policy base in West Germany. The rationale for small business support varies widely across Europe and includes elements of social (welfare, ownership and income distribution) as well as economic criteria (competition, balance of industrial power, source of innovation, etc.). Thus, policy in the Netherlands aims at providing equal opportunities in competition for small and medium business within the overall objective of socio-economic development.

The philosophy of "help for self help" pervades several European country support systems including those of Austria, West Germany and Switzerland. Increasingly, however, emphasis is being given to special area support such as high technology, new products and exports. These rationale provide a major base for the support systems in the Scandinavian countries, Ireland, Spain and Portugal.

Almost throughout Europe, **economic pragmatism** seems currently to have a stronger pull than **ideology**. Governments of very different political persuasions have developed extensive policies of support for the smaller business.

Nevertheless, ideologically in many countries, the small firm is still associated with the "market economy". Particularly among non-socialist governments this leads to criteria for intervention in support of small firms' development being ostensibly focused on "removing market disadvantages". Such governments tend to place heavy emphasis on the fact that there should be no "positive discrimination" in favour of small business which might distort market forces.

In reality, close examination of most of the assistance measures taken to help small businesses across Europe indicates clear discrimination in favour of the small firms' sector. Such discrimination is often justified in terms of preserving, in the long run, the dispersion of economic power and the sustaining of business competition.

In summary, therefore, the key factors which seem to be of importance in shaping small firms' policy include:
  * the length of the **tradition** of support for small firms;
  * the relative **political power distribution** between central, regional and local governments;
  * the **strength** of the existing small firms' sector;
  * the **balance** of industrial and political power between large industry and small business, reflected in the degree of "small firm orientation" of trade and business associations
  * the overall economic and social **rationale** for policy;
  * the basic **ideology** of governments;
  * and perhaps least importantly of all, the existence or otherwise of a formal comprehensive **policy statement**.

THE SHAPE OF INSTITUTIONAL SUPPORT

Institutional support for small business development can be classified in a variety of ways. These include:
  * the degree to which delivery is through **privately** or **publicly** owned organisations;
  * the degree to which the institutional support is **standardised** throughout the country or **differentiated**;
  * the degree to which all types of support are **integrated** into one organisation as opposed to provided by a number of **separate** institutions;
  * the degree to which institutions are **specialist** for small firms or **open** to all companies;
  * the **age** of the institutions;
  * the relative importance of **national**, as opposed to **regional** or **local** institutions.

It has been noted above that certain countries have a long tradition and framework of support for small business. In these countries, for example, the Federal Republics of Germany and Austria, much of the recent upsurge of further support for small business has naturally been channelled through existing support institutions. In other countries, where traditional institutional support has been weak, for example, Spain, Portugal, the United Kingdom and perhaps also France and The Netherlands, a variety of new, usually public, institutions have been developed over the past decade. The major sources of small business support are shown in Diagram 3.

In the majority of European countries, the chambers of commerce and/or the trade and industrial associations play a major role, particularly in the delivery of "software" support for small business. The most notable exceptions to this seem to be the United Kingdom and Ireland. The ubiquitous nature of the chambers of commerce and their statutory authority in a number of countries means that they can form the basis for a standard service throughout the country. Where membership is compulsory by law, as in West Germany and Austria, and where there are also special chambers and associations for craft industries as in these countries and also in The Netherlands, their coverage is substantial although they can scarcely be described as solely "private organisations". Only in Switzerland does provision seem to be almost wholly in the hands of the private sector. Elsewhere assistance is provided mainly through regional development funds or agencies which are public sector funded and of relatively recent origin, at least insofar as their capability to deliver small firm support is concerned. Few of these regional development agencies are specialist to the small firm, but a number provide integrated "software" and hardware" support. Examples of this are the National Swedish Industrial Board (SIND), the Norwegian Regional Development Fund (DU), the regional assistance agencies in Finland and the regional delegations for industry in France.

In many European countries, for example, Greece, Spain, Portugal, the United Kingdom and most of the Scandinavian countries, there are specialist small business organisations with substantial, if not national, coverage. These tend to offer information and counselling services. However, as has been noted earlier, the degree of standardisation of institutional provision varies considerably according to whether there is either a federal system of government with considerable power vested in the constituent states, or devolution of economic and social power as in Belgium, Italy, Scotland, Wales and Northern Ireland. Local or community authorities also play an important role in most countries and there is a variety of special local development initiatives (often involving joint private and public capital) throughout Europe. The Enterprise Agencies in the United Kingdom are a major example of this but there are also other examples in Italy, The Netherlands, the Federal Republic of Germany and Sweden.

All of this leads to wide differentiation in types of assistance. Nowhere does the unique "one-stop-shop" standardised provision exist, rationalising and coordinating all services. Such a situation is often beloved of bureaucrats: yet it can be argued that widely differentiated local

DIAGRAM 3

MAJOR SOURCES OF SUPPORT FOR SMALL
BUSINESS DEVELOPMENT IN EUROPE*

CHAMBERS OF
COMMERCE

PRIVATE
BANKS

TRADE ASSOCIATIONS &
OTHER BUSINESS FEDERATIONS

SPECIAL LOCAL
DEVELOPMENT
INITIATIVES

EDUCATION SECTOR

REGIONAL DEVELOPMENT
AUTHORITIES

FEDERAL
GOVERNMENT

SPECIALIST NATIONAL
FINANCIAL AGENCIES

STATE/REGIONAL (AS OPPOSED
TO FEDERAL) GOVERNMENT

SMALL BUSINESS
CLUBS

LOCAL
GOVERNMENT

*Excluding "informal" support systems (eg, family and
friends and acquaintances) and support obtained in the
normal pursuit of business (eg, through accountants). Banks
have been included because they are often the channel for
special measures.

assistance offering choice, some overlap and a little competition may be more effective in reaching a wide and miscellaneous customer base (such as is constituted by the small firm) than standardised provision - even though the latter may seem to be more efficient.

New institutions, mainly public, have emerged in the last ten years in many countries aimed particularly at improving technical and innovation support to the small firm. In at least half of the European countries studied, the major publicly funded institutions in support of small business have been established in the last ten years. Most of these relate to the provision of "software" support. The private banks remain the major source of "hardware" support and the major channel through which specialist subsidised loan schemes are operated. Several of the countries, however, have specialist credit organisations for the support of small businesses, with soft loans, often organised at a regional level. Some of these are traditional sources of finance, for example, the Fund for Handicrafts and Small Scale Industry in Norway, and the specialised funding agencies in Denmark. In several countries, for example, Ireland and parts of the United Kingdom, specialised financial provision is through regional development agencies.

Diagram 4 provides an "assessment" of the relative importance of the types of institution by country. This "assessment" is, however, particularly subject to the limitations outlined at the beginning of this chapter.

TYPES OF ASSISTANCE

This study has concentrated particularly on "software" (e.g. information, counselling, training) with only a minor acknowledgement of financial assistance and other "hardware" support. In many of the European countries, there is a long tradition of "hardware" support for small business development. In the majority of cases, some kind of **loan guarantee scheme** operates and most countries operate **"soft loan"** support schemes involving reduced interest rates for certain types of development and also delayed repayment scheduling. Such schemes exist, for instance in West Germany, Denmark, Italy, France, Spain and more widely particularly in relation to technology and research and development services. In many countries, soft loans funded by the European Coal & Steel Community and the European Investment Bank are also available. The range of such soft lending and its volume varies enormously from one country to another.

There are also a number of interesting experiments in the provision of **equity capital**. For example, in The Netherlands, equity guarantee schemes have been introduced which have stimulated the growth of small firm equity capital companies but as yet have not led to a great deal of investment. The Business Expansion Scheme in the United Kingdom

DIAGRAM 4
TYPES OF INSTITUTION AND ASSESSMENT
OF THEIR RELATIVE IMPORTANCE
IN THE PROVISION OF SMALL FIRM SUPPORT

INSTITUTION	VERY IMPORTANT	IMPORTANT
Official Specialist State Agencies/Services	Belgium Denmark Sweden UK Portugal Finland Norway	Switzerland France Spain Netherlands
Regional Development Authorities	Belgium Norway Italy UK	Switzerland France Sweden Germany Portugal Finland Netherlands
Specialist National Credit Agencies	Germany Belgium France Portugal Finland	Netherlands Denmark Switzerland
Private Banks	All Countries	
Chambers of Commerce	Germany France Austria Italy	Switzerland Denmark Spain
Trade and other Business Associations	Switzerland Germany Portugal Netherlands	Belgium Denmark France Spain Finland Norway
Local Authorities	Switzerland Germany Norway	Netherlands UK
Local Development Initiatives (Private and public funds)	Switzerland Sweden Germany UK	France Finland Norway
Education Sector	--	UK Denmark France Spain Finland Norway
Small Business Clubs	Switzerland Sweden	France

provides special tax incentives for individuals with incomes
in high tax brackets to invest in small businesses; and
Ireland in particular provides major tax incentives for
small business development.

The **major growth area** in small firms assistance throughout
Europe in the past decade has, however, been in the field of
software. Virtually every European country now has a network of **specialist information provision** and **counselling
or consultancy schemes** for small firms, usually organised
on a national basis but with a local delivery system. It
has been noted above that where the private sector agencies
are prominent nationally they constitute the main delivery
agents (for example, the chamber of commerce). Provision
for **training**, however, is rather more variable outside of
the traditional short courses provided by the chambers or
trade associations. Only in the United Kingdom is the education sector the major delivery vehicle for training, although there the emphasis is very much on start-ups.

Support for small business development can be characterised
in relation to certain "target" populations as follows:
- Support for business start-ups
- Support for business growth and development (including
  new product, new market, innovation and exports)
- Support for existing small businesses in difficulty

Nowhere in Europe does there seem to be a sustained programme of support for enterprise or entrepreneurship education in general - more fundamentally concerned with stimu-
lating entrepreneurial behaviour among the population at
large.

SUPPORT FOR START-UPS

In virtually every country in Europe national ministries
and/or regional and/or local governments provide **brochures
and booklets** on setting up one's own firm and relevant
sources of advice and assistance. Such booklets are also
provided by regional development authorities and, in a number of countries, by trade associations for particular industrial sectors.

Subsidised **counselling or consultant services** for wouldbe
entrepreneurs exist in most European countries but there are
substantial differences in their organisation. In Germany,
for example, the service is provided by subsidising the private sector consultancy market to encourage special start-up
services. In many European countries, the initial counselling is provided by trade associations or chambers of commerce which traditionally have always been the first port of
call for advice. But in a number of cases these have been
complemented by schemes provided by Regional Development
Funds or Authorities or regional councils as in the Scandinavian countries. In the U.K., the official counselling
scheme is based upon the American S.C.O.R.E. model with semi

or retired executives providing a network of assistance throughout the country organised on a regional basis. In all countries, however, the diversity of information and counselling support for start-ups is tremendous.

Within this diversity there are a number of interesting experiments. The Enterprise Development Programme in Ireland, for example, endeavours to provide sustained counselling matched with financial assistance for executives still in employment in large companies but with ideas of substance which they intend to make into an independent business. In France, the Boutiques de Gestion or "advice shops", seem to be expanding throughout the country to provide specialist counselling expertise on a local basis. There are also many schemes aimed specifically at the unemployed. Some, as in Sweden and the United Kingdom provide financial assistance to encourage the unemployed to set up on their own. Of particular interest are the schemes aimed at youth. In Ireland, a special Youth Employment Agency has been established which provides self-employed programmes for young people linked with Bank of Ireland financial support for the participants. Special youth project schemes also exist in Sweden.

Generally the emphasis in Europe for support of start-ups is on counselling rather than training. Many **training programmes** do, however, exist. They range from the short two-day programmes, as run through the Swedish Regional Development Funds and the Chambers of Commerce in France, to the four-day "check ups" undertaken under the umbrella of Chambers of Commerce in Italy, to the eighteen week start your own business courses funded by the Swedish Board of Labour alongside the Regional Development Funds, to the twenty week start-up course provided by the Industrial Training Authority (ANCO) in Ireland, and the four month New Enterprise Programme sponsored by the Manpower Services Commission in the United Kingdom.

There appears to be a growth in longer start-up programmes in Europe which aim to take the individual with a business idea through the various stages of converting it into a business. In Norway and Denmark the technological institutes, located in regions throughout the country, are very active in running a variety of such start-up programmes. The higher education sector in the United Kingdom seems to be much more active in this sphere than elsewhere in Europe. There, a whole hierarchy of programmes has been developed, aimed at different levels of start-up ranging from the New Enterprise Programmes mentioned above at five major business schools in the country, to the small business courses lasting between six and ten weeks run at many polytechnics and colleges throughout the country, down to self-employment and awareness programmes run on a part-time basis by numerous Technical Colleges and Colleges of Further and Higher Education. In Sweden, several of the universities provide short-term information-type courses as well as longer training programmes for potential entrepreneurs and in France and Italy business schools are beginning to offer start-up programmes.

Of particular interest in terms of hardware support for start-ups are the **"managed workshops"**, involving provision of premises linked with advice, information and associated services. Such workshops exist in France (the Hotels d'Entreprise), in The Netherlands and in the United Kingdom.

Outstanding among the **financial provision** for start-ups is the German start-up loan and risk capital scheme providing twenty year low-interest loans without security for start-ups with very low interest rates and delayed repayment facilities.

SUPPORT FOR EXISTING BUSINESSES

Generally the same **counselling and information support services** available for business start-ups are also available for existing businesses. Most of these have a regional or local orientation although they may be nationally organised. Examples include the Institutes for Economic Development in Austria, the Centres Agrees de Gestion in France, the Technological Centres in Denmark, the Dutch R.N.D. (the State Service for Industry). And in Germany the National Productivity Organisation (R.K.W.) provides a national state-funded consulting service for small business. In fact, in many cases, these counselling or consultancy services are subsidised: for example, in Sweden, Belgium, Denmark and the United Kingdom.

There is also a variety of **training programmes**, although in general there is no standard "nationwide" provision. Examples of individual institutions providing small scale industry training programmes include:
   * The Swiss Small Business Research Institute at St. Gallen, which provides a variety of training for existing businesses as well as facilities for interfirm comparison and for "experience-exchange" groups;
   * The Technological Institutes in Scandinavia, and the Training Development Associations within the Chambers of Commerce in Italy;
   * The Irish Management Institute which offers eighteen-month long Business Development Programmes;
   * The German National Productivity Association (R.K.W.) which provides a range of programmes, not necessarily specifically for the small firm;
   * The Danish Employers' Association which through its Small Business School runs a number of locally run business development programmes;
   * The Swedish Employers' Confederation which has developed a series of well-regarded materials entitled "Look After Your Own Firm".
These are implemented with the assistance of other organisations including educational institutions.

21

TECHNOLOGICAL INNOVATION & R & D

The major focus of support for small business development in Europe in recent years has been on technical innovation and research and development. In this respect, new **specialist small-business institutions** have been created. One example of these is the technologyoriented establishment centres in West Germany. These usually rely upon public support although they may be based in private institutions and can provide a mixture of software and hardware. Most of the software support schemes aim at providing either an information/awareness or a counselling/ consulting service on a local or regional basis. Schemes where an awareness criterion is important include the Athena Project in Belgium, the Technological Information Centres in Denmark and the work of ANVAR in France with its twenty two local agencies. Virtually every European country now provides examples of support for counselling/ consultancy in the field of innovation, often at subsidised rates.

Not every country at this stage, however, has a nationwide network of **local innovation, advice and consulting services.** In the United Kingdom, for example, certain specific enquiries and advisory services can only be reached by liaison with a centrally-located institution, although the ultimate provider may be local.

The technical consultancy services in Europe seem to vary widely in terms of:
  *their degree of **proactivity** (measure of the extent to which they are prepared to be actively concerned to visit companies);
  *the **emphasis** they place upon information signposting as opposed to intensive counselling;
  *the extent to which they assist in **problem identification and analysis.**

Alongside these services mechanisms have been developed in some countries, designed to encourage the transfer of technology from research institutes and large companies into small businesses. One means towards this has been the appointment of **liaison officers** in research institutions whose task is to provide the "point of access" to the small firm. The Transfer Point Mechanism in The Netherlands is one example of this, providing for a special liaison officer in a number of research and educational institutions. There is also now a burgeoning interest across Europe in the development of innovation and technology centres and science parks.

In most European countries there are special schemes aimed at providing **subsidised finance for small firm research and development, prototype development and innovation,** with increasing emphasis on computer-aided design and manufacture.

EXPORTS

There are a number of interesting programmes in the field of export development. Included among these are: programmes for **group cooperation** among small business for exporting (as in Switzerland and Sweden); special arrangements for small businesses to take on, at a subsidised salary, **export managers** (as in The Netherlands and Denmark); and **student support programmes** for market research and new product development as in Ireland and Portugal. Most of these training programmes are organised through "traditional" sources of export support including ministries, chambers of commerce and special foreign trade institutes, although they may be implemented (as in France) in collaboration with the education sector.

SUB-CONTRACTING

In the area of sub-contracting, attempts have been made in a number of countries, particularly West Germany, Portugal, Switzerland and Sweden to provide means by which all businesses might obtain information about opportunities for sales to public agencies and government departments. In Germany, this is attempted through eleven regional information centres; and in Portugal there are three such sub-contracting centres.

COOPERATION

Business cooperation for purposes of purchasing and business development is now well established in certain countries such as Switzerland, Germany and Austria and is growing in others (The Netherlands and France). These cooperative attempts can extend into a wide range of activities including marketing, technological development and business promotion.

TRANSFER PROGRAMS

An alternative supplementary approach to small business development has been explored in a number of European countries, namely, that of linking, by means of a training or retraining programme, an additional managerial resource to the small business. Graduate programmes in Portugal, Ireland, Denmark, The Netherlands and the United Kingdom, aim to support business development by linking graduates into small firms at a subsidised rate for periods of up to six months. These "transfer programmes" may have training and education components, both for the participant involved in the transfer and the participating company.

An outstanding example of this type of programme in the technology field is the "Technology Transfer Programme" operated by the Technological University of Berlin, by which Berlin science graduates are transferred into small and medium businesses for a period of up to a year to work on particular innovations.

Similar programme using either unemployed managers or graduates have also been launched in Ireland, Italy, Norway and
Austria (in the last-mentioned case through collaboration
between chambers of commerce and universities) aimed to support a sustained attempt by small business to exploit export
markets. Typically, such programmes are in short blocks
with interim associated counselling support.

SUPPORT FOR FIRMS IN DIFFICULTY

There are few major national schemes to help small companies
in difficulty in Europe. Many of the programmes that exist,
in Italy and in Ireland for example, are available for both
large and small firms alike and mainly concentrate on the
larger firms. There are, however, a number of schemes
operated by specialist development agencies, for example,
through the national government's small firms agency in
Portugal (I.A.P.M.E.I.), the National Swedish Industrial
Board (S.I.N.D.) and the association to help small firms
diagnose recovery when facing difficulty (A.P.R.O.D.I.) in
France.

GAPS AND TRANSFER POSSIBILITIES

It has been argued above that only through detailed comparison and investigation of needs can activities be analy-
sed and possibilities for transfer be explored in order to
indicate "gaps" in service provision in certain countries
which might be filled by the transfer of ideas from others.
Comparisons of supply provision can, however, lead to useful
discussion as to whether needs have been properly identified
and how they can be met in different ways. With these
points in mind, some general observations can be made short
about the potential for transfer:

* Start-up Support: whereas there is a variety of counselling schemes and no general lack of promotional programmes, it would seem that there is, as yet, no com-
  pletely comprehensive provision across the full scale of
  training opportunities in most European countries.

  The scope for the establishment of a more comprehensive
  programme portfolio lies in the face that in the start-
  up process a variety of different needs arise not only
  in relation to the skills of the business entrepreneur
  but also according to the stage of development that the
  start-up process has reached. Such a portfolio of programmes would cover a range of needs with different potential "customers" ranging from the population as a
  whole, or segments of it, such as youth or the unemployed or the retiring manager, to the person with a craft
  of other skill that might be used in self employment
  and/or mini-enterprise, and the person (persons) with a
  larger scale business idea or objective.

Moreover, there is as yet little evidence that prestart-up training aimed at developing broader-based "enterprise cultures" among the population has permeated the schools and colleges, although attempts are being made at this in the U.K. and France.

There is, therefore, still great scope for exchange and collaboration on the development of: **awareness and appreciation programmes**; **start-up programmes for smaller (craft-type) businesses**; **start-up programmes for potential employment creating businesses in manufacturing and industrial services**; and **education for enterprise** programmes at school, graduate and undergraduate levels aimed at developing enterprising capabilities among youth as part of the education system.

On the hardware side, it is evident that there is a wide range of soft loan and "managed workshop" type provision for new small businesses. There would, however, seem to be scope for a **closer comparative evaluation of a number of major lending schemes** such as the "risk loan" scheme in Germany and exchanges concerning the success or otherwise of the "managed workshops" as in France and the United Kingdom.

*Existing Small Business Support: software support is widely differentiated across Europe. There do, however, seem to be a number of areas of potential for transfer of ideas, particularly in the training field. Significantly, key programmes always address needs in terms of business development and by this means approach management development with the resultant accent on learning by, through and while doing. Areas of potential collaboration include:

- **Business development programmes** aimed at taking existing businesses through phased development of product, process and/or market as for example in the Business Development Programme of the Irish Management Institute.
- The use of **audit-type approaches** such as the "Look After Your Firm" material in the Scandinavian countries as a basis for encouraging firms to explore their own development potential.
- Programmes to **supply managers to companies** at either free or subsidized rates for purposes of expansion through exporting and/or new product development as per the Management Extension Programme in the United Kingdom and the Hire An Export Manager Scheme in Sweden.
- **Action-Learning programmes** of the kind organised by the Chambers of Commerce in Italy and variants of these in terms of experience exchange groups in Switzerland, Scandinavia and the United Kingdom.

- **Group cooperation and collaboration** for the purposes of purchasing, marketing, technology development as particularly in the Federal Republic of Germany.
- The **keeping of registers** as a basis for succession negotiations to ensure the survival by transfer of companies as in Austria and the Federal Republic of Germany;
- Information centres of **subcontracting possibilities** and public procurement as in Portugal and the Federal Republic of Germany;
- Special **technology and innovation centres** for "incubating" new business development with integrated financial and software assistance (sometimes Science-Park-based),as spread unevenly throughout Europe but particularly in Belgium, the Federal Republic of Germany and the United Kingdom.

TOWARDS IMPROVED COLLABORATION: A CAUTIONARY NOTE

The review above has demonstrated that there are many "ideas" for the support of small firms' development, the transfer and/or joint development of which might be explored by European countries contributing to this project. For those who pursue this, it is important, however, to add a further cautionary note.

The work has demonstrated a plethora of assistance and a variety of support for small business development within each country. There is a breed of entrepreneur who will actively but critically seek out a wide variety of assistance (both private and public). But the "average" entrepreneur may well be overwhelmed by this plethora of assistance and the variety of booklets, promotions and institutions with which he is bombarded. Perhaps the majority of small firms will respond to this book with the comment that "money, particularly public money, could be better spent in promoting more direct incentives in terms of reduced taxes to the small businessman rather than subsidised support which many entrepreneurs are reluctant to use."

The research cannot answer questions about the desirability of using resources differently. Indeed it has produced little evidence of measures of effectiveness which would assist in deciding how to allocate resources between one type of assistance and another. Moreover, it cannot provide a profile of the "best" type of institution, if any, needed for small firm support.

Nevertheless, it is important to reflect on a number of major principles which might be considered in designing or redesigning support measures. These should take into account that despite the variety of information, booklets and advice available, the typical small business is frequently not aware of assistance resources, nor yet inclined to use them. It is, in fact, insulated from official assistance sources by a variety of more familiar sources of advice and help which are used more regularly and in which it places more confidence. These include: family and friends; business acquaintances and members of the company; professional advisors, including the banks, accountants and lawyers; and those officials who **must** be dealt with as part of the normal business routine. Only after consulting these sources may the entrepreneur look for further particularly "official" sources of assistance of advice.

In designing or redesigning small business support systems therefore, attention might well be paid to the characteristics of those whom the small business uses as sources of regular advice. For it is these characteristics that could well be adopted by those seeking to design new forms of help. Some of these characteristics are shown in Diagram 5.

Further research needs to be done to validate the list of criteria in Diagram 5. This may aid greatly in determining which organisations should take up new forms of assistance and how they need to be tailored to the task if maximum effectiveness is to be achieved. Notwithstanding this cautionary note, it is clear that the research provides the basis for the next stage of collaboration between European small business support institutions. A great deal can, however, be left to individual initiative. For it is evident that in recent years a number of programmes or programme ideas have been effectively transferred across Europe by the process of individual personal contact and exchange alone. There is evidence to support the view from transfers already undertaken that results can be achieved more readily by individual entrepreneurial behaviour within agencies rather than by government or official interchange. Hopefully, the results of this work, which provide a major guide to small firms assistance as well as addresses and telephone numbers of relevant agencies, will form a sound basis and stimulus for further initiative and collaboration on an individual basis.

Nevertheless, it is evident there is scope for organisations sharing similar approaches to be brought together to share systematically their experience and in particular any programme evaluations that have been carried out. It was not possible during the project to identify in total all those measures that have been evaluated and the results thereof. It is clear that some of the support services have a long track record and have been monitored carefully over time.

Others are more innovative and there is as yet little information to provide effective evaluation. This is another peripheral area for comparison and for further investigation. Hopefully, these opportunities will be taken up by the EANPC, EFMD and/or others, such as the EEC, which have a vested interest in encouraging the flow of information across Europe.

DIAGRAM 5

SOME KEY FACTORS IN THE DESIGN OF EFFECTIVE
SMALL BUSINESS SUPPORT SERVICES

LOCAL

INFORMAL   HIGHLY VISIBLE

CONFIDENTIAL   RELEVANT

EASILY UNDERSTOOD   SMALL   CHEAP

                        FIRM
PROBLEM/OPPORTUNITY   EASILY ACCESSED
ORIENTED   INTEREST

ACTION ORIENTED   QUICKLY ACCESSED

UNOFFICIAL

WIDE
COVERAGE OF
NEEDS

.

Part II

Country Overviews

Austria

Materials prepared through the
Hernstein Institut for
Unternehmensfürung, Vienna

AUSTRIA

Population: 7.5 million
Area: 83,800 sq. km.

In Austria, small business is defined as those employing between 0 and 99 people and medium-sized firms as employing between 100 and 499. Together, they represent 99.8% of the total economy and account for 69% of the labour force.

As in Germany and Switzerland, there is a long tradition of support for small business development through the Federal and Land Governments, the regional authorities and the Federal and Regional Chambers of Commerce.

Financial support is provided through a number of mechanisms including: European Recovery Programme (ERP) funds for industry, trade and tourism; investment project financing (coordinated by the Federal Ministry of Finance and administered through the banks); federal schemes for export financing and new business establishment; and cooperative, jointly organised financial support programmes such as the Beteilingungsfinanzierungs AG (BFAG) for equity capital (a joint project of the Chambers of Commerce, Industry Associations and the Banks) and the Burges schemes (e.g. for start-ups, take-overs, machinery/equipment purchase, guarantees/interest subsidies for the tourist trade) which are coordinated through the Federal Ministry of Trade and Industry and administered through the banks; and the FFF scheme, supported by the Federal Ministry of Education and Science and providing research support.

Much of the software assistance, particularly in the areas of information, advice and counselling is provided through the Chambers of Commerce, especially through the Institutes for Economic Development (Wirtschaftsforderungsinstituten - WIFI). These institutes offer a wide range of training activities for small business both nationally and regionally, as well as counselling services. Special training for entrepreneurs is provided by Hernstein Management Center and Management Center Vorarlberg, among others. These programmes/institutes are financially supported by the Chamber of Commerce.

Also worthy of mention are the three state research institutes, subsidized by the Federal Ministry of Trade and Industry which provide, among other services, trend and performance data and cyclical observations to their member firms on an annual basis. Research is also effected through the Institutes of Small Industry at the universities of Vienna, Linz, Graz, Innsbruck and Klagenfort.

ORGANISATION	NATURE OF ORGANISATION	SOFTWARE			HARDWARE	
		Information/ Advice	Counselling/ Consulting	Training & Education	Finance	Other
BUNDESMINISTERIUM FUR HANDEL, GEWERBE, U. INDUSTRIE (BMGHI), Stubenring I 1010 Wien Tel: 43.222.75000	*Federal Ministry of Trade & Industry *Main Government ministry responsible for SMEs	*Through BMGHI Information Service, provides small firm infor- mation (classi- fied by type of trade & size) *Provides special two year reports on the effects of decisions based on the law con- cerning measures to increase small firm performance *Also offers information service on public purchasing	*Provides special consultancy *Promotes young entrepreneur schemes, co- operation, sub- contracting, exports and tourism (part. with the Chambers of Commerce/WIFI- see below) *Promotes manage- ment development in cooperation with management institutions		*Responsible for the SME-oriented Burges scheme, administered through the Banks (see section on Pri- vate Banks below) and the Burges (Burgschafsfonds) -GesmbH	
INNOVATION- SAGENTUR Address as above	*Federal Ministry of Commerce, Trade and Industry (to- gether with the institutions of social partnership, etc)	*New organisation to encourage small and medium sized enterprises in all areas of innovation, technological transfer, cooper- ation and manage- ment of informa- tion. Cooperation with all insti- tutions engaged in the promotion of innovation and with universities				
BUNDESMINIS TERIUM FUR FINANZ (BMF), Himmelpfortgasse 4-8 1010 Wien Tel: 43.222.53330	*Federal Ministry of Finance				*Through ERP fund provides credit & loans for in- dustrial & busi- nesss investment; & special credits for the tourist industry *Provides export funds, refi- nancing & guarantees (see Export section) *Provides credits for new business establishment in developing countries	Finance Cont. *Offers credits to manufacturing, research & transport enter- prises with guarantees from Finanzierungs- garentie Ges. m. b. h. *Provides investment & acquisition asssistance
PRIVATE BANKS	*Major private banks include Zentralsparkasse Wien, Erste Osterreichische Sparkasse, Lander bank, Creditanstalt- Volksbanken, Raiffeisenbanken				*Administer various aspects of the federal Burges financing, Burges scheme For example: -for the estab- lishment of new firms & take- overs by SMEs -For machinery & equipment purchase & construction work -for the hotel & restaurant trade	Finance Cont. *Operates joint credit scheme for SMEs in trade & industry for investment & equipment upgrading

ORGANISATION	NATURE OF ORGANISATION	SOFTWARE			HARDWARE	
		Information/ Advice	Counselling/ Consulting	Training & Education	Finance	Other
BETEILIGUNGS- FINANZIERUNGS-AG (BFAG), 1037 Wien Tel: 43.222.7296 950	*Joint financial support programme of the: -Austrian Savings Banks -Austrian Federal Chamber of Trade and Industry -Austrian Indus- trialist's Association				*Provides equity capital (limited for a certain time) to enter- prises with good prospects. This is done to en- courage invest- ments, open up new markets, launching new products and to facilitate the establishment of new business	
O.INVESTITION- SKREDIT AG, Renngasse 10 1010 Wien Tel: 43.222.666 00	*Subsidiaries of Austrian savings banks				*Offer "top" credits for erection or ex- tension of premises & change over to new lines of production	
WIENER INNOVATIONSGES- M.B.H. (INNOVA), Beatrixgasse 1 1030 Wien Tel: 43.222.756 6660	*A subsidary of the "Zentral- sparkasse und Kommerzialbank, Wien"		*Innovation consulting		*Innovation credit to finance build- ings, land, machinery and installations necessary work- ing equipment	
TECHNOVA KORBLERGASSE 111-113 8021 Graz Tel: 43.316.6010	*Styrian govern- ment, Chamber of Commerce	*Innovation and Consulting				
BUNDESKAMMER DER GEWERBLICHEN WIRTSCHAFT (BK), Stubenring 8-10 1010 Wien Tel: 43.222.650 50	*Federal Chamber of Commerce *Eight regional Chambers (see list R) each with six sec- tions (commerce, handicraft, industry, banking, and insurance, transportation, tourism) *Trade sections of BK	*Offers wide range of infor- mation & advice including: -Foreign trade & trade policy -List of foreign firm & products -statistics -technology standards lists of sources of purchase -literature on competition, eco- nomic problems taxation -lists of firms wishing to export *Carries out market research *Organises exhi- bition/PR campaigns	*Offers services on: -successor identification -exports -legal aid (some- times taking over costs of legal represen- tation) -business admin. (finance, cost- ing, production marketing, etc.) *In-co counselling visits arranged to individual firms (up to six days, half a day free, rest sub- sidized 25% by Chamber)	*Organises "exchange of experience" sessions between groups of businessmen in the same line	*Financial support for export- orientated research projects	

ORGANISATION	NATURE OF ORGANISATION	SOFTWARE			HARDWARE	
		Information/ Advice	Counselling/ Consulting	Training & Education	Finance	Other
WIRTSCHAFTSFOR-DERUNGS INSTI-TUT DER BUNDES-WIRTSCHAFTSKAMMER (WIFI) Wiedner Hauptstrasse 63 1045 Wien Tel: 43.222.650 50	*Institute for Economic De-velopment of the Federal Chamber of Commerce and 9 regional Institutes (in the fields of the counselling each with sections for 1) manufacturing 2) commerce 3) tourism 4) transportation 5) technics 6) innovation	*WIFI provides and subsidizes about 10.522 (p.a.) advisory assignments in the sections shown above (own staff both in the Federal Institute and the regional institutes and cooperation with about 500 free consultants) *Information: -special film services and audiovisual centre -publications e.g. "New Learning" -Specialised publication -practice oriented treatment of themes (150 publications-"Rationalisieren"		*Biggest Austrian adult education institution (1983: 9800 events/173,500 participants). The focal points oriented towards specific branches of profession or towards specific problems: -further training for managers and employers e.g. "Manfort" -elementary train-ing for young entrepreneurs -training in tech-nology such as micro-processors and in -export management	*Some special programmes are subsidized by Ministry of Commerce, Indus-try and Trade, Ministry of Social Affairs Ministry of Educational Affairs; Main burden of finan-cing: the Eco-nomic Chambers themselves and direct contri-butions of the participants	
HERNSTEIN-INSTITUT FUR UNTERNHEMNS-FUHRUNG DER WIENER HANDEL-SKAMMER, Berggasse 16 1091 Wien Tel: 43.222.345 611	*Management training centre supported by the Vienna Chamber of Commerce			*Special manage-ment training on e.g.: -Modern infor-mation tech-nology in small industry -Early warning signals -Cooperation in trade -The successor in business enterprises		
MANAGEMENT-CENTER VORARLBERG Bahnhofstrasse 24 6850 Dornbirn Tel: 43.557.267 971	*Management training centre supported by the Vorarlberg Chamber of Trade and Industry			Offer: -lectures by guest speakers -Business training -specialized courses for small industry subdivided by lines of business -Personality training		
MANAGEMENT-INSTITUT FUR INDUSTRIE, Schwarzenberg-platz 4 1010 Wien Tel: 43.222.752 5820	*This management center is sub-sidized by the Austrian Indus-trialist's Association					
OSTERREICHISCHE AKADEMIE FUR FUHRUNGSKRAFTE, 8020 Graz-Metahof Tel: 43.222.2491 563319	*This organization is supported by the Styrian Chamber of Trade and Industry					
BERUFSFORDERUNGS-INSTITUTE (BFI), Grillparzerstr. 14, 1001 Wien Tel: 43.222.5371 11	*Federal Chamber of Labour Unions *Coordinates activities of 11 regional development institutes (see list A)		*Training for workers and employees in e.g. business administration, EDP, micro-processors			

ORGANISATION	NATURE OF ORGANISATION	SOFTWARE			HARDWARE	
		Information/ Advice	Counselling/ Consulting	Training & Education	Finance	Other
INSTITUTES FOR SMALL INDUSTRY e.g. Wirtschafts- universitat Wien Augasse 2 - 6 1090 Wien Tel: 43.222.6371-11 (also at the Universities of Linz, Graz, Innsbruck and Klagenfort)	*Department of Vienna University of Economics	*Supply of inter- national litera- ture *scientific studies con- cerning small industry *contribution to discussions con- cerning economic development of small industry *research work concerning management and data processing *soft-ware development *studies con- cerning coopera- tion and coopera- tives		*training of economists for small industry *advanced and continuing courses for businessmen and executives		
FORSCHUNGSFOR- DERUNGSFONDS FUR DIE GEWERBLICHE WIRTSCHAFT, (FFF) Karnter Strasse 21 - 23 1010 Wien Tel: 43.222.524 584	*Research fund organization supported by Federal Ministry for Education & Science					*Support to research projects, including the erection of installations and provision of research equip- ment if directly necessary to certain research projects. Also gives interest subsidies on other bank loans, assumes guaran- tees and direct subsidies
INSTITUT FUR GEWERBEFORSCHUNG, Althanstrabe 14 1090 Wien Tel: 43.222.659 761	*Institute for Empiric Research *Specialising in handicraft	*Participating firms receive regular infor- mation on: -their firm's performance (comparative information)				
INSTITUT FUR HANDELSFOR- SCHUNG (IFH) Esslinggasse 9 1013 Wien Tel: 43.222.6344 0	*Institute for Empiric Research specialised on commerce at the Wirtschafts- universitat Wien	-cyclical obser- vations (to increase aware- ness of the market situation) *Expert opinion on SME develop- ment prepared for government				
INSTITUT FUR FREMDENVERKEHR Augasse 2-6 1090 Wien Tel: 43.222.4375 41	*Institute for Empiric Research specialised on tourism at the Wirtschafts- universitat Wien *These Institutes are all subsidized by the Federal Ministry of Commerce, Trade and Industry and the Federal Chamber of Commerce					

SMALL FIRMS ASSISTANCE IN AUSTRIA: GENERAL

LIST A - REGIONAL BFI

BFI Niederosterreich
Grillparzerstrasse 14
1010 Wien

Tel. 43 (222) 43 12 24

BFI Oberosterreich
Grillparzerstrasse 50
4020 Linz

Tel. 43 (997) 56 4 31

BFI Karnten
Bahnhofstrasse 44
9020 Klagenfurt

Tel. 43 (994) 57 0 70/401

BFI Steiermark
Sudtirolerplatz 13
8020 Graz

Tel. 43 (993) 91 36 50/206

BFI Salzburg
St. Julien-Strasse 2
5020 Salzburg

Tel. 43 (996) 74 3 37

BFI Tirol
Salurnerstrasse 1
6020 Innsbruck

Tel. 43 (995) 20 8 95

BFI Vorarlberg
Reutegasse 11
6900 Bregenz

Tel. 43 (055 74) 34 7 18

BFI Burgenland
Lehargasse 5
7400 Oberwart

Tel. 43 (33 52) 23 56

LIST B - REGIONAL CHAMBERS OF COMMERCE

Niederosterreich
Herrengasse 10
1014 Wien

Tel. 43 (222) 63 66 91

Oberosterreich
Hessenplatz 3
4010 Linz - Postfach 253

Tel. 43 (997) 78 4 44

Karnten
Bahnhofstrasse 40 - 42
9021 Klagenfurt

Tel. 43 (994) 57 5 55

Steiermark
Korbiergasse 111 - 113
8021 Graz/Postfach 1038

Tel. 43 (993) 60 10

Salzburg
Julius Raab-Platz 1
5027 Salzburg

Tel. 43 (996) 71 5 71

Tirol
Meinhard Strasse 14
6021 Innsbruck/Postfach 570

Tel. 43 (995) 35 6 51

Vorarlberg
Wichnergasse 9
6800 Feldkirch/Postfach 5

Tel. 43 (5522) 22 55 11

Burgenland
Ing. Julius Raab-Strasse 1
7001 Eisenstadt

Tel. 43 (998) 25 80

LIST C - REGIONAL WIFI.

WIFI Handelskammer Niederosterreich
Herrengasse 10
1014 Wien

Tel. 43 (222) 63 66 91

WIFI Handelskammer Oberosterreich
Wiener Strasse 150
4-24 Linz

Tel. 43 (997) 46 2 31

WIFI Handelskammer Karnten
Bahnhofstrasse 40
9021 Klagenfurt

Tel. 43 (994) 57 5 55

WIFI Handelskammer Steiermark
Korblergasse 111 - 113
8011 Graz

Tel. 43 (993) 60 10

WIFI Handelskammer Salzburg
Julius Raab-Platz 2
5020 Salzburg

Tel. 43 (996) 71 5 71

WIFI Handelskammer Tirol
Egger-Lienz-Strasse 116
6021 Innsbruck

Tel. 43 (995) 25 1 81

WIFI Handelskammer Vorarlberg
Bahnhofstrasse 24
6850 Dornbirn

Tel. 43 (5572) 64 1 94

WIFI Handelskammer Burgenland
Golbeszeile 1
7001 Eisenstadt

Tel. 43 (998) 25 86

WIFI Handelskammer Wien
Wahringer Gurtel 97
1180 Wien

43 (222) 34 66 22

Belgium

Materials prepared by

Paula Pahlawan
EANPC

in cooperation with

Tony Hubert
EANPC

and

Dirk Deschoolmeester
Rijksuniversiteit Gent

BELGIUM

Population: 9.8 million
Area: 30,500 sq. km.

In Belgium there is no universally recognised definition of
SMEs: generally, however, small industrial firms are taken
as those employing less than 50 people. Almost 2 million of
the 4.1 million working population are engaged by private
sector companies in manufacturing and services. Of these,
some 37% is engaged in firms of 0-49 employees and a further
30% in firms employing between 50 and 499. Small firms account for some 48% of turnover.

The vital role of small business to the Belgian economy has
long been recognised - indeed, Belgium is one of the few
countries to have a national ministry, the Ministry of the
Middle Classes, dedicated to small business and the self-
employed. A number of measures have been passed nationally
aimed at encouraging investments in small companies through
financial support such as subsidized interest rates, capital
premiums, employment incentives and reduced social security
payments. At present, particular emphasis is being given to
the areas of job creation and technological innovation.
Also at the national level, the Small Firm Economic and
Social Institute (created in 1946 by the national small
firms' ministry) carries out a wide range of studies, publishes numerous booklets and offers a comprehensive information service and consulting services. In addition, the
National Employment Office offers vocational training services and financial support for the unemployed to establish
small firms.

Implementation of the national fiscal measures is the responsibility of the regional authorities. Each of the three
has its own government with important powers in regional
planning, enterprise assistance, applied scientific research
and education training. In the Walloon region, for instance, the Regional Government's Economic Expansion Service
provides written information and operates a network of information centres as well as implementing financial support: the Regional Ministry of New Technologies offers information and advisory services and through the CGTC (Manag-
ing Unit for Technological Contracts) and CPTEI (Unit for
Technical Promotion of Industrial Companies), provides project financing support and interest free capital for innova-
tion/job creation initiatives. Similar bodies (such as the
FIDC (Flanders Investment Opportunity) exist in the Dutch-
speaking part of the country.

Supplementary software services are organised through the
Chambers of Commerce and the Professional Associations.
Vocational training services are offered through the small
business institutes. Management training is offered through
the Industry-University Foundation and some of the universities - it is not, however, generally specifically geared
to SMEs with the exception of the counselling programme for
small businesses at Ghent University and the Small Business
Study Centre recently created at UFSAL (the University
Faculty of St. Aloysius) in Brussels.

ORGANISATION	NATURE OF ORGANISATION	SOFTWARE			HARDWARE	
		Information/ Advice	Counselling/ Consulting	Training & Education	Finance	Other
MINISTERE DES CLASSES MOYENNES/ MINISTERIE VOOR MIDDENSTAND 12, Blvd. de Berlaimont 1000 Bruxelles Tel: 32.2.2194150	*Government Ministry for the Middle Classes *Middle classes cover small business, inde- pendent workers and independent professionals (architects, doctors, lawyers, etc.) *Responsible for implementation of the legislation on economic expansion					
INSTITUTE ECONOMIQUE ET SOCIAL DES CLASSES MOYENNES/ (ECONOMISCH EN SOCIAAL INSTI- TUUT VOOR DE MIDDENSTAND 33 Rue du Congres 1000 Bruxelles Tel: 32.2.2193434	*Economic and Social Institute for "Middle Classes" *Created in 1946 by the Ministry of Middle Classes as a research and information body; provides techni- cal assistance since 1965 information body; provides techni- cal assistance since 1965	*Carries out: -Studies-general, sectoral, regional *Runs library open to public *Publishes monthly booklets and press reviews, brochures. Runs TV and radio programmes *Publishes perio- dically updated loose-leaf guide on the rights and duties of inde- pendent workers, before and after starting a business	*Technical assistance: -individual assistance by consultants to firms of up to 40 persons (dis- tribution, ser- vice) and 100 (production) 1st interview free of charge; dura- tion of the con- sultancy varies according to the difficulty (aver- age 3 days). Approximately 400 firms receive counselling each year -collective assistance to professional federations and associations through study days, seminars	*Training of consultants: -Consultants are university graduates who have followed post-university training sessions organised by the IESCM -Sessions last 6 months and are geared on on business' every day practice *Training and ongoing education of managers of small companies. The training system is based on practice in companies supple- mented by theore- tical and general training in seminars		
FONDS DES PROTOTYPES, MINISTERE DES AFFAIRS ECONO- MIQUES/MINISTERIE VOOR ECONO- MISCHE ZAKEN 28, Sq. de Meeus 1040 Bruxelles Tel: 32.251.118 30 Tel: 32.2.5111830	*Prototype fund within Ministry of Economics					*Advances inter- est free funds to finance up to 80% of research costs of companies. These funds are refunded as soon as the products are marketed successfully
MINISTERE DE L'EMPLOI ET DU TRAVAIL/ MINISTERIE VOOR TEWERKSTELLING EN ARBEID, 51-53 Rue Belliard 1040 Bruxelles Tel: 32.223.341 11 Tel: 32.2.2334111	*Ministry of Employment & Labour			*Vocational training		*Finance for setting up one's own by the unemployed

ORGANISATION	NATURE OF ORGANISATION	SOFTWARE			HARDWARE	
		Information/ Advice	Counselling/ Consulting	Training & Education	Finance	Other
OFACE NATIONAL DE L'EMPLOI (ONEM)/RIJKS- DIENST VOOR ARBEIDSVOOR- ZIENING 7, Blvd. de L'Empereur, 1000 Bruxelles Tel: 32.2.51382 80	*National manpower services body, ONEM, has net- work of regional offices					
MINISTERE DE LA REGION WALLONNE-SERVICE DE L'EXPANSION ECONOMIQUE DES PME, 10 Sq. Frere Orban, 1040 Bruxelles Tel: 32.2.2305951	*Economic expansion service of the Ministry of the Walloon region imple- menting the various laws on economic expansion focusing on SMEs	*Publishes a booklet on "Helps to SB" showing a card index, the assistance provided for the creation and ex- pansion of SB in the framework of the recovery legislation of 1981 as well as the assistance provided by other organisations *Has a network of information services in various towns			*Interest rates subsidy -An interest rebate of 7% is granted for in- vestment loans made by specified commercial banks credit insti- tutions to finance invest- ments in fixed assets and in some intangible assets. This rebate is granted for a period of 1 to 3 years on 75% of the investments eligible for aid, to companies em- ploying up to 40 or 50 persons (according to their category). This 7% rebate includes the cyclical aid of 2%. -Other conditions for special cases cases include: -First settlement For young people (under 35 years) 8% during 5 years on 90% investment limited to 5.000.000 Bfrs or 75% (for a society) For others: 8% or 7% (according to category) for 3 years -Innovating Companies For enterprises with an invest- ment project for the production of a new product or the design of a new process in Wallonia the rebates is of 7% for 5 years on 75% of the investment eligi- ble for aid. *Capital premiums If the investment is made on own resources for up to 50% the sub- sidy on interest is replaced by a non-repayable capital grant of an amount equiva- lent to the sub- sidy on interest	Finance Cont. *Extension of the period of interest sub- sidy or in- crease of the capital grant -For job creation The period can be extended for 1, 2, 3 or 4 years for the hiring of additional employees -Export efforts Extension of one year for com- panies which have increased their exports by 20% during a period of 12 consecutive months *Fiscal relief a) exemption for real estate taxes can be granted for a period up to 5 years for enter- prises making in- vestments in fixed assets which bene- fit from interest subsidies or capital premiums b) double straight depreciation can be taken by enter- prises during a maximum period of 3 consecutive years for assets covered by a sub- sidized investment programme c) exemption for registration taxes of 1% for increase of the share capital of a company *Premiums for additional employment Companies employ- ing less than 15 persons can be granted one or more grants (60.000Bf and 50.000Bf) for each additional job

ORGANISATION	NATURE OF ORGANISATION	SOFTWARE			HARDWARE	
		Information/ Advice	Counselling/ Consulting	Training & Education	Finance	Other
MINISTERE DES TECHNOLOGIES NOUVELLES ET DES PME POUR LA REGION WALLONE, 19h, Avenue des Arts, 1040 Bruxelles Tel: 32.2.2194620	*Ministry of New Technologies & Small business for the Walloon Region (MNTSB) *Executive authority for Walloon region *Launched "Athena programme" in 1982 (see special section: technological innovation R&D)	*Covers a wide range of assistance: -information on new technologies through infor- mation's days and a Bulletin -information on patents -Club Athena (see special section: technological innovation R&D)	*Programme RIT Provides a company for a period of up to 1 year with a consultant to assist the company with the design and elaboration of innovation projects		*80% of the remuneration of the consultant is paid by the RIT programme *Subsidy for the introduction of micro-electronics *Subsidies covering 50 to to 80% of R&D costs for indus- trial projects *Awards	
CELLULE DE GESTION DES CONTRATS TECHNOLOGIOUES, (CGTC), 3 Place Josephine Charlotte 5100 Jambes Tel: 32.81.3040 23	*Managing Unit for technological contracts *Created in 1979 by MTNSB above				*Finances projects aimed at elaborating new products and processes likely to lead within 5 years to a profitable economic activity in Wallonia *Finance covers 50% to 80% of research costs	
CELLULE DE PROMOTION DES INNOVATIONS TECHNOLOGIOUES (CPTI) 6, Rue du Temple 5000 Namur Tel: 32.81.223454	*Unit for Technological Promotion of Independent Companies *Established through MTNSB above				*Advances interest free capital to finance the pur- chase of in- tangible invest- ments of up to 60% of research costs of enter- prises employing less than 100 persons which are innovative, competitive and job creating	
GEMEENSCHAPPS MINISTER VAN ECONOMIEX EN WERKGELEGENHEID, 30, Jozefstraat, 1040 Bruxelles Tel: 32.2.2181210	*Flemish ministry of Economic Affairs & Work Opportunities for the Flemish region				*Similar aids as for the Walloon region	
FIOC 30, Jozefstraat, 1040 Bruxelles Tel: 32.2.2181210	*Flanders Investment Opportunity Council *Within the Flanders Govern- ment, a strategy has been de- veloped called "Third industrial revolution in Flanders" giving priority to three basic tech- nologies and 7 growth areas	*A brochure "Flanders, the investment opportunity: has been sent to 7000 foreign companies *A major publicity campaign has been mounted & an international conference/ exhibition held			*Similar aids as for the Walloon region	
MINISTERE POUR LA REGION BRUXELLOISE, 21-23 Building au Regent, 1000 Bruxelles Tel: 32.2.51382 00 (French speaking) or 32.2.5138300 (Flemish speaking)	*Regional authority for Brussels				*Similar aids as for the Walloon & Flemish regions	

ORGANISATION	NATURE OF ORGANISATION	SOFTWARE			HARDWARE	
		Information/ Advice	Counselling/ Consulting	Training & Education	Finance	Other
CAISSE NATIONAL DE CREDIT PROFESSIONAL (CNCP),/NATIONAL KAS VOOR BEROEPKREDIET 16, Bld. de Waterloo 1000 Bruxelles Tel: 32.2.41126 73	*National Bank for Professional Credit *Public institution. Its statutes have recently been adapted in order to ease the access of SB to venture capital				*Guarantee Fund: This fund guarantees the repayment of loans granted to independent workers who present sufficient personal guarantees *Participation Fund: created in 1978 to enbale SB to have access to venture capital. Became operational in 1984. Can take minority share in a company and can grant loans under special conditions	
INSTITUT POUR LA RECHERCHE SCIENTIFIQUE DANS L'INDUSTRIE ET L'AGRICULTURE/ INSTITUUT AANMOEDIGING WETENSHAPPELIJK ONDERZOEK IN NIJVERHEID LANDBOUW 6, rue Crayer 1050 Bruxelles Tel: 32.2.64881 45	*Institute for Scientific Research in Industry & Agriculture *Financially dependent on the Ministry of Economic Affairs and Ministry of Agriculture. Main task to subsidize basic research in companies or universities. Only its technological guidance is of interest to SB		*Technological guidance and free consultancy			
FONDATION INDUSTRIE UNIVERSITAIRE (FIU)/STICHTING INDUSTRIE UNIVERSITEIT Rue de la Concorde 53, 1050 Bruxelles Tel: 32.2.51345 80	*Industry/University association *Set up jointly for business & the universities for further training of managers (mainly large enterprises)			*Associated university centres run postgraduate and post-experience courses for managers; some directly aimed at SB		
INSTITUT BELGE DE FORMATION ET DE TRANSFERT DES TECHNOLOGIES, (IBFTT) 63, rue Montoyer, 1040 Burxelles Tel: 32.2.23011 80	*Belgian Institute for Training and Transfer of Technology *Aims at promoting technological transfer in Belgium and abroad		*Analysis by a group of experts of products, markets industrial potential and suggestion		*Consultants fees are covered by government -1st day: free -2nd day: 50% of cost covered	
DESIGN CENTRE (DC), 51, Galerie Rawenstein 1000 Bruxelles Tel: 32.2.51162 35	*Design Centre *Depends on the Federation of Belgian Enterprises. Aims at improving design	*Information on products and industrial design *Exhibitions				

44

ORGANISATION	NATURE OF ORGANISATION	SOFTWARE			HARDWARE	
		Information/ Advice	Counselling/ Consulting	Training & Education	Finance	Other
UNIVERSITAIRE FACULTEITEN ST. ALOYSIUS (U.F.S.A.L.), 17, Av. de la Liberte 1080 Bruxelles Tel: 32.2.42799 60	*University faculty	*Created a small business study centre in 1983 to carry out research on SMFs		*Organises seminars and study days	*Competition for "most promising Flemish company". This contest, created in 1983, is open to all Flemish companies employing up to 50 persons which have started their activities between 1980 and 1981. The enterprise is selected by a special jury and receives: 150.000Bf to be used for deplacement costs useful for the development of the company	*Free advertising in an economic review: De Markt

Denmark

Materials prepared by

Per Ronnau
Jutland Technological Institute

in cooperation with

Bjarne Haastrup and Jane Wickman
Handvaerkstradet

DENMARK

Population: 5.1 million
Area: 43,000 sq. km.

In Denmark, small business is traditionally defined as: 1)
firms in manufacturing/employing than 50 persons; 2) the
construction sector; 3) firms related to a craft in the
trade, service and maintenance sector. This sector currently employs 1/5 of the total labour force and accounts
for 1/5 of the total value added and some 15 percent of the
turnover. Most Danish manufacturing firms are small. Only
about 80 manufacturing firms employ a staff of more than
500, while there are more than 5,000 manufacturing firms
employing between 10 and 500. These firms employ approximately 200,000 persons. Another 125,000 are working in
14,000 even smaller production firms.

While there is no clearly defined small firms policy, the
Ministry of Industry is presently emphasizing: a) increased
exports (through inter-firm cooperation); b) renewal and
growth of high technology firms; c) post start-up product
development. Among politicians and in society at large, the
importance of small firms, and thus the necessity to promote
the possibilities of small companies through the general
legislative framework is widely recognized. During the last
25 years, therefore, resources including an extensive network of technological service institutes have been built up
from which Danish industry - in particular the small firms -
can benefit.

Emphasis is also placed upon the regionalisation of services
to small firms and, to this end, the National Agency of
Technology has established Technological Information Centres
in each of Denmark's 13 countries. As well as providing
information and advisory services, these centres act as a
coordinating mechanism between the small firm manager and
other service providers.

Important in the provision of "software" support are the
Danish Council for Crafts, Trades and Small Industry, The
Federation of Danish Industries, The Danish Employer's
Association, and the network of technological service institutes, especially the two technological institutes, which
both put more than 50 per cent of their efforts into supporting small firms (less than 50 employees) on technological and managerial issues. As well as the banks, important sources of financial support include: The Danish Export
Credit Council, The Export Promotion Council (both part of
the Danish Trade Fund), The Financing Institute for Industry
and Craft, The Industry Research of Technology and The
Directorate for Regional Development, 60 per cent of whose
financial aid goes to firms with less than 50 employees.

ORGANISATION	NATURE OF ORGANISATION	SOFTWARE			HARDWARE	
		Information/ Advice	Counselling/ Consulting	Training & Education	Finance	Other
TEKNOLOGI-STYRELSEN Tagensvej 135 D. 2200 Copenhagen N Tel: 45.1.851066	*National Agency of Technology *A directorate in the Ministry of administrating: -The Council of Technology: a body created in 1973 to advance the technological development in Denmark. This is achieved through The Danish Technological Network which consists of 28 approved institutes and 13 minor information centres - one in each county, employing a staff of 3,000, and a total annual turnover of approximately 1 billion D.kr. 70% of income are companies payment for work performed. The Council of Technology budget is approx. D.kr. 350 million	*Through the Technological Information Centres (one in each county) free of charge information and contact service is offered to the small firms in the county. The technological institutes receive basic grants of which a part is spent on the informative assistance - reaching-out as well as ordered *The Technological Information Centres inform of various support schemes and project results on a broad basis (see below)	*Various schemes in order to make the consultative assistance performed by the institutes in The Technological Service Network - The Technological Institute, The Jutland Technological Institute, The ATV-institutes - less expensive (see finance column)	*Provides financial support to a large number of short teaching and training courses (technical and managerial) carried out by the technological institutes. (See finance column & section on technological institutes)	*Grants for General Counselling from the Technological Institutes: -Consultancy service of a technical, environmental or management nature. For firms with less than 50 employees -Up to 100 hours of service at approximately 50% of the normal rate (120-210 D.kr) plus any travel expenses that are involved *Provision of Assistance in Completing Applications: -Grants of up to 20 hours service. Support covers 80% of total cost, not exceeding D.kr. 7000 exce. VAT *Provision of Consulting Service in the area of Micro-Electronics: -Up to 40 hours of assistance free of charge -Service provided by The Technological Institute. The Jultand Technological Institute, and Elektronikcentralen plus 6 authorized electronic consultants. -Counselling for firms interested in applying micro-electronics to their products. The consultant assesses how micro-electronics can be introduced, and counsels the firm as to how this development can be planned and carried through in the best possible manner	Finance Cont. *Consulting Service for Entrepreneurs starting new production: -300-500 projects a year grants usually cover 75% of consulting expenses (See Instruments) *Busary for Entrepreneurs starting new science-based productions/ firms. -Amounts and durations are individually stimulated. The framework maintains maximum of contribution to 15,000 D.kr. monthly, in 12 months. *Grants for the Development of Ideas for Products beneficial to Society *Grants of up to 100% of all costs including general expenses during the idea development stage. The projects should be of D.kr. 200,000 to 2 million. (Not specifically for small firms) *Programme for promotion of Product ideas from Private Inventors: -Up to 100% of the expenses associated with experimentation functional investigations, testing, etc. As a rule, the maximum sum is D.kr. 80,000 - 100,000 per project. -R&D projects are granted up to 100% equalling approximately D.kr. 120 million a year

ORGANISATION	NATURE OF ORGANISATION	SOFTWARE			HARDWARE	
		Information/ Advice	Counselling/ Consulting	Training & Education	Finance	Other
	-The Productivity and Consultancy Scheme aims to advance the management and cooperation in the firms. The scheme comprises approximately 450 consultants placed in various organizations: °trade unions °industrial associations and employers' associations °crafts °trade °institutions Approximately 70% of the consultants are estimated to work with small and medium-sized firms primarily. Budget: D.kr. 60 million	*Through the consultancy services, information and contact services are offered *Current information on service and subsidy schemes *The scheme runs its own film service on management and technical education	*Approximately 150 consultants work with labour market tasts, approximately 170 consultants deal with management tasks and approximately 130 consutants work with mercantile tasks (sales organization, marketing and export)	*A number of courses related to productivity improvement are offered. *An education programme for consultants is also available.	*Grants for productivity projects of different kinds (75% of external costs). Financial support is provided for education of shop stewards and other labour management cooperation arrangements. *Education of consultants fully supported	
	-Industrial Research and Development Fund				*Public Development Contracts with Industry: -Grants of up to 100% of all costs, including indirect expenses, during the development process, but not for initial investments, production or marketing. Repayment in accordance with utilisation of results. (Not special for small firms)	Finance Cont. *Loans for Research and Development in Industries -Loans of 50-70% of the accumulated costs
	-The Product Development Scheme: The purpose is to advance new Danish production by granting financial support for product development in the firms.				*State Grants for Product Development -Grants of up to 40% of the extra costs connected with product development. Grants of maximum 1 million D.kr. 20,000. The grant is tax free. Total amount in 1983 approximately D.kr. 150 million on 900 projects	

ORGANISATION	NATURE OF ORGANISATION	SOFTWARE			HARDWARE	
		Information/ Advice	Counselling/ Consulting	Training & Education	Finance	Other
DIREKTORATET FOR EGNSUDVIKLING Soendergrade 25 DK 8600 Silkeborg Tel: 45.6.825655	*The Directorate for Regional Development *Part of Ministry of Industry *Purpose: to assist the pro- motion of indus- trial and other business develop- ment financially in regions where it is judged necessary in order to achieve ordinary eco- nomic, social and cultural pro- gress. Approxi- mately 60% of financial aid is granted to firms with less than 50 employees. Budget: approxi- mately D.kr. 400 millions *Responsible for HMI loan scheme (see Finance section)	*N.B. The law will probably be changed in January 85. Budgets are likely to be reduced to D.Kr 200 and HMI loans will be moved to another organisation			*Loans/Grants for promotion of Regional Development: -Initial invest- ments, (build- ings, machines) related to start- ing a business, moving, expansion rationalization, product change- over, etc. of the firm's production machinery. The investment must promote employ- ment and improve the income level in the area -Grants for industrial and service firms in regions with adverse conditions. -Grants for the moving of firms and moving grants for staff	Finance Cont. *HMI Loan scheme: -For small industry and craft -Budget: approxi- mately D.kr. 150 millions financing approximately 45% of the total number of affected investments -HMI-loans are granted at a particularly low rate of interest fixed by the Minister of Indus- try for industry & craft firms with less than 75 em- ployees. The loans may be granted for investment in new buildings, re- building, exten- sions, and machin- ery in connection with the estab- lishment of new firms as well as the expansion of existing firms. The scheme empha- sizes technologi- cal novelty, job creation, export increase, and import reductions (See selected instruments)
DANMARKS ERHVERVSFOND Codanhus Gl. Kongevej 60 DK-1850 Copenhagen SV Tel: 45.1.313825	*Danish Trade Fund *A directorate in the Ministry of Industry administrating: -Danish Export Credit Council -Export Promotion Council (For details, see special section: Exports)				*Export Credit scheme *Grants in support of collective exports *Financing of long-term export credit (for details, see special section: Exports)	
UDENRIGSMINI- STERIETS HANDELSAFDELING Asiatisk Plads DK-1448 Copenhagen V Tel: 45.1.920000	*The Trade Division of the Ministry of Foreign Affairs	*Foreign Ministry offering export promotion services to individuals and groups of exporters - Market Research, Contact Arrangement, Collection and Distribution of information on Export Markets -If a company wants to export its products, the Trade Department of the Foreign Ministry may assist in finding the right markets, in establishing a contact to potential customers and in solving other export problems -The assistance is confidential and free of charge (only for definite, ordered services the cost price is paid). Moreover, the assistance is individual and adapted to solving the problems of the individual company				

ORGANISATION	NATURE OF ORGANISATION	SOFTWARE			HARDWARE	
		Information/ Advice	Counselling/ Consulting	Training & Education	Finance	Other
DIREKTORATET FOR VIDEREGAENDE UDDANNELSER Frederiksholms Kanal 26 DK-1220 Copenhagen K. Tel: 45.1.925300	*The Directorate of Higher Education *Part of Ministry of Education			*Grants for Hiring Unemployed Persons who have completed an Education: -Support for projects with partici- pation on the part of long-term unemployed who have completed an education, particularly higher education. Some possible projects: °product development °introduction of new methods °personnel trends °market trends °starting a new business -The projectmust involve the hiring of additional staff in order to peform a project that would other- wise not be carried out -Grants per participant, correspond- ing to the maximum maintenance allowance, approximately D.kr. 100,000 per year. Limited to one year.		
FINANSIERINGS- INSTITUTTET FOR INDUSTRI OG HANDVAERK (FIH) Nyropsgade 17 DK-1602 Copenhagen V. Tel: 45.1.131321	*Financing Insti- tute for Industry and Craft, Ltd. (Danish Export Finance Corpor- ation) *Private-national *Purpose: to effect advanta- geous long-term investment funds for investment in buildings, machinery, pro- duct developoment and marketing. *The owners are: The National Bank of Denmark, banks and savings banks, insurance companies, plus industry and craft firms. *6000 loans p.a. amounting to a total of D.kr. 4.2 milliards				*FIH-loan charac- teristics: -high lending limit -long-term loan -possibility of non-payment arrangement -advantageous rate of interest *Four loan-types: -Ordinary loans: °construction or purchase of buildings °purchase of production equipment °change-over of production, product develop- ment or marketing -H-loans: as above, but effected quickly through custo- mers' own bank -K-loans for Export: for expansion of firms	Finance Cont. -EM-loan for Export, Environ- ment and Energy purposes: For export firms and firms whose production can compete with imported products. Loans to be used for: °starting new production °expanding pro- duction °electronics °change-over of production °sales drive in new markets °environmental investments °energy conser- vation invest- ments Loans with inter- est at a rate of 3/4 of the market interst rate, presently 12 1/2% Machinery invest- ments: up to 6 years. Building investments: complete with machinery: up to 10 years. Loan limits: up to 80% of the amount invested

52

ORGANISATION	NATURE OF ORGANISATION	SOFTWARE			HARDWARE	
		Information/ Advice	Counselling/ Consulting	Training & Education	Finance	Other
BANKS AND SAVINGS BANKS	*Private, mostly national, with many branch offices.	*Provide information on borrowing facilities, subsidy and service possibilities with the state as well as private persons and institutions, e.g.: -Regional development -Export -Technological service -Arranging information -meetings and conferences -Referring to relevant consultants	*Some large branch offices have consultants available for advisory service to the bank's customers.		*There are various funds, established by banks, making venture capital available to small and medium-sized firms working with ideas for new productions. The condition for the investment is most often partnership through the purchase of shares	
HANDVAERKSRADET Amaliegade 15 DK-1256 Copenhagen K. Tel: 45.1.123676	*Danish Council for Crafts, Trades and Small Industry *A national trade and industry organization. An "umbrella frame" organization for a number of employers' organizations within the traditional crafts and small industry.	*Widespread information service for members. Cooperates with the TICs in the local areas. Informs about technological service, possibilities of subsidies, etc.	*Marketing and Export consultants: -Hire an export manager scheme (see special section: Exports & Selected Instruments) -Manages a number of consultants partly financed by the "Productivity and Consultancy Scheme"			
DEN DANSKE SAMMENSLUTNING AF KONSULENTER I VIRKSOMHED- SLEDELSE (DSKV) c/o Dansk Teknisk Oplysningstjen- este Rygaards Alle 13:A DK-2500 Hellerup Tel: 45.1.181711	*The Association of Danish Management Consultants		*Provision of Assistance in Completing Applications -Grants of up to 20 hours service. Support covers 80% of total cost, not exceeding D.kr. 7,000 excl. VAT			
INDUSTRIRADET H.C. Andersens Boulevard 18 DK-1596 Copenhagen V. Tel: 45.1.152233	*The Federation of Danish Industries *Principal organisation and 2300 member companies representing 80% of manufactured exports *Tasks: policy making (business policy) & member servicing activities	*Economic analysis, forecasts, economic policy *Commercial and industrial legislation *Technical issues *Export promotion *Contact service for buyers of Danish know-how and industrial products *Public relations and information services for member-companies and organizations	*Advisory assistance and individual service in matters pertaining to trade and other international problems *Export counselling	*Seminars and conferences		

ORGANISATION	NATURE OF ORGANISATION	SOFTWARE			HARDWARE	
		Information/ Advice	Counselling/ Consulting	Training & Education	Finance	Other
DA SKOLE FOR LEDELSE AF MINDRE VIRKSDMHEDER Dester Alle 54 DK-8400 Ebeltoft Tel: 45.6.344000	*The Danish Employers' Association School for Managing Small Businesses *See selected Instruments			*The school arranges courses in the large provincial towns for managers of small businesses. The courses take place at intervals and are held outside normal working hours so that the busy manager may participate in the course without having to be away from his firm for too long. The main subjects of the course are: -finance, accounts and budgets -sales -management, - delegating, motivating and strategies *Follow-up consultancy assistance is offered in connection with the course. *800 participants p.a.		
TEKNOLOGISK INSTITUT (TI) Gregersensvej DK-2630 Taastrup Tel: 45.2.996611 **JYDSK TEKNOLOGISK INSTITUT (JTI)** Marselis Boulevard 135 DK-8000 Aarhus C Tel: 45.6.142400	*The technological institutes *Independent non-profit organizations. Polytechnological industrial and research experience and include engineers, economists, and certified technicians in lines of subject- or trade-oriented departments *Main function is to transform theoretical research results into applied technology by -commenting on technological and managerial issues -running industrial training courses -testing new products, processes and materials. -performing research and development projects *TI founded 1906; staff 650; turnover D.kr. 200 million; 17 departments *JTI founded 1943; staff 475; turnover D.kr. 150 million; 11 departments	*For trade and small industries: -provide general information about subsidy schemes and possibilities of assistance -answer questions, especially on technical matters	*Variety of services as detailed in section on National Agency of Technology above for: -New or intending start-ups. Topics include: °public restrictions/ requirements °marketing °financing °product development -Existing small firms. Topics include: °product policies/assortment °introduction of new or altered production °expanding production capacity °marketing and export *Also assistance in completing grant/loan applications, & range of technical, environmental, management services (see National Agency & Technology)	*Runs short courses for: -entrepreneurs who wish to start new productions -skilled workers, technicians, and engineers advances/new technologies -managers/owners of small firms. Trade-oriented *JTI runs courses for approximately 8,000 participants p.a.		

ORGANISATION	NATURE OF ORGANISATION	SOFTWARE			HARDWARE	
		Information/ Advice	Counselling/ Consulting	Training & Education	Finance	Other
TECHNOLOGICAL INFORMATION CENTRES (TIC)	*A technological information centre has been established in each of Denmark's 13 counties. Their purpose is to strengthen the developoment of local busi- ness - expecially trade, craft and small industry - by serving as intermediaries of contact *The staff of the TIC's are gen- eralists with different edu- cational back- grounds and ex- periences. They usually include an engineer, an economist, an industrial con- sultant and a secretary. The TIC's consul- tancy, informa- tion and contact services are all free of charge. *Since the foun- dation of the TICs, there has been a marked increase in use of the techno- logical insti- tutes on the part of local industry. *The TICs have been developed by TI and JTI. (see above and selected instruments)	*Answer queries *Assist in evalu- ating and recog- nizing problems and needs *Undertake small tasks *Bring attention to and initiate contacts with suitable special- ists/consultants *Provide general information about subsidy schemes and possibilities of assistance *Cooperate with local authori- ties, organi- zations, the trade department, educational institutions, fi- nancal insti- tutions, etc. on questions of relevance to the local industry *Initiate contacts with subcon- tractors				
DANISH INVENTION CENTRE Gregersensvej DK-2630 Taastrup Tel: 45.2.996611	*Departments at TI and JTI (see above) *Established in 1973 as a tech- nological service institute subsi- dized by the Council of Tech- nology. Main function: -Identifying new ideas -Advisory service for inventors -Prototype work- shop -Licence agency -New product service and *Secretariat for Produktideudval- get (The Product Idea Development Committee) of the Council of Tech- nology. Approxi- mately 25 employees		*Provides assis- tance for private Danish inventors/ entrepreneurs with regard to: -project manage- ment, coordina- tion and follow- up, including -prototype production -functional investigation -advisory service on licencing and contract negoti- ations		*Programme for Promotiono of Product/ideas from Private Inventors: (see section on National Agency of Technology above *Busary for Entre- preneurs starting new Science- based Produc- tion/firms: amounts and dura- tions are indi- vidually deter- mined. The frame- work maintains maximum of con- tribution to D.kr 16,000 monthly in 12 months. (Also financed by Council of Technology)	

ORGANISATION	NATURE OF ORGANISATION	SOFTWARE			HARDWARE	
		Information/ Advice	Counselling/ Consulting	Training & Education	Finance	Other
ATV-INSTITUTES The Council of ATV Institutes Venlighedsvej 2 DK-2970 Hoersholm Tel: 45.2.867055 Elektronik- Centralen Venlighedsvej 4 DK-2970 Hoersholm Tel: 45.2.867722	*20 independent, non-profit re- search and devel- opment institutes *The main objec- tive is to con- tribute to tech- nical development to the benefit of society, trade and industry. Working areas of the institutes: research, devel- opment, consul- ting, testing, training and information. *Only in few areas are the ATV Institutes especially involved with small firms		*8 ATV-Institutes are providing services under the general coun- selling scheme (see section on National Agency of Technology above). Besides the Elektronik Centralen (see below), these are: the Danish Acoustical Insti- tute; the Danish Corrosion Centre; The Danish Insti- tute of Fisheries Technology; the Danish Packaging Research Insti- tute; the Danish Welding Insti- tute; and the Danish Aqua- culture Institute *ElektronikCentra- len is involved in the provision of Consulting Service in the area of Micro- electronics: (see section on National Agency of Technology above)			

Finland

Materials prepared through

Reijo Maunula
*Finnish Employers' Management
Development Institute, Oitmaki*

FINLAND

Population: 4.8 million
Area: 337,000 sq.km.

In Finland, approximately 21% of the labour force is employed in manufacturing firms employing less than 100
people. Some 40% of value added in manufacturing is ac-
counted for by organisations with less than 500 employees.
In the service sector, the respective percentages are 39%
and 60%.

Principally through the Ministry of Trade and Industry, the
Government plays an important role in the provision of services to small firms. The Ministry has a network of nine-
teen local assistance agencies across Finland: these provide both advisory training and consulting services. In
addition, it grants loans for product and research development, now particularly encouraging developments in high
technology areas. Other Ministries and para Governmental
bodies providing services to SMEs include: the Ministry of
Labour (plant location and start-up training); the State
Guarantee Fund, the Regional Development Funds and the
Export Guarantee Board (financial support); and the Foundation for Small and Medium Enterprises which provides counselling and advisory services. In addition, in 1980, the
Council of State (in association with the Ministry of Trade
and Industry) appointed a Council for Small and Medium-Sized
Industries. A major report, detailing a number of recom-
mendations for improvement in the services to SMEs, was issued by the Council in 1983. The most important of these
were in the areas of taxation, finance, R&D and marketing.

The Finnish Employers' Confederation and its member federations also play an important role, particularly in the provision of software services to SMEs: specialised training
programmes are offered through the Confederation's training
Institute, Johtamistaidon Opisto. Universities and institutes of higher education are also increasing their specialised training for small firms and the Institute for the
Development of Occupational Skills provides a wide range of
technical courses as well as providing advisory and consulting services.

An increasing emphasis is being placed on start-up and technical innovation support. In addition, exports remain a
constantly high Finnish priority with a range of support
services provided including the recent development by firms
and local communities of regional organisations aiming
specifically to develop small firm export activity through
the provision of advisory and consulting services particularly aimed at forming contacts, obtaining contracts, and
implementing market research and technical feasibility markets.

ORGANISATION	NATURE OF ORGANISATION	SOFTWARE			HARDWARE	
		Information/ Advice	Counselling/ Consulting	Training & Education	Finance	Other
KAUPPA-JA TEOLLISUUS-MINISTERIO (KTM), Etelaesplanadi 8 00130 Helsinki Tel: 358.0.1601	*Ministry of Trade & Industry & its 19 Regional Offices *Wide range of support measures for SMEs, some in collaboration with other organisations *Some 120 employees assist SMEs through the national & regional offices *Also funds the Technical Research Centre (see special section, Technological Innovation & R&D)	*Information contact with companies by letters, personal contacts & telephone - approximately 50,000 enquiries p.a. *Help with applications for grants & loans	*Free counselling & consulting visits to companies *Assistance on all areas (marketing, administration, finance, production, product development, etc. *Approximately 5,000 visits made each year	*Offer range of subsidized courses including: -Starting one's own company (1-2 days, 75% subsidized - 2000 participants p.a.) -Corporate & Financial Analysis (2x2-4x2 days, 50% subsidized) -Administration (1-2x2 days) -Accounting (2-2x2 days) -Product Development & Marketing (1-3x2 days) -Export Marketing (-2x2 days) -Production (1-4x2 days) -Above 5 courses, 50% subsidized, approximately 5000 participants, p.a.	*Product Development grants & repayable loans for up to 50% of project costs *In 1978, some 37% of the Ministry's total grant & loan budget went to SMEs (approx. 17 mill. FM) *In a separate scheme, a wide range of export promotion loans & grants, some 80% of which go to SMEs (see special section on Exports)	
KEHITYSALUERA-HASTO (KERA), P.O. Box 127, 70101 Kuopio Tel: 358.71.1241 00	*Regional Development Fund of Finland Lts. *Established in 1971 to promote the economy of development regions through incentives to private enterprise *Administratively linked to KTM, above *Bulk of funds go to SMEs		*Counselling services available through KERA's local offices		*Finances investments & development projects in least prosperous areas in development regions *In 1984, 70% of of these loans (420 Mill FM) went to SMEs with a turnover of less than FM 5 million	
TYOVOIMAMINISTE-RIO, Kalevankatu 13 00100 Helsinki Tel: 358.0.644706	*Ministry of Labour			*Arranges start-up training courses	*Has financed establishment of "industrial villages," offering low cost facilities & financing for start-ups	*Helps new firms identify areas in which labour force & buildings are available
TEOLLISUUDEN KESKUS-LIITTO (TKL) Etelaranta 10 00130 Helsinki Tel: 358.0.18091	*Confederation of Finnish Industries & its 23 branch organizations	*On special matters such as taxation, business legislation and environmental questions	*CFI Service Ltd, Tax and Business legislation information service of CFI	*Taxation & bookkeeping seminars		
SUOMEN TYONAN TASIEN KESUUSLIITTO (STK) Etelaranta 10 00130 Helsinki Tel: 358.0.17281	*Finnish Employers' Confederation	*Software services include: advice on negotiation & labor legislation; information on new collective agreements & legislation; coordination of regional member cooperation				

59

ORGANISATION	NATURE OF ORGANISATION	SOFTWARE			HARDWARE	
		Information/ Advice	Counselling/ Consulting	Training & Education	Finance	Other
JOHTAMISTAIDON OPISTO (FEMDI), Aavaranta 0 2510 Oitmaki Tel: 358.0.81411	*Finnish Employers' Management Development Institute *Created in 1946, back up organi- sations are STK (above) & the Confederation of Finnish Commerce Employers. (21 Confederations are members) *Aim: training in leadership skills & other areas to raise industrial productivity *1983: 96 employees *Specialist SME training approx- imately 5%		*Fee paying services provided for individual firms on: -training requirements; -planning of training programs; -managerial climate analysis; -work study	*Offered mainly for: -supervisors -middle management -personal manage- ment -rationalization, production & work planning -organizational development -business development -SME management training *Both open courses & tailor-made courses offered (Duration 1-20 days) *1983: 495 courses, 10,000 participants		
PIENTEOLLISUUDEN KESKUSLIITTO Kansakoulukatu 10 A 00100 Helsinki Tel: 358.0.69438 66	*Central feder- ation of handi- craft and small industry, created in 1898	*To member firms free of charge by telephone, letters, personal assistance on -legislation -taxation -financing -labour & training *Magazine				
KASI-JA PIENTEOLLISUUDEN KOULUTUSSAATIO Fredrikinkatu 57 B 00100 Helsinki Tel: 358.0.69434 15	*Established in 1973 to develop small firms through training, education, information and advice *Administratively linked to Pienteollisudden Keskusliitto	*Information by letters, personal contacts & telephone *Publishes books on marketing administration, finance product development, etc.	*Counselling services available for individual firms	*Offers courses mainly for management of small firms in all business areas		
SUOMEN METAL- LITEOLLISUUDEN KESKUSLIITTO, (FFMEI) Etelaranta 10, 00130 Helsinki Tel: 358.0.1709 22	*Federation of Finnish Metal & Engineering Industries	*Technical & statistical information & a magazine *General infor- mation on new technologies (see special section: technological innovation)		*Wide selection of courses suited to SME needs, e.g. -business development -marketing -R&D -production -accounting (Duration, 1-12 days)		
PKT-SAATIO, Uudenmaankatu 25A, 00120 Helsinki Tel: 358.0.6488 33	*Foundation for small & medium Industry *Aim: to make SMEs aware of the benefits of out- side management consultancy & to subsidize con- sulting projects	*Advice & information on all kinds of management consulting questions		*Offers courses for management consultants *Subsidizes the consulting services & seminars *Provides subsi- dized courses & seminars		
KESKUSKAUPPA KAMARI Fabianikatu 14 00140 Helsinki Tel: 358.0.6501 33	*Chambers of Commerce	*Information on start-ups and various forms of entrepreneurship				

60

ORGANISATION	NATURE OF ORGANISATION	SOFTWARE			HARDWARE	
		Information/ Advice	Counselling/ Consulting	Training & Education	Finance	Other
OSTERBOTTENS FORETARGAFORENING (OF), Radhusgaton 19 A 26 65100 Vasa Tel: 358.61.1150 18	*Regional asso-ciation of Swedish speaking entrepreneurs at the Botnian coast *Created in 1951 *Funded partly by the Government of Finland, partly by members *Backup organi-sation is PTK, the Central Federation of handicraft and small industry	*Advice given on economic & legal affairs, adapting to new technologies in written form and personally *Information and assistance on all areas (marketing, administration, production, etc.)		*Arranges seminars to support family-owned firms		
HELSINGIN KAUPPAKORKEA-KOULU, Runeberginkatu 22-24 00100 Helsinki Tel: 358.0.43131	*Helsinki School of Economics (HSE) *Specialist SME centre at Helsinki School of Economics and Business administration *Founded for SME consulting, training and research			*All students in the four year Masters of Economics and Business Admini-stration under-take a special small business study programme. This involves intensive cooper-ation between the student, the HSE contact person and the small firm manager. *Services offered: -general management programmes (about 500 hours) for bigger companies as well as related seminars and activities -small business programmes (about 150 hours) 100 participants yearly -Start up your business - programmes (about 400 hours within 2 years time) 30 participants yearly		
AMMATTIENEDIS-TAMISLAITOS, (AEL), Kaavnatic 4 00410 Helsinki Tel: 358.0.53071	*Institute for the Development of Occupational Skills	*On technical matters	Counselling in special fields	*Technical courses in 21 different areas including: -electrical engineering -metal and machinery -textile and cloting -automobile and motor -building -waterworks -printing -paper, pulp and wood industries		
ELINKEINOELAMAN TUTKIMUSLAITOS, Lonnrotinkatu 4B, 00130 Helsinki Tel: 358.0.601322	*Research Insti-tute of the Finnish Economy	*Biannual short term & annual medium term economic forecasts	*Carries out research projects			

ORGANISATION	NATURE OF ORGANISATION	SOFTWARE			HARDWARE	
		Information/ Advice	Counselling/ Consulting	Training & Education	Finance	Other
TEKNOLOGIAN KEHITTAMISKESKUS (TEKES), Yrjonkatu 36A 00100 Helsinki Tel: 358.0.6940 11	*Technology Development Centre *Financed by Ministry of Trade and Industry *Coordinates and promote techno- logical develop- ment in Finland to ensure inter- nationally com- petitive products		*Provides consult- ing help to companies in product develop- ment & marketing problems. This is provided through small consulting units in different parts of the country and specializes in studying the technical and economic feasi- bility of new product ideas *Consulting services of up to 5 days are free		*Finances product development work (loans and grants). Priority is given to such projects which include a sig- nificant rise in technology in Finland	
UNIVERSITIES & TECHNICAL UNIVERSITIES	*Financed by Ministry of Education	*R&D of interest to industry particularly carried out at Helsinki; Tampere; Vaasa (see selected Instrument No. 3); Oulu & Lapeenranta. Information services also offered either free of charge or at subsidized rates				
VIEXPO- OSUUSKUNTA, Strenberginkatu 1 68600 Pietarsaari Tel: 358.67.131 00	*One of a number of regional organisations to develop SME export activity	*See Special Section: Exports				
SUOMEN ITSENAISYYDEN JUHLAVUODEN 1967 RAHASTON (SITRA), Uudenmaankatu 16-20 B 00120 Helsinki Tel: 358.0.6418 77	*Finish National Fund for Research and Development (Basic capital 400 mill. FM Annual yield, approx. 34 mill. FM) formed in 1967 *Operates in association with the Bank of Finland *Particular empha- sis on technical product development *Staff: 19	*Surveys and transfer of know-how *Regular bulletin on current projects and available reports			*Finances product development within companies & the development of products bought under license from abroad. Also provides design funding. *In addition, provides: guarantees to companies introducing new equipment or technologies; financial support for the purchase of licenses; investment financing where new technology is used; and contract research funding *In 1983, FM 14.2 was spent on projects in firms with less than 100 employees, particularly for equipment & apparatus *Applications for funding are received and evaluated in the SITRA office and final selection is made by Bank supervisors	
KEKSINTOSAATIO, Atomitie 5C 00370 Helsinki	*The Foundation of Finnish Inventions was established in 1971 to support and promote the development and commercial ex- ploitation of inventions and know-how *Financed mainly by the Finnish Government and the Finnish National Fund for Research and Development SITRA	*See Special Section: Technological Innovation and R&D				

ORGANISATION	NATURE OF ORGANISATION	SOFTWARE			HARDWARE	
		Information/ Advice	Counselling/ Consulting	Training & Education	Finance	Other
SPONSOR Or, Mannerheim-minitie 14 B 00100 Helsinki Tel: 358.0.6081 33	*Venture capital corporation *Established in 1967 to promote the formation of Finnish industrial enterprises with a high level of international competitiveness *Listed in the Helsinki Stock Exchange in 1984				*Permanent equity investments in medium-sized enterprises, which are generally required to be profitable and growth-oriented *In 1983 the total turnover of the firms in the Sponsor group amounted to 100 mill.	
TEOLLISTAMIS-RAHASTO OY (TR), Lonnrotinkatu 13 00120 Helsinki Tel: 358.0.6447 06	*Industriali-zation Fund of Finland Ltd. *Development finance corporation *Established in 1954 to promote Finnish industrial enterprises through mobilizing resources for their use *Shareholders include the Bank of Finland and domestic as well as foreign financial institutions *Major source of long term loans to SMEs in manufacturing industry and tourism in Finland *Two regional offices (Tampere, Turku) in addition to the main office in Helsinki	*Sectoral studies on the development and prospects in different industries in Finland *Annual sectoral surveys on 12 industries	*Advisory services in analysing and planning of investment projects as well as in general business development to SMEs	*Some seminars and handbooks for SMEs (product development, marketing)	*6 to 12 year loans for investment projects in manufacturing industry and tourism up to 50% of the value of the investment, including the increase in working capital *Especially favourable loan rates to small firms in the context of a small-scale industry and tourism programme *Minority equity investments to SMEs *In 1983 the financing provided amounted to 550 million FIM, of which 60% SMEs	*Is a shareholder of three different venture capital companies, the Technology Village Ltd. in Otaniemi and the Finnfund (joint-ventures with companies in developing countries)
SAVINGS BANKS & REGIONAL BANKS					*Important in credit operations for SMEs *"Soft" loans to industry provided through the State Investment Fund, administered by POSTIPANKKI, the state-owned savings bank *Risk capital also provided by the Scandanavian Investment Bank (PIP)	
SUOMEN GALLUP Lauttasaarentie 28-30 00200 Helsinki Tel: 358.0.69231 25	*Finnish Gallup	*Provides regular consumer & industrial survey				

63

France

Materials prepared by

Christophe Dupont
*Institut de Preparation
aux Affaires (IPA-IAE)
Universite de Lille 1*

FRANCE

Population: 54 million
Area: 552,000 sq.km.

In France, some 5.3 milion people are presently employed in "pme's" (manufacturing and service firms employing more than 10 and less than 500): of these, 43% work in firms employing 10-49 people; 34%, 50-199 and 23%, 200-499. Turnover from pme's amounted to 1800 billion FF in 1980.

Although there is a degree of regional devolution appearing in France, political power remains highly centralised. Within the specialised agencies, major decisions are generally taken in Paris. There are very few comprehensive policy statements on small business and there is considerable dispersion of authority - and activity - regarding small business problems; indeed the "small business sector" falls under several Ministries - particularly Industry and Research, and Commerce and Crafts. The limited support given to small business up to the late 70s was mainly in response to pressures from the "small business sector" to restrain the monopoly power of big business. More recently, the main rationale for small and new business support has been to reduce unemployment directly and to create new jobs, with the development of exports, the stimulation of technological innovation and a better regional balance as secondary themes.

Public support is typically financial, generally in the form of loans at below market rates (channelled through specialized agencies and through the banking system) and grants (notably for employment creation). In addition, a number of institutions and agencies have been established at the national level to provide both software and financial support: typically these are specialized by type of activity (CEPME for finance, ANVAR for innovation, ANCE for startups). Representative of the governmental policy to encourage decentralisation has been the creation of regional local branches of these agencies and the establishment of regional agencies within the Ministry of Industry and Research (Delegations Regionales pour l'Industrie et la Recherche).

The powerful, private Chambers of Commerce and Industry, and the Craft Chambers play a key role in software support systems, especially information, advice and training. The future role of these institutions has sometimes been questioned in certain government quarters but no major change has been made. In addition, several new initiatives have been taken in the public and private sectors oriented towards small business development and new firm creation, e.g., small business "clubs" or networks for start-ups, associations designed to provide information or other assistance to SMEs (e.g., for innovation, export or reconversions) and the Boutiques de Gestion.

ORGANISATION	NATURE OF ORGANISATION	SOFTWARE			HARDWARE	
		Information/ Advice	Counselling/ Consulting	Training & Education	Finance	Other
DIRECTION(S) REGIONALE(S) DU MINISTERE DU INDUSTRIEL ET DU REDEPLOIEMENT COMMERCE EXTERIEUR (DRIR'S), 101, Rue de Grenelle, 75007 Paris Tel: 33.15563636 Generally located at main city of the "region" *Are part of the Government's decentralization effort with a number of specific responsibilities, e.g. with regard to pollution, mines, metrology, energy savings, etc. In addition, most DRIR's have set up a "DDI" (Direction de Developpement Industriel) - (Department of Industrial Development), whose function is to provide information/advice, counsel and expertise on such subjects as: -diagnosis of the firm, -quality control -automation -design and value analysis, -start-up, -turn arounds/reconversions *These actions are not entirely, but substantially designed for small firms which often find themselves "isolated" from the industrial environment and know little about public support schemes. They are supported by a budget derived from allocations of the State budget (Fonds d' Industrialisation et de Modernisation). These funds are often combined and/or supplemented by local authorities' budgets ("Conseil Regional", E.P.R.: Etablissement Public Regional) *Employment: Ile de France: 314 people, total: 3000 people	*Regional Agencies of the Ministry of Industrial Redeployment & Trade	*DRIR's supply free brochures on their activities *Their staff of industrial experts (often transferred from a previous entrepreneurial career) - some fifteen people for the Paris area, for example - are available to answer enquiries on subjects within the scope of DRIR's activities *Some of the staff are assigned a territorial unit in which they organize initiatives such as: -visits to office and factory sites, -information meetings -seminars *To give an idea of the magnitude of these activities, DRIR - Ile de France visited approximately 1000 firms (mainly small) in 1983 and contributed to approximately 600 concrete actions	*DRIR's are initiating some specific programmes of counselling/consultancy (principally for small firms) described in column 2 *The machinery used for these purposes is described in the selected instruments in which a description is given of a specific quality control programme *Particular attention has been given to several factors: -costs should be minimal to the firm, at least in the initial stage of devising the programme, -experts should be carefully selected and some control on their work should be effected -firms should show a willingness to "modernize" and show potentialities for development	*DRIR's organize activities within their field responsibility (see column 2) These activities can 'include: -information meetings, -seminars At times they are combined with those undertaken by the local Chamber of Commerce	*Supporting schemes for finance take the form of grants/subsidies for the tivities mentioned in 2. A typical ample is given in the selected instrument on quality control. This type of assistance from DRIR would likely cost approximately 6000 - 8000 F. for a "first stage" diagnostic and 40 - 50,000 F. for a "second stage" diagnosis (e.g. a market research study)	
COMITE INTER-MINISTERIEL POUR LE DEVELOPPEMENT DES INVESTISSE-MENTS ET LE SOUTIEN DE L' EMPLOI, (CIDISE), 151 Rue Saint-Honore 75056 Paris Cedex 01 Tel: 33.1.29723 50 33.1.2972106	*A government ad hoc Committee designed to provide finance for all firms - especially small and medium sized in two specific situations: -inadequacy of equity at a crucial time of growth, especially because of an increase in exports, -weakness of the financial structure due to increased foreign competition				*Provides special loans ("prets parti-patifs": some sort of subordinate loan) through money allocated to FDES (Economic & Social Development Fund) *Study of the request for assistance is made by local agencies of such organizations as Credit National, CEPME, SDR's (see below) etc. *Procedure in non-administrative and quick (less than 2 months)	

ORGANISATION	NATURE OF ORGANISATION	SOFTWARE			HARDWARE	
		Information/ Advice	Counselling/ Consulting	Training & Education	Finance	Other
CREDIT D' EQUIPEMENT DETITES ET MOYENNES ENTREPRISE (CEPME), 14 Rue du 4 Septembre 75002 Paris Tel: 33.1.298800 00	*Bank for SMEs *This is a large public organisa- tion whose main function is to be the principal provider of special finance (i.e. other than ordinary finance by banks) to small (and medium size) firms *CEPME was estab- lished on Jan. 1, 1981 to take over the activities of Caisse Nationale des Marches (created: 1936), Credit Hotelier, Commercial et Industriel, and Groupement Inter- professionnel des PME *Although funding is CEPME's major "raison d'etre" and core activi- ty, it has de- veloped extensive services of in- formation, re- search, and ex- pertise mostly centered on SME problems *Finally, it often acts as a Secre- tariat for gov- ernment commit- tees providing finance to firms (including small) for specific purposes, e.q. CODEFIS (see below)	*CEPME has set up special divisions of economic studies and re- search and has a "Service Rela- tions Publiques" (14, Rue du 4 Septembre - 75002 Paris - Tel. 298.80.85) These services are well equipped to give infor- mation to SME enquirers al- though observed practice show that such firms often prefer to channel their requests through their local banker *CEPME has set up regional branches to be closer to the small firms *CEPME publishes a Journal "Eco- nomie et PMF" three or four times a year This provides rather intensive information on selected segments of its activi- ties, statistical data and research articles	*CEPME "counsels" some government agencies on the attribution of loans, grants, etc. provided by such agencies (i.e. CODEFIS, CIDISE, see below)		*CEPME provides loans for short- term and long- term purposes. In addition, it provides advances on government contracts (see selected : instruments and/or guarantees *Most of these operations are at market rates, yet a number of loans are at special prefer- ential rates. This is the case especially for: -"Prets speciaux aux investisse- ment's (PSI) - (special loans for equipment). Such investments have to result in an increase in employment or be concerned with specific fields, notably: inno- vation, auto- mation ("robo- tique") and savings in energy or raw material requirements. Such loans are at rates (end 1983) of 9.75%. Amount involved in 1983: about 4 bil- lion F. -"Prets aides aux entreprises" (PAE). (Subsi- dized loans to firms) - Same as above but involv- ing more flexi- bility as regards commitments of the firm. Rate: 11.75%. Approxi- mate amount in 1983: 2.1 bil- lion F.	Finance Cont. -"Prets supple- mentaires de refinancement" (PSR) - (addi- tional refinan- cing loans) These are re- served to firms showing a high ratio of finan- cial charges to debt. Rate: 9.75% -"Prets Partici- patifs" (subordi- nate loans). There is a variety of these, totalling a little more than 1 billion F. in 1983. Specifi- cally created for small firms (in 1978) their main advantage is to forego the pro- vision of guaran- tees (a National Fund of Guarantee has been set up in this respect) There are several types of such loans, their rates vary but the most advantageous are (end 1983) at 7%
SOCIETE(S) DE DEVELOPPEMENT REGIONAL (SDRs) Generally lo- cated in the main city of the "region"	*Regional Devel- opment Companies *Semi-public fi- nance companies, regionally based, financed by bor- rowing on the market *Mainly designed to alleviate the lack of equity and loan capital of "regional" firms, especially SMEs				*Provide finance either through: -subscription of shares (up to 30% + total equity), -loans (medium or long-term) up to 75% of capital requirements, -subsidies (under certain condi- tions) to newly created small firms	

ORGANISATION	NATURE OF ORGANISATION	SOFTWARE			HARDWARE	
		Information/ Advice	Counselling/ Consulting	Training & Education	Finance	Other
INSTITUT DE DEVELOPPEMENT INDUSTRIEL (IDI) et SOPROMEC, 4 rue Ancalle 82200 Neuilly Tel: 31.1.74771 17	*Industrial Finance Company *Government-backed Company designed to reinforce - on a revolving basis - the capital structure of firms. Has an affiliate: "SOPROMEC" more specialized in small business financing				*IDI and SOPROMEC may subscribe to shares up to 49% of equity *Provides financing for joint venture capital *May also lend medium or long term capital. *Most IDI financing is to large firms	
COMITE(S) DEPARTEMENTAL POUR L'EXAMEN DES PROBLEMES DE FINANCEMENT DES ENTREPRISES (CODEFIS), Located at offices of "Tresorier payeur du Departement" &/or "Directeur de la Banque de France (Local Office)	*Regional Committees for the study of firms' financial problems *CODEFI's are one of several "cellules d' animation financiere regionales", (e.g. CORRI's: Comites regionaux de restructuration industrielle, commission des chefs de Services Financiers) consisting of ad hoc representatives of government agencies and/or having jurisdiction on certain matters, e.g. in tax or social security and of certain public (Credit National, CEPME) or semi-public (SDR's: Societes de Developpement Regional) financial institutions. These Committees decide on how to assist firms for certain given purposes: employment, avoidance of closure or bankruptcy, etc.		*Counselling is indirect - through recommendations and "software assistance" to implement the solution: e.g. organizing the contacts and procedures to meet the financial plan, etc. *CODEFI's may help a small firm to actively find other firms interested in taking over the firm in difficulty, or they may on occasions recommend special procedures and actions to set up a SCOP (Societe Cooperative Ouvriere de Production) or SAPO (Societe Anonyme a Participation Ouvriere)		*While CODEFI's and other similar committees have no special money of their own, they may recommend use of public funds (such as these derived from the central budget (FDES - Fonds de Developpement Economique et Social and FIM: Fonds d'Industriali- sation et de Modernisation), the local (regional) budgets or through special procedures of the financial institutions involved (see for example special loans of CEPME above)	
AGENCE NATIONALE DE LA VALORI- SATION DE LA RECHERCHE (ANVAR), 43 Rue Caumartin, 75946 Paris Cedex 9 Tel: 33.1.26693 10 (Has 22 regional offices)	*Nation Agency for Applied Research *Public organi- zation designed to facilitate the transfer of fun- damental research into commercial operations *Not specific to small enterprises but particularly useful for them	*Has developed a data bank on technology, patents, etc. (BCT: Banque des Connaissances et des Techniques) *Organize or support various information de- vices, e.g. con- ferences, exhi- bition, national meetings (e.g. "Journees Nation- ales de l'ANVAR")	*May take part in feasibility studies of inven- tions and inno- vations, inclu- ding design		*Provides no- interest loans to innovating firms for 50 per- cent of the amount of the programme. These loans are reim- bursable only in case of success. The most impor- tant regional agency (Delega- tion of Ile-de- France) has gran- ted 403 such loans since 1980 mostly to small firms and 32 laboratories for an amount of 128 million F	Finance Cont. *Recently (1983) ANVAR's field of action has been substantially enlarged to cover many types of "modernization" loans (granted at 9.75% rates). ANVAR has been designated to manage the funds allocated to the FIM (Fonds d' Industrialisation et de Moderni- sation) *See also special Matrix: Techno- logical Innovation & R&D

ORGANISATION	NATURE OF ORGANISATION	SOFTWARE			HARDWARE	
		Information/ Advice	Counselling/ Consulting	Training & Education	Finance	Other
THE BANKING SYSTEM	*A complex and well developed network of bank and finance institutions covers the country. The legal status of these organi- zations is not uniform, ranging from state institutions (e.g. Credit National), nationalized banks, coopera- tive banks and the private sector	*Banks (especially local branches) are generally ready to assist client firm to get information and advice on the financing, or even the economic management side of their business. Some banks tend to develop point actions with their clients, e.g. EDP, cash management pro- grammes, etc.			*An extremely complex system (more than 100 different types) of credit grant- ing has developed over the years almost leading to confusion as to the appropriate alternative a- vailable for a specific purpose. *For a complete list of credits, see: "Les princi- paux mecanismes du credit" - Banque de France, Service de l' Information (yearly issue)	
CHAMBRES DE COMMERCES/ CHAMBRES DES METIERS 27, Avenue Friedland, 75382 Paris Cedex 08 Tel: 33.1.56199 00 *Semi-public structures composed of representatives elected by member firms, and employing a rather large professional and technical staff *Funded largely by dues, taxes and duties *Act as official authorities for a large variety of activities (indus- trial estates, professional training, congress halls, indus- trial fairs, arbitration, etc.) *Are regionally and locally organ- ized. Chambres des Metiers include handicrafts, agriculture, retail trade and small individual businesses (less than 10 employees)	*Chambers of Commerce/Chambers of Crafts	*Extensive activities.	*Although not indulging in consulting, may be involved in selection of (and provision for) experts *Have recently set up special ser- vices designed to provide consult- ing to small firms on "reason- able" terms (see Centres Agrees de Gestion)	*Extensive ac- tivities in this field	*Chambers of Com- merce do not normally inter- vene in pro- viding direct finance to firms, but may be indirectly in- volved in certain "joint actions" (e.g. financing of exhibitions, export promotion schemes, etc.)	
CONSEIL NATIONAL DU PATRONAT FRANCAIS, 31 Ave. Pierre ler. de Serbie, 75016 Paris Tel: 31.1.72361 58	*Main "official" representative body and spokes- man for industry as a whole *Constituted by representatives of sectoral and geographic feder- ations of employers *Well staffed and has a wide range of activities *Has more recently set up a special commission in charge of Small Business	*Informations mainly channeled in information letters and periodicals		*Organizes semi- nars, meetings and conferences on economic, social and man- agement matters. Some of these are of particular interest to small firms		
CONFEDERATION GENERALE DES PME (CGPME)	*Smaller pro- fessional organi- zation than CNPF Represents mainly retailers and the commerce sector	*As above		*As above		

ORGANISATION	NATURE OF ORGANISATION	SOFTWARE			HARDWARE	
		Information/ Advice	Counselling/ Consulting	Training & Education	Finance	Other
SYNDICAT NATIONAL DE LA PETITE ET MOYENNE INDUSTRIE (SNPMI), 63 Ave. de Villiers, 75017 Paris Tel: 31.1.76601 28	*A somewhat rival organization of CNPF, but with a much lower number of affiliates - small business is main member- ship	*As above		*As above		
CENTRES TECHNIQUES PROFESSIOELS CENTRES DE RECHERCHE INDUSTRIELLE COLLECTIVE	*Technical Centres, many in number providing technological information and supporting technological research and transfer	*See Special Section: Technological Innovation & R&D				
PROFESSIONAL ASSOCIATIONS	*Very diversified organizations which group firms on a sector and/ or geographical basis. Act as a "secretariat" for the profession and have a variety of activities					
CENTRES AGREES DE GESTION Federation des Centres agrees de Gestion, 60 Blvd. Malesherbes 75008 Paris	*Regional net- works of special management assis- tance centres *Joint initiatives of local Chambers of Commerce, pro- fessional associ- ations and/or chartered accountants *Firms can join the centres upon payment of an annual fee	*Available at moderate cost & yearly perform- ance diagnosis prepared *Centres are particularly strong on accounting & financial advice			*Tax deduction possibilities (for details see selected instru- ments	
ASSOCIATION PUR FAVORISER LA CREATION D'ENTREPRISES (AFACE), 56 Rue de la Boetie, 75008 Paris Tel: 31.1.56305 61	*Private associ- ation designed to promote the creation of new enterprises *See also special section on start-ups	*For those wishing to start a new firm *Quarterly infor- mation letter on start-ups		*Joint activities with Chambers of Commerce Regional Councils	*Start-up Grants (See special section: Start- ups)	
RESEAU INTER- OPPORTUNITIES D'ENTREPRISES, (RIO), 142 Rue du BAC, 75007 Paris Tel: 33.1.54438 25	*Opportunity & Acquisition Network -Private network *Confidential data file for members	*On transactions relating to interfirm co- operation e.g. buying/selling a firm, distribu- tion networks, etc.				

ORGANISATION	NATURE OF ORGANISATION	SOFTWARE			HARDWARE	
		Information/ Advice	Counselling/ Consulting	Training & Education	Finance	Other
ASSOCIATION POUR LA PROMOTION ET LE DEVELOPPEMENT INDUSTRIEL (APRODI), 87, Ave. Kleber, 75016 Paris Tel: 31.1.72751 49	*Association to stimulate Industrial Development *Non-profit association founded by various public and semi-public (e.q. Chambers of Commerce) & private organisations	*Diagnosis of the economic & financial problems of firms, particularly SMEs. *Proposals to help overcome present difficulties and prevent insolvency *Some 600 firms have benefitted to date				
BOUTIQUES DE GESTION, c/o Comite de Liaison des B.G., 559 Ave. de la Republique, 59700 Marcq-en-Broeul	*Management "boutiques" information "shops" *Local associ- ations each with own staff of ex- perts to help individuals or groups wishing to start a business	*Assistance & Counselling provided to 1405 firms in 1983				
FONDATION NATIONALE POUR L'ENSEIGNEMENT DE LA GESTION DES ENTREPRISES, 2, Avenue Hoche 775008 Paris Tel: 31.1.76603 08	*National Foun- dation for Management Training & Education *Part of the French civil service, created in 1968. *Plays an impor- tant role in all activities re- lated to the teaching of management. *Although not designed specifi- cally for small business, this field is viewed as an appropriate field for its manifold activi- ties, parallel to other users	*Supplies infor- mation in many areas. Publishes a monthly letter of information, two reviews (Revue Francaise de Gestion, Enseianement et Gestion) *Orqanizes and/or supports many meetings, con- ferences and seminars, facili- tates or organ- izes contacts with similar institutions abroad		*Assists in training manage- ment professors through finan- cial aid for visiting uni- versities and centers abroad, for participation in seminars, etc. *Helps create new courses, metho- dologies, tools and more gener- ally any valuable project in the field of management		*Gives financial assistance for research projects (e.q. EANPC/EFMD Small Business Project)
TRAINING AND MANAGEMENT EDUCATION CENTRES			*Intensive activities in these areas, traditionally not SME specific although now paying some- what more attention to this area			

Federal Republic of Germany

Materials prepared by

Dieter Ibielski
RKW Rheinland/Pfalz, Mainz

FEDERAL REPUBLIC OF GERMANY

Population: 61.4 million
Area: 248,700 sq.km.

In the Federal Republic of Germany, small business is generally defined as manufacturing and service firms with up to
49 employees and an annual turnover of up to 1 million DM:
medium sized business numbers 50 to 499 employees with a
turnover from 1 - 100 million DM. Within these classifi-
cations, small and medium sized firms account for some 64%
of employment in firms and some 48% of total GNP.

There is a tradiion of Federal support to small business
developing going back to early post war policy and the
European Recovery Programme. Federal policy for small firms
- as an integrated part of the general economic social-
oriented market policy - is set out in a small firms assistance based upon the concept of balance: in competition; in
job opportunity; and in social class. The philosophy is
"help for self help" and emphasis has been placed upon
financial measures and improved productivity although recently start-ups, employment creation, technological innovation and export promotion have received increasing attention.

At the Federal level, the Ministry of Economics houses a
Small Business Secretariat and publishes numerous booklets,
provides financial support for advisory, counselling and
training services administered through the business associations and chambers of commerce, as well as of the crafts
industries, provides grants for applied research projects,
has overall responsibility for the ERP fund loan schemes
(administered through the Kreditanstalt fur Wiederaufau (Re-
construction Loan Corporation) and the Deutsche Ausgleichs-
bank (German Equalization Bank) and schemes to strengthen
small firm R&D activities (administered mainly through the
Confederation of Industrial Research Associations). The
Ministry of Research and Technology also plays a role,
particularly through the financial support of a number of
comparatively recent technological information and advisory
centres, technological parks and innovation projects. The
Ministry of Economic Cooperation and its agencies promote
small business activities with partners in the Third World.

Since Germany is a Federal State, the various Lander have
considerable influence alongside the Federal Government over
the direction of industrial policy. However, there is some
difference in small firms policy between various Lander,
dependent upon regional demands.

Much of the software assistance is channelled through the powerful Chambers of Commerce and Chambers of Crafts industries which emphasise both help for existing companies and start-ups. Assistance is linked in a number of cases with RKW, the national productivity and management organisation. In addition, supplementary support is proprovided through a large number of professional trade and industry associations.

Private banks are the main delivery mechanism for public loan schemes. There is a tradition of "soft" loan support for small business startups through the ERP duplicated and expanded by various land schemes in cooperation with the private banks to which the applicants have to apply. Also credit guarantees and small business lending provide links between starters and consultants who are asked to appraise propositions.

ORGANISATION	NATURE OF ORGANISATION	SOFTWARE			HARDWARE	
		Information/ Advice	Counselling/ Consulting	Training & Education	Finance	Other
BUNDESMINIS-TERIUM FUR WIRT-SCHAFT (BMWI), Villemobler Str. 76, 5300 Bonn Tel: 49.228.6151	*Federal Ministry of Economics *Government Department housing small business secretariat *The secretariat employs three people, but several other departments are charged to administer the different promotion programmes	*Several booklets to inform the public about policy and assis-tance programmes. For example: -Brochure: aids for small businesses -Guidebook: start-up assis-tance -Guidebook: Credits of the ERP-Fund -Flyer: Manage-ment Consultancy Support -Brochure: Small business Export-ing Aids	*Based upon pre-determined operating rules, the Federal Ministry (to-gether with the State Ministries of Economics) have charged the top business as-sociations & RKW (in cooperation with freelance consultants) to manage, without commercial interest, publicly spon-sored advisory services spread over a limited time period (within 5 years 40% of the assignment costs, but not more than DM 7.500 - per applicant) *The scheme also comprising start-up, energy saving and export consulting grants *In addition, supports a wide range of "produc-tivity studies" including inter-firm comparisons, sector analyses, market research projects, etc.	*Occasional support provided to the business associations to: promote develop-ment of training guides; conduct selected semi-nars, courses or in-house train-ing; train the trainers *ERP secures low interest long term loans for establishment of vocational training facilities	*Overall responsibility for ERP fund loan schemes (admini-stration as de-scribed below) *Offers R&D Man-power grants for small manufac-turing firms of up to 500 employ-ees and less than 50 Mill. DM annual turnover interested in strengthening their R&D ac-tivities. Appli-cants may contact the Confederation of Industrial Research Associ-ations (AIF) Bayenthalgurtel 23 5000 Koln 5 Tel: 49.221.3720 91 and receive a 40% grant (but not more than 120 000 DM annually) calcu-lated in terms of taxable personnel expenditure for R&D *A special start-up loan scheme as well as risk capital programme also exists to encourage the own business (see start-up section)	*Together with the State Govern-ments, offers "Improvement of the Regional Eco-nomic Structure" investment incentive. *Financial assistance is given for the location, estab-lishment, exten-sion & modernization of firms (ERP fund)
BUNDESMINIS-TERIUM FUR FOR-SCHUNG UND TECH-NOLOGIE (BMFT), Heinemann Str.2 5300 Bonn 2 Tel: 49.228.591	*Federal Ministry of Research & Technology *Government de-partment with some special project-orien-ted interest in the pro-motion of smaller firms	*Publishes a series of infor-mation booklets, e.g. -Advisor on Research and Technology (pro-motional pro-grammes and advisory help) -Information technics -Production technics -BMFT journal *Research and Technology Infor-mation services provided by the Chambers, Busi-ness & other Associations	*The Chambers, several Business Associations and specialised cen-tres offer inno-vation consul-tancy, partly by providing public subsidies up to 50% of the costs of an assignment but not more than 12,500 dm. annually *The scientific supervision of the publicly sponsored bodies is carried out by the Institute of System Technics and Innovation Research (ISI) of the Fraun-hofer Society for the Advance-ment of Applied Research (FhG), Breslauer Str. 48 7500 Karlsruhe 1 Tel: 49.721.6809 102	*Financial sup-port is provided from time to time for selected training measures	*A number of specialised agencies are commissioned to administer vari-ous R&D innova-tion projects including: -two tax relief laws: special depreciations on R&D investment -BMFT Pilot Ex-periment, Tech-nological Orien-tated Business Establishment (TOU) has been launched recently (see selected instruments)	*Stimulated and partly finan-cially assisted by the BMFT about 30 recent initia-tives either from municipalities or universities, chambers, banks, bigger firms, etc. have based the preconditions for the establishment of "Technology Parks"

ORGANISATION	NATURE OF ORGANISATION	SOFTWARE			HARDWARE	
		Information/ Advice	Counselling/ Consulting	Training & Education	Finance	Other
BUNDESMINI- STERIUM FUR WIRT- SHAFTLICHE ZUSAM- MENARBEIT (BMZ), Karl Marx Str. 4-6, 5300 Bonn Tel: 49.228.5351	*Federal Ministry of Economic Cooperation *Government de- partment with some special SME initiatives	*In order to promote and to expand small business relations with partners in the developing countries and to cover the particu- lar risks German enterprises could incur in the case of private direct investment, advice and know-how are provided as well as financial joint venture assistance through the government owned: -German Financing Corporation of Participation in Developing Coun- tries (DEG), Belvederestr. 40, 5000 Koln 41 Tel: 49.221.49861 *Another government agency: -German Corporation for Technical Cooperation (GTZ), Dag Hammarskjold-Weg 1 6236 Eschborn, Tel: 49.61.96790 encourages trade relations and technical cooperation projects (free of charge) by acquiring partners and by hiring part-time experts to assist during the planning and implementation period			*Offers low interest loans for technology transfer by German small firms to develop- ing countries. This scheme is ad- ministered through: -Reconstruction Loan Corp. (KFW), Palmengartenstr, 5-7, 6000 Frankfurt 1, Tel: 49.69.74310 *Also responsible for programme for the establish- ment, expansion or take over of a subsidiary which facilitates par- ticipation in a developing country (Niederlassungs- programme)	
KREDITANSTALT FUR WIEDERAUFBAU (KFW), Palmengartenstr. 5-9 6000 Frankfurt 1 Tel: 49.69.74310	*State owned Reconstruction Loan Corporation, with the objective of providing loan finance mainly to the smaller firm from the ERP-Fund or own resources. Applicants have to contact their private banks	*Publishes infor- mation materials			*Investment in less developed regions *Private equity investment in productivity projects *Small business loans for inno- vation investment projects to meet personnel and equipment costs, product intro- duction expendi- tures, and ex- penses of opening a new market *Low interest loans for evnironment protection investments	
DEUTSCHEAUS- GLEICHS BANK (DAB), Wielandstr.4 5300 Bonn 2 Tel: 49.228.8311	*State owned "Equalization Bank, with the objective of providing loan finance mainly to the smaller firm and in particular to starters. The means are pro- vided from the ERP-Fund or own resources. App- licants have to contact their private banks	*Publishes information materials			*(Re-)location including investment *Setting up of vocational train- ing facilities *Establishment of environment pro- jection equipment *Provides risk capital in form of long term low interest loans as well as loans of the special ERP start- up scheme *Offers addition- al investment loans to secure the start-up activities and to facilitate selected follow- up expansion projects	

77

ORGANISATION	NATURE OF ORGANISATION	SOFTWARE			HARDWARE	
		Information/ Advice	Counselling/ Consulting	Training & Education	Finance	Other
GEMEINSCHAFTSAUS SCHUSS DER BUNDESKREDIT- GARANTIE GEMEINSCHAFTEN, C/O Zentral Verband des Deutschen Hard- werks (ZDH), Johanniterstr. 1 5300 Bonn 1 Tel: 49.228.5451	*Private based joint committee of loan and participation guarantee associations				*The Federal and State Governments grant back-to- back guarantees as well as guarantee finan- cial loans from the FRP Fund	
LANDER (STATE) GOVERNMENT MINISTRIES, DEPARTMENTS AND DEVELOPMENT AGENCIES (See List A)	*Public authori- ties of the state *Assistance provided varies from state to state *Development Agen- cies are mainly concerned with business premises & local invest- ment aids as charged by the Ministries and partly by the Chambers of Industry & Commerce	*A number of Lander minis- tries/agencies have issued small business brochures	*Provide finan- cial support & cooperate with business advisory services of the associations & RKW	*Some Lander governments provide subsi- dies/financial support for seminars	*Offer various loans, interest subsidies, guarantees & grants: these differ from one Lander to another	
DEUTSCHE WAGNIS FINANZIERUNGS GESELLSCHAFT (WFG), Ulmenstr. 37-39 6000 Frankfurt 1 Tel: 49.69.7205 61	*Government backed Venture Capital Corp., linked to a major group of commercial banks				*Provides equity capital for high risk technologi- cal innovation projects through time-limited minority partnerships	*Recently, several privately sponsored Venture Capital Corps. have been established *Some regional savings banks also undertake these types of initiatives
PRIVATE BANKS	*All the bigger corporations, including the trade unions bank as well as the smaller insti- tutions operate independent from state influence	*A wide range of publications cover small business issues *Some banks publish special series of brochures	*Financial counselling is an important service	*Occasionally offer information seminars, in cooperation with third parties	*Several small business loan schemes are provided *Private banks also act as partners to the public banks in the government financial assis- tance programmes (incl. ERP)	*Occasional local local involvement in special small firm premises
DEUTSCHER SPARKASSENUND GIROVERBAND, Simrockstr. 4 5300 Bonn 1 Tel: 49.228.2041 BUNDESVERBAND DER DEUTCHEN VOLKSBANKEN U, RAIFFEISEN BANKEN (BVR), Heussallee 5 Tel: 49.228.5091	*Savings banks & credit coopera- tives based on special legislation *Are the immediate partners of the small firm at the local level	*Publish directly small business related infor- mation sheets or brochures	*Financial counselling mostly in cooperation with the publicly sponsored business advisory services of the trade associa- tions & RKW (see below)		*Special small business credits & execution of the publicly sponsored programmes	*Occasional local involvment in special small firm premises

ORGANISATION	NATURE OF ORGANISATION	SOFTWARE			HARDWARE	
		Information/ Advice	Counselling/ Consulting	Training & Education	Finance	Other
BUNDESVERBAND DER DEUTSCHEN INDUSTRIE (BDI), Gustav-Heinemann Ufer 84-88, 5000 Koln 51 Tel: 49.221.37081	*Federation of German industry with special small business policy department *36 member associations	*Publications include the half yearly "Mittelstands- information"	*These associations and their member associations and the individual Chambers of Commerce Industry and the Chambers of the Craft Industries, are entrusted by the Government to operate publicly sponsored business advisory services (management consulting) in cooperation with free-lance experts *From time to time, they also carry out advanced training programmes or even selective small business research *Also publish commentaries on small business policy statements and discuss small business related legislation			
DEUTSCHER INDUSTRIE UND HANDELSTAG (DIHT), Adenauer Allee 148, 5300 Bonn 1 Tel: 49.228.1040	*German Associa- tion of Chambers of Industry & Commerce *Represents 69 regional chambers	*Publishes information leaflets and guidebooks				
ZENTRALVERBAND DES DEUTSCHEN HANDWERKS (ZDH), Deutscher Hand- werks Kammertag (DHKT) Johanniterstr. 1 5300 Bonn 1 Tel: 49.228.5451	*Central Associa- tion of Arts & Crafts/Chamber of Crafts *Represents 52 central technical associations, & 42 chambers with a total of 492000 businesses *Runs the applied research insti- tutes shown in list B	*Publishes a series of periodicals, guidebooks, brochures and other informa- tion documents				
OTHER MAJOR BUSINESS ASSOCIATIONS (see List C)						
RATIONALISIER- UNGS-KURATORIUM DER DEUTSCHEN WIRTSCHAFT (RKW), Dusseldorfer Str. 40 D-6236 Eschborn (nr. Frankfurt) Tel: 49.61.9649 51	*German Manage- ment & Produc- tivity Associa- tion *State supported antonomous centre with 11 regional offices partly funded by business & individual membership fees, offering servi- ces on a fee basis	*Publishes, mainly as guide books, the re- sults of applied research of con- cern to the smaller manu- facturing firm *Publishes monthly newspaper "Economy & Pro- ductivity" *Intermediates in interfirm cooper- ation (partner- ships, licences, patents, innovation *Technical advice and information upon request	*A management consulting service, publicly recognised & sponsored, and a wide range of training activities related to small firm needs are the principal daily activities of the regional centres			
RATION ALISIERUNGS- GEMEINSCHAFT DES HANDELS (RGH), Spicherinstr. 55 D-5000 Koln Tel: 49.221.574 90	*Private insti- tute funded by trade associa- tion member fees and state support (to carry out applied research projects)	*Publishes a newsletter on a quarterly basis *Publishes study results	*A management consulting service & advancement training programmes are offered			

ORGANISATION	NATURE OF ORGANISATION	SOFTWARE			HARDWARE	
		Information/ Advice	Counselling/ Consulting	Training & Education	Finance	Other
INSTITUT FUR MITTELSTANDS- FORSCHUNG (IFM), Maximilianstr. 20 D-53000 Bonn 1 Tel: 49.228.729970 ---------------- MITTELSTANDSINS- TITUT NIEDER- SACHSEN, Augustinerweg 20, D-3000 Hannover 21 (Marienwerder) Tel: 49.511.7913 03 ---------------- BETRIEBSWIRT- SCHAFTLICHES FORSCHUNGS- ZENTRUM FOR FRAGEN DER MITTELSTANDI- SCHEN WIRTS- CHAFT (BFM) AN DER UNIVERSITAT BAYREUTH, Bahnhofstr. 21 D-8580 Bayreuth Tel: 49.921.261 81	*Institutes for SME research	*Publish research results in condensed or detailed scripts				
FACHHOCHSCHULEN	*Polytechnics, technical department	*In a few states (e.g. Hamburg, Baden-Wurttenberg, Northrhein, Westfalen and Rheinland-Pfalz), the governments have introduced short- term advisory schemes in coopera- tion with the polytechnics				

SMALL FIRM ASSISTANCE IN THE F.R. GERMANY: GENERAL - SUPPLEMENTARY ADDRESSES

LIST A: LANDER (STATE) GOVERNMENT MINISTRIES AND DEVELOPMENT AGENCIES

		Telephone
* BADEN-WURTTEMBERG		
- Ministerium fur Wirtschaft, Mittelstand und Technologie Baden-Wurttemberg,(Ministry for Economics, Small Business and Technology) Theodor-Heuss-Str.4, D - 7000 STUTTGART 1		49(711) 20201
- Landesgewerbeamt, Kienestr. 18, D-7000 STUTTGART		49(711) 20201
* BAVARIA		
- Bayerisches Staatsministerium fur Wirschaft und Verkehr (Bavarian State Ministry of Economics and Transportation) Prinzregentenstr. 28, D - 800 MUNCHEN 22		49(89) 21620
* BERLIN		
- Senator fur Wirtschaft und Aussenhandel, (Ministry for Economics and Foreign Trade) Martin Luther Str. 105, 1000 BERLIN 62		49(30) 7831
- Berliner Wirtschaftsforderungsgesellschaft, (Berlin Economic Development Corporation) Budapester Str. 1, D - 1000 BERLIN 30		49(30) 26361
* BREMEN		
- Senator fur Wirtschaft und Aussenhandel, (Ministry for Economics and Foreign Trade) Bahnhofsplatz 29 2800 BREMEN 1		49(421) 3611
- Wirtschaftsforderungsgesellschaft der Freien Hansestadt Bremen (Economic Development of the Free Hanseatic City of Bremen) Rembertiring 2, D - 2800 BREMEN 1		49(421) 328275
* HAMBURG		
- Behorde fur Wirtschaft, Verkehr und Landwirtschaft-Amt fur Wirtschaft (Senate of Economic Affairs Transport and Agriculture of the Free and Hanseatic City of Hamburg) Alter Steinweg 4, D - 2000 HAMBURG 11		49(40) 349121
* HESSE		
- Hessisches Ministerium fur Wirtschaft und Technik, (Ministry for Economics and Technology) Kaiser-Friedrich Ring 75 6200 WIESBADEN 1		49(6121) 8151

- Hessische Landesentwicklungs-und Treuhandgesellschaft HLT   49(6121)7742
0   (The HLT Group, State of Hesse)
   Abraham-Lincoln-Str. 38-42,
   D - 6200 WIESBADEN 1

* LOWER SAXONY
- Niedersaschisches Ministerium fur Wirtschaft und Verkehr   49(511)1201
   (Ministry of Economics and Transport)
   Friedrichswall 1,
   D - 3000 HANNOVER

* NORTH RHINE - WESTPHALIA
- Ministerium fur Wirtschaft, Mittelstand und Verkehr,   49(211)8370:
   (Ministry of Economics, Small Business & Transport)
   Haroldstrasse 4,
   4000 DUSSELDORF 1

- Gesellschaft fur Wirtschaftforderung,   49(211)8085
   (Economic Development Corporation for North Rhine-Westphalia)
   Kavalleriestr. 8-10,
   D - 4000 DUSSELDORF

* RHEINLAND-PFALZ
- Ministerium fur Wirtschaft und Verkehr des Landes Rheinland-   49(6131)161
   Pfalz,
   Ministry of Economics and Transport)
   Bauhofstr. 4,
   6500 MAINZ

- Gesellschaft fur Wirtschaftsforderung,   49(6131)620

   (Economic Development Corporation of Rhineland-Palatinate)
   Erthalstr. 1,
   D - 6500 MAINZ

* SAARLAND
- Ministerium fur Wirtschaft, Verkehr und Landwirtschaft des   49(681)5011
   Saarlandes
   (Ministry of Economics Transport and Agriculture)
   Hardenbergstr. 8
   D - 6600 SAARBRUCKEN

- Gesellschaft fur Wirtschaftsforderung Saar m.b.H.   49(681)654(
   H An der Romer brucke 22,
   D - 6600 SAARBRUCKEN

- Wirtschaftsforderungs-Gesellschaft Schleswig-Holstein   49(431)630(
   (Economic Development Corporation of Schleswig-Holstein)
   Sophienblatt 60,
   D - 2300 KIEL 1

- SCHLESWIG-HOLSTEIN
   Ministerium fur Wirtschaft und Verkehr   49(431) 59(
   (Ministry of Economics and Transport)
   Dusternbrooker Weg 94-100,
   D - 2300 KIEL

SMALL FIRM ASSISTANCE IN THE F.R. GERMANY: GENERAL -
SUPPLEMENTARY ADDRESSES

LIST B: APPLIED RESEARCH INSTITUTES RUN THROUGH THE DEUTSCHES
HANDWERKS-INSTITUT
(CENTRAL ASSOCIATION OF GERMAN CRAFT INDUSTRIES)

- Institut fur Handwerkswirtschaft
  Otto-Str. 7, D - 8000 Munchen 2, Tel: 49(89) 593671

- Forschungsinstitut fur Berufsbildung im Handwerk an der
  Universitat zu Koln, Haedenkampstr. 2, D - 5000 Koln 41

- Seminar fur Handwerkswesen an der Universitat Gottingen
  Gosslerstr. 10, D - 3400 Gottingen

- Heinz-Piest-Institut fur Handwerkstechnik an der Technischen
  Universitat Hannover, Wilhelm-Busch-Str. 18, D - 3000 Hannover

- Institut fur Technik der Betriebsfuhrung im Handwerk
  Karl-Friedrich-Str. 17, D - 7500 Karlsruhe

- Institut fur Kunststoffverarbeitung im Handwerk an der
  Technischen Hochschule Aachen, Pontstr. 49, D - 5100 Aachen

LIST C: OTHER MAJOR BUSINESS ASSOCIATIONS - F.R. GERMANY

o Hauptgemeinschaft des Deutschen Einzelhandels (HDE) with 29 member
  associations
     Betriebswirtschaftliche Beratungsstelle fur den Einzelhandel
  (BBE-Unternehmensberatung)
  - Confederation of German Retail Associations -
  Lothringer Str. 56 - 68, D - 5000 Koln 1, Tel: 49(221) 3397325/328210

o Bundesverband des Deutschen Gross - und Aussenhandels (BGA) with 70
  member associations
  Bundesbetriebsberatungstelle fur den Deutschen Gross - und
  Aussenhandel (BBG)
  - Federation of German Wholesale and Foreign Trade -
  Kaiser-Friedrich-Str. 13, D - 5300 Bonn 1, Tel: 49(228) 211041

o Zentralarbeitsgemeinschaft des Strassenverkehrsgewerbes (ZAV) with 5
  member associations
  - Central Association of the Road Transport Industries -
  Breitenbachstr. 1, D - 6000 Frankfurt am Main 93, Tel: 49(69)79191/775719

o Centralvereinigung Deutscher Handelsvertreter- und Handelsmakler-Verbande
  (CDH) with 24 member association
  - Central Association of the German Commercial Agents and Brokers -
  c/o Unternehmensberatung fur die Wirtschaft (UBW)
  Landgrafenstr. 16, D - 1000 Berlin 30, Tel: 49(30) 2611826

o Deutscher Hotel- und Gaststattenverband (DEHOGA) with 14 member
  associations
  - German Hotel and Restaurant Association -
  Kronprinzenstr. 46, D - 5300 Bonn 2, Tel: 49(228) 362016

o Deutscher Reiseburoverband - German Association of Travel Agencies - D - 6000 Frankfurt am Main
Leimenrode 29, Tel: 49(69) 550806

o Bundesverband der Selbstandigen - Deutscher Gewerbeverband (BDS)
- Federation of Self-Employed Business -
Coburger Str. 1 a, D - 5300 Bonn 1 with about 60,000 individual members,
Tel: 49(228) 232026

o Arbeitsgemeinschaft Selbstandiger Unternehmer (ASU) with about 7,000 individual members
- Association of Independent and Entrepreneurs - and Bundesverband
Junger Unternehmers (BJU)
- Federation of Young Entrepreneurs -
Mainzer Str. 238, D - 5300 Bonn 2, Tel: 49(228) 343044

o Aktionsgemeinschaft Wirschaftlicher Mittelstand (AWM)
Adenauer-Allee 11B, D - 5300 Bonn 1, Tel: 49(228) 219077

o Bundesverband Mittelstandische Wirtschaft
Adenauer-Allee 13b-c, D - 5300 Bonn 1, Tel: 49(228) 218339

o Vereingung Mittelstandischer Unternehmer (VMU)
Maximiliansplatz 20, D - 8000 Munchen Z, Tel: 49(89) 292420

o Bundesverband der Freien Berufe (BFB)
- Federation of the Independent Professions -
Godesberger Allee 54, D - 5300 Bonn 2, Tel: 49(228) 374369

Greece

Materials prepared by

Tony Hubert
EANPC, Belgium

and

Emmannel Xanthakis
Advisor, Ministry of
National Economy, Greece

GREECE

Population: 9.7 million
Area: 131.957 sq. km.

It is not clear in Greece what constitutes a SME. In the recently published industrial survey for 1980 from a total of 128.000 manufacturing establishments, 93,3% of them employed less than 10 persons, 3,6% between 10-19 persons and 3,1% more than 20 persons. However, the last group gave two-thirds of all jobs in the manufacturing sector, provided over three-quarters of the total labor remuneration, produced nearly the three-quarters of the manufacturing output, was almost three times more productive than the small family units and contributed about 85% to the formation of gross investment in manufacturing. The first group, being mostly family units, provided a total of 274.000 jobs, of which only 114.000 referred to hired labor.

The group of establishments employing 10-99 persons, being the nearest to what could be determined as SME, represented in 1980 91% (9%) of the manufacturing companies with more than 10 workers and employed 46,7% (53,3%) of the labor used. It represented 31,1% (67,9%) of gross production, 34,5% (65,5%) of the value added from industrial activity (the percentages in parentheses give the share of establishments employing more than 100 persons).

The main source of support for the development of the SMEs is the Hellenic Organization of Small and Medium sized Industries and Handicrafts (EOMMEX). This is a state financed organization which through its offices across the country offers complete packages of assistance and finance to small and medium scale industries and handicrafts. The assistance and advisory services of EOMMEX cover the whole range of the firm's operation such as training and education, management programs, market research for new products, technical assistance in creation of new products, evaluation of new investments and provision of grants for them, financial and technical assistance for participation in exhibitions at home and abroad, brochures, and general information concerning the firm's activities.

The banking system in Greece offers special capital to finance SMEs with subsidized interest rates (4-5 units) provided by the Central Bank according to the purpose of use.

This special capital is available to SMEs when they are interested in:

1. Construction, expansion or modernization of industrial plants.

2. Purchase of new machinery and equipment.

3. Working capital.

4. Imports or exports of raw materials, semi-finished goods or finished goods.

Also, the Greek Government passed in 1982 the Law 1262 which offers incentives for new investments. This Law is applicable to all business enterprises and it offers grants ranging from 10-50% of investment cost depending on the activity and the area in which the firm is going to settle.

Beyond the above sources of support there are several organizations or institutions not especially for SMEs, which offer assistance related to the fields of training and education, consultancy and information (e.g. information on how to export, computer applications, financial analysis, brokerage functions, seminars for management).

ORGANISATION	NATURE OF ORGANISATION	SOFTWARE			HARDWARE	
		Information Advice	Counselling/ Consulting	Training & Education	Finance	Other
EOMMEX 16 Xenias Str. GK-115 28 Athens Tel: 30.1.770.2636	*Hellenic Organisation of Small & Medium sized Industries & Handicrafts *State financed organisation to provide assistance to small and medium-scale industries and handicrafts *Provides services in Athens and through provincial offices. 600 staff	*Innovation offices (including consultancy) since 1983 *Brochures *Information on major contracts up for tender	*Techno-economic studies especially for banks *Product development up to and including market research *Help creation of small firms' consortia, especially for access to large state projects *Technical assistance in creating coops: -juridical -organisational *Technical assistance for handicrafts	*Technological Development Training Awareness program - 6-8 units x 4hr or 3hr + foreign missions *Long-term management program (100 hrs) *Would-be entrepreneurs *Technical problems of SMEs (methodology, QC, etc.) *SME assistance in management of co-ops and placement	*Evaluation of start-up projects and provision of grants for Drs. 1-40m investment projects as follows: -50% grants + 50% long term loans -100% grants for innovative products -100% grants for young people (<30 years) *Support for exhibitions on a selected line of products basis *Financial support for creation of cooperatives	*Exhibition centers in Frankfurt, Brussels and New York *Financial and other assistance to SMEs for exhibitions in Greece and abroad *Assistance for sub-contracting of Greek SMEs with Greek or foreign firms *Services through PROMET, an affiliate, for provision of materials for production in better prices and quality
OΠE 24 Stadion Str. Athens 105 64 Tel: 30.1.322.687 18	*Greek Export Promotion Organisation *Official body financed through state budget *+/- 100 staff - not solely for small firms	*Information on how to export *Brokerage function between foreign buyers and Greek smaller companies	*Proactive market research of main trading partners	*General awareness workshops for SMEs on international marketing (30 days, 100 participants since 1982) *4-month international marketing seminars for unemployed language graduates + paid attachments to smaller companies (35 participants per course)		*Provides space in own pavilions at a selected number of foreign trade fairs *Provides finan- cial assistance for participants in other trade fairs
BEA 18.Academias Str. 10671 Athens Tel: 30.1.363.15 72	*Athens Chamber of Small Industries *Independent membership organisation having 55000 members	*Taps groundswell opinions to advise government on proposed legislation *Guide on export promotion	*Analyses (5-days) members' credit worthiness			*Helps members participate in public procurement tenders *Helps members obtain subsidized interest rates (14% cfr 24% market rate) for 70% of investments to be paid back over 8-15 years (available from main banks)
EΛKEΠA/ELKEPA 28, Kapodistriou Str. Athens 147 Tel: 30.1.350.04 11	*Greek Productivity Centre *Semi-state agency employing +/- 200 in Athens X 5 regional offices. Not specifically for smaller companies but mainly dealing with them	*Brochures	*Computer applications *Micro-electronics' applications	*Seminars for unemployed graduates on management *Courses in functional areas of management (not necessarily for small firms)		*Micro-electronics prototype development for SMEs

ORGANISATION	NATURE OF ORGANISATION	SOFTWARE			HARDWARE	
		Information Advice	Counselling/ Consulting	Training & Education	Finance	Other
OAE OAED Thrakis 6-Trahones	*The National Manpower Commission *State employment agency	*Provides range of employment services for individuals *Publications for the Greek labor force		*Training seminars for unemployed and retraining for employed individuals		
EEΔE 27 V. Sophias Ave. GR-Athens 138 Tel: 30.1.723.5545	*Greek Management Association *Private organisation, catering for large firms except for ESF seminars			*In-company seminars		
BANKS AND PRIVATE CREDIT INSTITUTIONS e.g. ETBA	*The banking system consists of a central Bank, thirty-five commercial banks, three investment banks and five specialized credit institutions. The National Bank and the commercial Bank which are under the state control, accommo-date the 80% of the total banking activities		*Information and assistance on how to finance various economic activities		*Construction of industrial plants *Purchase of new machinery *Importation of new technology *Working capital *Exportation or importation of finished goods, semifinished goods, etc. It should be noted that the interest cost of domestic borrowing of SMEs from the banks is subsi-dized by the Government through the Central Bank	
TECHNOLOGICAL EDUCATION INSTITUTES	*Up-graded secondary schools giving courses in several technical fields		*Research on introducing technologies into SMEs			
EEBE 20 Solomou Str. Athens 10682 Tel: 30.1.360.75 32	*Private organisation not solely for small companies	*Brochures *Library on managerial topics		*Seminars on management functions and on current economic problems		
ITCO 44B. Konstantinou Ave. Athens 11635 Tel: 30.1.721.73 73	*International Trade Co. *State financed Organization to provide assis-tance to Greek firms in exporting their goods	*Information on ways and means of exporting in different countries *Brochures *Brokerage function	*Market research			

Iceland

Materials prepared by

The Technological Institute
of Iceland

ICELAND

Population: 238,000
Area: 103,000 sq.km.

In Iceland most firms are small: only one firm in the country employs more than 500 employees. Currently firms with up to 50 employees provide over 50% of the jobs. Those firms represent 95% of all Icelandic manufacturing companies. Firms with up to 10 employees represent 64% of all Icelandic manufacturing companies and they employ 18% of the workforce. The assistance available to small firms in Iceland is therefore the same as applies generally for all manufacturing companies. In the past, the Icelandic economy has depended heavily on fisheries and agriculture. Agriculture provides all the meat and dairy products needed in Iceland but export has been very unprofitable due to the high production costs in the country. Fishing and fish processing makes up 20% of GNP but contributes 75% to exports. In 1910 fishing and agriculture employed 63% of the workforce but that ratio has gone down to 11.2% in 1981. Fish processing and other secondary industries employed 12.2% of the workforce in 1910 but 37.1% in 1981. Services employed 28.8% in 1910 but 51.7% in 1981. It is clear that primary industries will employ fewer people in the future and that services will play a more important role in employment than ever before. At the same time it is of utmost importance that secondary industries are strengthened and their output increased in value even if they may not employ a higher percentage of the workforce in the future than they now do. Because of this outlook the Parliament of Iceland approved a parlimentary resolution on the 3rd of May 1982. Its main emphasis is the following:

- Increased productivity in the manufacturing industry.

- Strengthened industry in areas where Icelandic firms are competitive.

- Strengthened funds to finance industrial projects.

- Increased financial sources for research and development.

- Strengthened service institutions working with industry in order to increase productivity, innovation and export of industrial products.

- Strengthened industry in the outlying regions.

- Development of industrial parks.

- Companies encouraged to develop production technology and products that can be sold in foreign markets.

In a white paper on the vitalization of the economy issued by the Icelandic government in September 1984 increased support to manufacturing industries is emphasized. Specifically the government proposes to provide 500.000.000 Ikr (approx. 17.000.000 US$) for the following:

- Establishment of a development agency to support innovation in industry.

- Establishment of a Regional development agency to strengthen development in less populated areas.

- Increased R & D activities.

- Adjustment of the educational system to the needs of industry and trade.

- Increased effort in export marketing.

ORGANISATION	NATURE OF ORGANISATION	SOFTWARE			HARDWARE	
		Information Advice	Counselling/ Consulting	Training & Education	Finance	Other
IDNADARRADU-NEYTI Arnarhvoli 101 Reykjavik Tel: 1.25000 Telex: 2224 isdoms is	*Ministry of Industry *Responsible for the performance of the parliamentary resol. of May '82 on main objectives and alternatives in industry *Initiates issues for productivity improvement, quality control and innovation	*Responsible for and/or supports a number of advisory, counselling and training schemes through financing and by participation in boards, such as regional industrial consultants, The Industrial Training Centre, The Supervisory Courses, The Export Board of Icelandic Industries and the Technological Institute of Iceland			*For a special "Start-Up" project for small firms in 1982-1983 3.7 mil. IKR was granted by the ministry and the Industrial Funds *Has regularly provided financial support for development projects in different branches amounting to 2.7 mil. IKR on the budget for 1984. Grants for regional industrial counselling service 1984: 3.5 mil. IKR	
IDNDROUNAR-SJODUR Austurstraeti 14 101 Reykjavik Tel: 1.20500	*The Industrial Development Fund. Established in 1970 with 15 million US$ contributed by the Nordic countries upon Iceland's entry into EFTA. The purpose is to promote the technological and industrial development of Iceland and facilitate its adjustment to free trade within EFTA; to promote cooperation between Iceland and other Nordic countries; to improve competitiveness for the domestic market. The fund provides investments credits, grants or loans at special terms for technological development, product development or market research	*The fund has set up special projects which it sponsors. Recent examples are projects in product development and export marketing. These projects are carried out in cooperation with other organizations and Icelandic and foreign consultants			*The main activity of the Fund is to provide credits for investment to industrial firms. In 1983, 440 loans were granted, amounting to 3 million US$ provided for purchase of equipment, the construction and renewal of factory space, and operational rationalization and organization. Credit is normally extended for up to 70 per cent of investment cost. Each year a certain sum is allocated to grants, amounting 1983 to 130.000 US$. These are provided for projects of importance for manufacturing industry as a whole or its individual branches. A limited amount is provided as product development loans, in 1983 150.000 US$. These loans may be converted into venture grants	

94

ORGANISATION	NATURE OF ORGANISATION	SOFTWARE			HARDWARE	
		Information Advice	Counselling/ Consulting	Training & Education	Finance	Other
FRAMKVAEMDA-STOFNUN Raudararstig 25 105 Reykjavik Tel: 1.25.133 Telex: 2318 defnei is	*The Economic Development Institute *An independent, state owned, institution charged with economic planning, regional affairs and lending. The Institute consists of three Departments: Development Planning Department, Regional Development Department and Development Finance Department	*The Development Planning Department draws up plans and programmes on the development and growth of the most important industrial sectors and the overall development of economic activity			*The Development Finance Department conducts research on the profitability and the national economic benefit of planned new industries and enterprises and evaluates enterprises already operating. It may also initiate the establishment of new enterprises *The Department evaluates loan applications to the Development Fund and the Regional Development Fund *The function of the Development Fund is to give financial support to desirable projects and to research aimed at innovations in industry *Funds may also be used for the preparation of new enterprises which the Institute intends to sponsor *The Regional Fund works towards a regional balance by financial support to projects and to the promotion of employment and the improvement of living conditions in different parts of the country	
IDNLANASJODUR Laekjargotu 12 101 Reykjavik Tel: 1.20580 Telex: 3003 ibank is	*The Industrial Loan Fund *Established in 1935 with limited funding, but in 1963 a special Industrial Loan Fund tax levied on all industries in Iceland increased its lending capacity. The tax was 0.5% of the total turnover of the payers ' involved, but was lowered in 1983 to 0.05% *The Board of the Industrial Loan Fund, which consists of three members, is appointed by the Minister of Industry				*The purpose of the Industrial Loan fund is to support the manufacturing and service industries in Iceland by granting loans for investments in buildings, machinery and equipment. In 1984 the fund has at its disposal for new loans about 13 mill. US$ *On July 1st 1984 a new division commenced operations within the fund, the Product Development and Marketing Division. It shall make loans and grants available for development of new products and for export marketing Funds for the new division are expected 2.5 mil. US$ 1985	

95

ORGANISATION	NATURE OF ORGANISATION	SOFTWARE			HARDWARE	
		Information Advice	Counselling/ Consulting	Training & Education	Finance	Other
IDNTAEKNISTOFNUN ISLANDS, Keldnaholti 110 Reykjavik Tel: 1.687000 Telex: 3020 istech is	*The Technological Institute of Iceland, founded in 1978 by merger of two former institutes for industrial development and research. A government sponsored institute with the objectives: 1) To enhance industrial development and productivity through education and training, consulting, managerial and technological services, testing, control and research 2) Utilization of Iceland's natural resources for industry *The main national machinery for "software" services to industrial firms and institutions	*Provides general information on subsidy schemes and possibilities of loans. Technical information through consultants and a technical library's information service *Monthly newsletter published	*To manufacturing firms, mainly in the textiles, furniture, chemicals, food processing, metals, electrical and electronics industry: counselling service on choice of materials and machines, processes and other technical matters *Also management counselling and consultative services in connection with loan applications *Quality Control	*Various courses, symposia and conferences on technical and management matters for managers and employees in different branches of industry and trade *Vocational training for employees in manufacturing firms		*Research laboratory for product development and testing of materials and products
FRAEDSLUMIDSTOD IDNADARINS KLeldnaholti 110 Reykjavik Tel: 1.687000 Telex: 3020 istech is	*Industrial Training Centre *Under supervision of the Technological Institute of Iceland			*Produced study and teaching materials, provides and runs courses in cooperation with institutes for applied research, technical schools, branch organiza- tions and trade unions *Provides courses for supervisors from all trades and industries as well as for students from certain schools		
VERKSTJORNAR- FRAEDSLAN Keldnaholti 110 Reykjavik Tel: 1.687009 Telex: 3020 istech is	*The Supervisory Courses *Run by a special board under supervision of the Technological Institute					
UPPLYSINGA- DJONUSTA RANNSOKNARADS Hjardarhaga 6 104-Reykjavik Tel: 1.29920 Telex: 2307 isinfo is	*The National Research Council Information Service	*On-line contacts - with information centres in Europe and USA *Provides and seeks information for institutions, trade organizations and individual firms				

ORGANISATION	NATURE OF ORGANISATION	SOFTWARE			HARDWARE	
		Information Advice	Counselling/ Consulting	Training & Education	Finance	Other
EMPLOYERS ORGANIZATIONS: **FELAG ISL. IDNREKENDA (FII)** Hallveigarstig 1 101 Reykjavik Tel: 1.27577 Telex: 2985 index is **LANDSSAMBAND IDNADARMANNA (LI)** Hallveigarstig 1 101 Reykjavik Tel: 1.12380 **VINNUVEITENDA-SAMBAND ISLANDS** Gardastraeti 41 101 Reykjavik Tel: 1.25455	*Federation of Icelandic Industries *Federation of Icelandic Craftsmen *Federation of Icelandic Employees	*All organizations publish regular letters with information of interest to members *All organizations hold regular meetings for members about topics of current interest *FII and LI publish a quarterly bulletin about economic outlook in industry *FII participates with other Nordic countries in the publication of Nordic economic outlook twice a year *FII publishes a product catalogue to provide information about industrial products manufactured in Iceland *All organizations employ economists which provide information on economic trends *All organizations provide members with information and advice in the areas of finance, import-export duties, taxes, labour contracts, etc.	*All organizations have technical departments which provide consulting services to members. In some cases, they are charged for. Areas of expertise include computerized labour negotiations, incentive pay schemes, product development and productivity improvement *The organizations organize often special projects partly carried out by their own staff, partly by outside consultants. Examples are: -Productivity improvement in the clothing industry -Productivity improvement and market adjustment in the furniture industry -Product development and market adjustment in the confectionary industry -Cost control in bakeries -Cost control and productivity improvement in the metal and shipbuilding industries -Cost control, productivity improvement, product development and market adjustment in the construction industry -Computerization of small firms	*All organizations sponsor regularly seminars of interest to members. Examples of recent are Packaging, Robotics, Computerization of small firms, logistics, innovation, etc.		
STJORNUNARFELAG ISLANDS Sidumula 23 108 Reykjavik Tel: 1.82930	*The Icelandic Management Association *A private training organization which gets most of its funding from seminar fees although a small part comes from members' fees and the government	*Distributes a monthly newsletter and training catalogues twice a year		*Offers a great selection of seminars and conferences with Icelandic and foreign speakers. Areas covered include finance, production, marketing, accounting, organizational behaviour, applications of computer, e.g. office automation, etc.		

ORGANISATION	NATURE OF ORGANISATION	SOFTWARE			HARDWARE	
		Information Advice	Counselling/ Consulting	Training & Education	Finance	Other
RESEARCH INSTITUTES (other than The Technological Institute of Iceland)	*National, non-profit applied research institutes. Objectives: Technical development and utilization of resources in the respective fields					
RANNSOKNASTOFNUN BYGGINGARIDNADAR INS, Keldnaholti 110 Reykjavik Tel: 1.83200	*The Building Research Institute	*General information and counselling on technical matters. Permanent exhibition of aggregates and other objects for the building industry *Quality control and testing of materials for builders of roads and houses. Publications: leaflets, technical notes		*Runs numerous courses on technical matters. Seminars and lectures in various parts of the country		*Research laboratories for product development and testing
RANNSOKNASTOFFNUN LANDBUNADARINS Keldnaholti 110 Reykjavik Tel: 1.82230	*The Agriculture Research Institute - Food Science Unit -	*Working area mainly farming, but the Food Science Unit provides information and advice on nutritional matters to the dairy and meat industry		*Courses for butchers and skilled labour in the meat processing industry		*Research laboratories for product development and testing
RANNSOKNASTOFNUN FISKIDNADARINS Skulagotu 4 101 Reykjavik Tel: 1.20240	The Icelandic Fisheries Laboratories	*Information on handling, processing and distribution of fish to the fish industry *Analytical work and technical service for freezing plants, canning and conserving firms and to producers of salted fish products, fish meals and oils				*Research laboratories for product development and testing
VEIDIMALA-STOFNUN, Hverfisgotu 116 105 Reykjavik Tel: 1.81811	The Directorate of Freshwater Fisheries	*Advice to small firms in a beginning trade, the freshwater fish aqua culture				
ORKUSTOFNUN Grensasvegur 9 108 Reykjavik Tel: 1.83600 Telex: 2339 orkust is	*The National Energy Authority	*Advice on the utilization of geothermal energy for industry				

ORGANISATION	NATURE OF ORGANISATION	SOFTWARE			HARDWARE	
		Information Advice	Counselling/ Consulting	Training & Education	Finance	Other
UTFLUTNINGS- MIDSTOD IDNADARINS Hallveigarstig 1 101 Reykjavik Tel: 1.27577 Telex: 2985 index is	*Export Board of Icelandic Industries. Semi-Governmental Agency. *The mandate of Export Board is the Following: -To promote Icelandic industrial products abroad by participation in exhibitions and information on export activity in Iceland -To provide consulting service to industrial firms -To organize and motivate export cooperation of industrial firms -To act as intermediary in export and establishment of business contacts	*Publications: -Occasional newsletter -Trade promotion catalogues for distribution abroad -Export statistics (monthly) -Computer printout from the Statistical Bureau of Iceland on export firms *Provides selected export information on ad hoc basis and upon request	*Export consultant for hire available to companies for marketing and promotional work *Export advisory service: Organization of trade fairs, exhibitions participation and publicity abroad, providing contacts for exporters abroad and advice on distribution channels. Chargeable consultancy service: Market research and market scanning -Coordination of sales promotion -Planning of itineraries, information on suppliers, consultancy services for overseas buyers	*The Export Board sponsors training seminars in various field of export marketing		

Ireland

Materials prepared by

Allan Gibb
Durham University Business School, UK

in cooperation with

Chris Park
Irish Management Institute

and

William Glynn
University College, Dublin

IRELAND

Population: 3.4 million
Area: 70,282 sq.km.

In Ireland, definitions of what constitutes a small firm vary between 50 and 100 employees. Currently manufacturing firms with up to 100 employees provide over 100,000 jobs and represent about 90% of all manufacturing firms. Firms employing less than 50 people represent 80% of all manufacturing companies and employ 65,000 people or 27% of total manufacturing employment. Small and medium sized firms together (i.e., employing up to 500 people) account for 193,000 industrial jobs. The 5,000 or so small manufacturing firms (up to 100 employees) account for: 90% of the total number of manufacturing firms; 40% of total manufacturing employment; 30% of total manufacturing output; and 25% of total industrial exports.

A major source of support for small firms development is the state controlled Industrial Development Authority (IDA) which, through offices across Ireland, offers a comprehensive package of advice and financial assistance to people interested in setting up or expanding small firms. In addition, two regional development agencies, Shannon Development and Udaras na Gaeltachta, have introduced a number of innovative hardware and software services such as the Innovation Centre at Limerick (to identify product opportunities and provide product development services) and Managed Workshops (to provide shared facilities for small businesses). An important role in the provision of software services is played by the state supported Industrial Training Authority, AnCO, which provides training both for start-ups and for existing firms. Also involved in specialist small firm training are: the Irish Productivity Centre; the Irish Management Institute and the National Institute for Higher Education.

Ireland has the largest percentage youth in population in Europe: 50% of its population is under 25 years of age. As a result, increasing attention is being paid to the problems of youth unemployment and a number of programmes have been introduced (e.g., by AnCo and the Irish Youth Employment Agency) to encourage youth self employment. In addition, organisations such as the Institute for Industrial Research and Standards (technical services), the Irish Goods Council (marketing support), the Irish Export Board (C.T.T. - trade and exports) and Kilkenny Design (design and promotion) service a large small firms clientele although their services are not specifically designed for SMEs.

102

The Industrial Credit Company (ICC), the state owned development bank, offers a range of financial facilities including short, medium and long term loans, hire purchase and equipment leasing. While not especially for small firms, two-thirds of ICC's lending is to firms with under 100 employees. Financial support is also provided through Ireland's "big four" banks. Of these, the Bank of Ireland appears the most actively concerned both through a small business policy programme involving higher gearing and lower security requirements than elsewhere and through sponsorship of business competitions and management seminars and courses.

Recently (July, 1984) the Irish Government issued a White Paper on Industrial Policy. Plans for the small firms' sector included greater selectivity in grants to small industries; further regionalisation of the IDA's Small Industries Programme with a "one stop shop" service available to small industries in each region; national application of successful initiatives developed to date by Shannon Development; the establishment of Small Industries Boards in all regions; further development of the National Linkage Programme (launched through the IDA in 1983) aimed at encouraging small firms to meet the raw materials/components supply requirements of large industrial projects; and, continuing emphasis on the Enterprise Allowance Scheme (launched by the Ministry of Labour in 1983) to assist the unemployed to set up their own firms.

ORGANISATION	NATURE OF ORGANISATION	SOFTWARE			HARDWARE	
		Information/ Advice	Counselling/ Consulting	Training & Education	Finance	Other
INDUSTRIAL DEVELOPMENT AUTHORITY (IDA), 42/47 Lower Mount Street, Dublin 2 Tel: 353.1.6866 33	*State supported 'autonomous' development agency respon- hle for all aspects of Irish industrial development. Has Small Industries Division with 70 staff (10% of total) Eight offices through- out Ireland. 200m budget	*Information Centres in nine regional offices *Product Ideas Centres to iden- tify product opportunities Prepares market opportunity/ economic surveys in each of the regional offices *Promotions in different loca- tions to en- courage business starters (22 in 1982) *Information clinics for small business (106 in 1982) *Booklets, e.g. Start Your Own Business	*Enterprise De- velopment Pro- gramme under which a limited number of high flying new projects are put together with clients for which extensive cash support is then provided. In 1982, 22 projects completed	*Provides finan- cial support to a number train- ing programmes of ANCO, IMI and others (see below) Administers new industry training grants (FEC sponsored)	*For manufactur- ing industry: -Feasibility Studies grant of up to 15,000 maximum. Available for new projects. (229 grants 1982) -Capital grants towards cost of sites, buildings and machinery (60% in special areas and 45% elsewhere) -Training grants of up to 100% of costs for training at all levels -Product and process develop- ment grants up to 50% (max. of 250,000). (77 grants worth 1m in 1982) -Special loan guarantees and interest subsi- dies available for working capi- tal loans under the Enterprise Development Programme -Grants scheme as above for inter- nationally trada- ble services (22 grants in 1982). Total grant assistance 1982 28m	*Incubator units with rent subsi- dies for start- ups. 1982 - 883 883 sq. metres constructed *Small industry centres at seven locations (1982) 27,000 sq. metres
UDARA'S NA GAELTACH TA, Na Forbacha Gaillimh Tel: 353.91.210 11	*Gaeltacht Development Authority *Specialist Development Agency for Irish speaking areas of Ireland with special measures for small and medium industry *Staff: 150	*Range of Services as Per the IDA above but more liberally applied				
SHANNON DEVELOPMENT CORPORATION, Shannon Town Centre Co. Clare Tel: 353.61.615 55	*Limited lia- bility company with shares held by three minis- tries. Has responsibility for promoting indigenous industry (under 50 employees) in in area surround- ing Shannon Airport *Staff: 250	*Matchmaker service to link products of small companies with larger firms needs throughout the country	*Runs Enterprise Development Programme simi- lar to IDA -Has 5 field officers throughout the region *Industrial clinics through- out region *Business Advisory service (staff of 15), a diag- nostic rather than intensive service	*Programmes include: -New Business courses -Financial Admin -Business Manage- ment courses -Cooperative Management course -Marketing courses placing graduates in small business for up to nine months *Entrepreneurship and High Tech- nology programme to encourage graduate engineers to set up their own business	*Cash grants available as with the IDA. Total- ling 4.9m for 135 projects in 1982. Covers site, buildings, real reductions, machinery, train- ing, feasibility studies and research and development *Loan guarantees and tax relief	*Managed work- space with shared facili- ties for small business *Factory building programme of small units throughout region. (11,000 sq. metres in 1982)

ORGANISATION	NATURE OF ORGANISATION	SOFTWARE			HARDWARE	
		Information/ Advice	Counselling/ Consulting	Training & Education	Finance	Other
INDUSTRIAL TRAINING AUTHORITY (AnCO) Nespil Road, Dublin 4 Tel: 353.1.6857 77	*State supported "autonomous" agency charged with the development of training through- out Ireland *Staff 2300 *Operates levy grant system to raise small amount of revenue *Funded by the European Social Fund and Youth Employment Agency and Irish government (see below) *Has now special Small Firms Division employ- ing a staff of 10	*Operates "hot- line" telephone service for small firms training problems and opportunities	*In-company "assignment units" for a number of manu- facturing indus- tries. The pro- gramme is based on analysis of the companies problems and actions by management with follow-up visits over a period of 6-8 months. Covers production and financial analysis in particular. (deals with 300 small companies - 10-30 employees a year) *"Retired Execu- tive Panel" for companies up to 20 employees. Available at 50 per day fee for short exercises in company. AnCO may subsidise fee up to 50%	*Marketing De- velopment Pro- gramme to place recent trained marketing gradu- ates free with a small company for 6 months. Linked with Universities (25 companies a year) *Product develop- ment and Export marketing pro- grammes. Link training pro- grammes for indi- viduals with specific company development project over six months paid by AnCO *Starting Your Own Business 20 weeks full- time (6 weeks formal tuition) For those with a feasible idea and demonstrated capacity to start a business *Shorter, part- time evening seminar courses of this nature are available for those in employment *Self Employment as a career, programme over 15 weeks for young people aimed at helping career choice and possible start-up in self employment	*Grant aids up to 50% of Training Courses in Management and Supervisory skills	
INDUSTRIAL CREDIT COMPANY (ICC), 32 Harcourt Street, Dublin 2 Tel: 353.1.7200 55	*State owned bank with objective of providing medium and long term loan and equity finance to industry *Not a specialist small business organisation but two-thirds of its lending (90% of projects) is to firms under 100 employees. Has special depart- ment for small and medium sized firms *Total staff 300- two regional offices	*Sponsors busi- ness compe- titions. Hosts regional seminars for businessmen to create awareness *Participates in various IDA Committees, e.g. Small Industries, Committee, Do- mestic Industries committee, Enter- prise Development Committee and Cork Small Industries Board	*A subsidiary, ICC Corporate Finance Ltd. pro- vides corporate financial advice advises on public share issues; share valuations; management buy- outs, mergers acquisitions and divestments fees charged	*Co-sponsors IMI Small Business Development Pro- gramme (see below) *Co-sponsors work- shops for small businesses arranged through the Small Firms Association with the Universities	*Short-term and long term (10 yrs.) lending and equity. Borrows from European Invest- ment Bank for lending to small and medium sized industry. Also lends working capital loans to exporters at Euro currency based rates *A small loan scheme in desig- nated areas. Loans up to 10,000 with minimum formality up to 5 years Cooperates with County Develop- ment Officers on this. Lending is at commercial rates *Borrows from the European Investment Bank for its lending to small firms	*Leases Indus- trial and warehouse property

ORGANISATION	NATURE OF ORGANISATION	SOFTWARE			HARDWARE	
		Information/ Advice	Counselling/ Consulting	Training & Education	Finance	Other
YOUTH EMPLOYMENT AGENCY, 3/4 Upper Pembroke Street Dublin 2 Tel: 353.1.7898 44	*Autonomous state owned company funded by special 1% levy on all declared income. Aims to provide training and work experience for young people and to develop new approaches to job creation (120m budget 1983)				*Youth Self-Employed Pro-gramme. Links with Bank of Ireland (see below) to offer loans of up to 3,000 towards new business projects. For those unemployed (over 3 months) and under 25. YEA provides 60%. *Funds AnCO 'Self Employment' programmes for young people	
COMMUNITY AND YOUTH ENTERPRISE PROGRAMME	*Administered by Youth Employ-ment Agency (above)	*Provides advice to community groups on enterprise initiatives		*Through funding for AnCO of Youth Self Employment Programmes	*Provides funding for recruitment by the Group of an 'Enterprise Worker' for up to 12 months to help get the project going *Provides planning grants for inves-tigating and developing the project *Direct financial aid for groups at point of 'start-up' (both capital and revenue)	
BANK OF IRELAND, Head Office Lr. Baggot St. Dublin 2 Tel: 353.1.7857 44	*Clearing (com-mercial) Bank. One of 'big four' in Ireland but the most actively con-cerned with small firms. Have Smaller Business Policy involving more liberal (higher gearing/ less security) lending	*Sponsor Business Competitions to create aware-ness. Business sector officers located through-out county. (advice to small firms)		*Management Seminars for Customers -Co-sponsor Youth Employment Agency -Community Enter-prise Programme -Sponsor IMI Small Business Develop-ment Programme	*Smaller Business Policy programme involving higher gearing and lower security require-ments	
FOIR TEORANTA 25, Adelaide Road Dublin 4 Tel: 353.1.7644 84	*State sponsored reconstruction finance company. Concerned with providing specialist fi-fance for 'turn-rounds'. Not particularly small firms oriented				*May provide equity and long term (10 years) lending at flat rate. Lenders of last resort	
THE INNOVATION CENTRE, Limerick Enterprise House, Plessey Techno-logical Park, Limerick Tel: 353.1.61481 77	*Funded by Shannon Develop-ment Corporation but with national responsibility *Autonomous organisation with Board of Direc-tors from range of relevant institutions	*Product ideas newsletter published *Sources of infor-mation on licen-cesor col-laborative possi-bilities *Market fact pack service or report on techni-cal research	Product Develop-ment Service -Assistance with development of prototypes -Assistance with the buying and selling of technology -Assistance with idea evaluation, business plan development, market testing, venture capital approaches, (have 70 cur-rently under way)	*Seminars on licencing new product develop-ment *Group Entrepre-neurship pro-gramme, aimed particularly at formation of multi-disciplin-ary partnerships to launch ambi-tious ideas in the U.S. venture market	*'Intern' scheme paying salaries of 'innovators' for up to 18 months. (Some external to Centre others internal). Company search, testing and other costs. 20 interns in December 1983	*Provision of work-shop space for prototype development and testing and pilot production

ORGANISATION	NATURE OF ORGANISATION	SOFTWARE			HARDWARE	
		Information/ Advice	Counselling/ Consulting	Training & Education	Finance	Other
IRISH MANAGEMENT INSTITUTE (IMI), Sandyford Road Dublin 4 Tel: 353.1.9839 11	*Independent management institute funded by member fees (with state and EEC support)	*Has monthly management magazine available free to members *Publishes annually "Who Helps Small Industry"		*Small Business Development Programme. 18 months programme for small business growth with carefully selected participants, monthly workshops and in-company counselling, 18 participants. A number of short courses (specialist) for small business		
IRISH PRODUCTIVITY CENTRE (IPC), 35 Shelbourne Road, Dublin 4 Tel: 353.1.6862 44	*Independent organisation with equal represen- tation of unions and employees supported mainly by fees of business and unions but with substantial minority govern- ment support. (Advisory staff of 14)		*Short term assignments in firms under 200 employees on: -Company evaluation -Development planning -Systems design/ installation -Management Organisation and Recruitment -Management Information -Fees charged *Also continuous contact service of 1-2 days per month	*Runs Start Your Own Business courses with AnCO and Youth Employ- ment Agency. *Assists with Irish Management Institute Business Develop- ment Programme		
COUNTY DEVELOPMENT TEAMS	*Groups made up of County Development Officers and representatives of Tourist Board, IDA, AnCO etc. under auspices of the County Councils in West- ern half of country	*Operate advice centres	*Help in prepara- tion of grant application to IDA	*Small discretion- ary grant of up to 3,000 in 'designated' areas		
IRISH EXPORT BOARD (CTT), Merrian Hall, Strand Road, Sandymount Dublin 4 Tel: 353.1.6950 11	*A state spon- sored limited liability company with major re- sponsibility of promoting export services to firms. Is not small firms specialist but 70% of enquiries are from firms under 100 employ- ees. Staff of *Staff of 330, 1/3 overseas. *Has small firms export department	*Information and research on markets from published sources and network of 25 overseas officers proactively con- cerned with plant visiting and advice on exports (1000 firms interviewed in 1982) *Special advisory service on design and product development for overseas markets. Support for exhibitions	*Are encouraging development of export groups. Seven group schemes at present. Fund salary for limited period of 'group' export salesman			*Generally avail- able financial support for exhi- bitions, promo- tions as per standard services

ORGANISATION	NATURE OF ORGANISATION	SOFTWARE			HARDWARE	
		Information/ Advice	Counselling/ Consulting	Training & Education	Finance	Other
IRISH GOODS COUNCIL, Ireland House Trade Centre Strand Road Dublin 4 Tel: 353.1.6960 11	*Company limited by guarantee. Largely state financed. Not specialist small business. Annual budget 1.3m. Responsible for market development and promotion of Irish goods in the home market	*National sub-contract capa-bility register *Market research reports *Marketing advice to companies (not counselling - only short visits) *Publish trade directories *Import substi-tution and can-you-make-it exhibitions and 'opportunities' publications (34m of orders placed in this way, 1982)	*Develops Product Strategy Groups in different sectors (17 such groups). Joint advertising, pro-motions, exhi-bitions, market research. Re-ducing funding support *Places marketing personnel through Youth Employment Agency with support of up to 3000 or 60% of first year cost of employment. For firms with less than 100 employees	*Trade Seminars	*Support for Product Strategy Group activities (exhibitions, etc.)	
INSTITUTE FOR INDUSTRIAL RESEARCH AND STANDARDS, Ballyman Road Dublin 9 Tel: 353.1.3701 01	*Is national technology grid for Irish Industry *Statutory body funded mainly by grants and by Ministry of Industry, Com-merce & Tourism *Objective is to encourage the use of science and technology in industry. Is not a specialist small business organisation but has special services	*Deals with technical infor-mation enquiries. Has limited scheme of liaison officers to take proactive approach to small companies especially *General service of technical consultancy, investigation, testing and analysing avail-able to small firms (fee paying services)	*Technical gradu-ates scheme to place engineering graduates in small firms for one year (60 places a year). Linked with Youth Employment Agency. 95% offered permanent employment			
KILKENNY DESIGN, Castle Yard Kilkenny Tel: 353.1.56221 18	*Government spon-sored agency with prime responsi-bility for advancement of good design in craft industry. Is limited lia-bility company *Does substantial part of its work with small indus-try and craft. Has retail out-lets in Dublin and Kilkenny (120 employees with 2m turnover)	*Runs exhibitions and promotions	*Retail and In-dustrial Design services on fee and sales royalty basis -Model making -Prototype development -'Soft' model development	*Some seminars on design and Work Experience Programme		*Have model making and prototype development work-shop (mainly craft)
NATIONAL BOARD FOR SCIENCE AND TECHNOLOGY, Shelbourne House, Shelbourne Rd. Dublin 4 Tel: 353.1.6833 11	*State financial organisation to advise government on Science and Technology Policy (Staff of 80 and budget of 3.3m). Is not small firms specialist. Funds mainly univer-sity research				*Has special cooperative de-velopment pro-gramme to en-courage joint ventures in research and development be-tween university and industry. Some small firms are benefitting	

Italy

Materials prepared by

Guiseppe Russo
Chamber of Commerce, Milan

in cooperation with

Roberto Artioli
*Agenzia Industriale Italiana (AII)
and ASSEFOR*

Maddalena Basile
(AII)

and

Vladimir Lodygenski
ASSEFIN

ITALY

Population: 56 million
Area: 302,225 sq.km.

In Italy, almost 59% of the manufacturing labour force is employed in firms with less than 100 employees and, in recent years, small firms (employing between 10 and 100 people) have performed well, particularly in comparison to their larger (1,000+ employees) counterparts: they have, for instance, shown the highest increases in employment, higher value added and higher gross profits per employee.

Government assistance, however, does not appear to be in proportion to the employment or output provided by SMEs and there is no national small firms policy. On the other hand, recent years have witnesses some positive changes: for instance, a fixed share of industrial incentives is now reserved for small and medium-sized firms.

The principal Ministry involved is the Ministry of Industry, Commerce, Trade and Handicraft. In cooperation with the Ministry, medium and long term loan support is provided through the Medio Credito Centrale and its regional branches and a number of other Industrial Credit Banks. Over the last few years, Medio Credito has significantly bolstered its financing activity through judicious cooperation with/use of both the European Investment Bank and the Ortoli Fund. The more than 600 rural and artisan banks also play an important role in small firm financing, particularly since some 60% of them represent the only credit institution in their communities. Some financial assistance to small firms is provided through the Regional Governments: their role in the provision of credit is, however, limited by law and their major activity towards small firms lies in the provision of sites and facilities, real estate leasing, factoring and joint guarantees.

The independent public Chambers of Commerce, Industry, Agriculture and Handicraft play a major role, particularly at the local level, and particularly through the provision of information, advice and training services. An important recent training initiative has been the specialised SME training programme, now coordinated by ASSEFOR (Association for Training and Assistance of SMEs) whose members comprise the Chambers and numerous business associations. A major informational data bank is provided through CERVED, a national network with eight computerised data banks, owned mainly by the Chambers of Commerce and the banks. Public Sector institutions such as FORMEZ (Institute for Vocational Business Training in the South), IASM (Institute for Development Assistance in the South), certain university level business schools, a number of private training institutions and consulting firms also offer some specialised SME training and counselling.

Industry associations also play a role in the provision of support to SMEs: Confindustria (Confederation of Industry), for instance, has established a National Small Firms Committee with regional branches serving both to represent member needs and to provide advisory and consulting services. CONFAPI is another independent association which offers an active service to about 20,000 small and medium businesses. The handicraft associations (CGA and CNA) with thousands of members are also particularly important for new firms.

ORGANISATION	NATURE OF ORGANISATION	SOFTWARE			HARDWARE	
		Information/ Advice	Counselling/ Consulting	Training & Education	Finance	Other
MINISTERIO INDUSTRIA E COMMERCIO, via Vittovio Veneto 33 00100 Roma Tel: 39.6.4705 MEDIOCREDITO CENTRALE, via Piemonte 51 00187 Roma Tel: 39.6.47911	*Ministry of Industry and Commerce and Handicraft *National Government *Public service corporation established July '52 to regulate & direct financial support to SMEs; coordinate the special credit system; provide for re-financing of banks/credit institutions in specified areas; & carry out a number of other operations together with the banks/credit institutions (see attached instruments)				*Ministerial Financial Support administered through Medio-credito Centrale & other Indus-trial Credit Banks (see List A) *Includes: -8 year moderni-sation loans. Assisted amount: up to 40% of fixed investments Interest rate 72% of "Reference Rate" as ruled every 2 months by treasury terri-torial & secre-torial priorities D.P.R. 902 9/11/76 *Provides medium term SME financing through EEC, European Investment Bank & "Ortoli Fund" *Through EIB provides 10 year loans for new equipment or machinery impove-ments to indus-trial firms with invested capital of less than 15 billion lire	Finance Cont. -10 year loans for product line changes &/or structural change Assisted amount: 40,50,60% of investment according to type of change & project costs. Interest rate: 40,50,60% of reference rate depending on areas. Law 12/8/1977 No. 675 Finance Cont. -maximum amount: 50% of the in-vestment (from 33 to 9.500 million lire). Assisted interest rate: ruled by Medio-credito according to the date of the contract
MEDIOCREDITO REGIONALE (See list A)	*Regional branch offices of Mediocredito providing a range of soft-ware and hard-ware services for SMEs	*Publish pamphlets on medium term credit opportunities	*Carried out through area officials		*Provide 10 year loans at going interest rate & other medium term financing to firms with in-vestment capital of under 15 bil-lion lire. Max-imum amount: 30 billion. Law 22.6.1950 n. 445 *Medium term loan support given to associations of at least 5 companies each with fixed in-vestments of less than 9.89 billion lire & a combined total of less than 500 employ-ees for joint purchase of raw materials, joint commercial net-work activity, joint EDP. Maxi-mum assisted amount 70% of investments to a maximum of 1 billion lire on fixed investments & 500 million lire on other investments. Law 21/5/82 n. 240	Finance Cont. *Also offers: -5 year loans to meet legal standards of waste water (latter not SME specific)

ORGANISATION	NATURE OF ORGANISATION	SOFTWARE			HARDWARE	
		Information/ Advice	Counselling/ Consulting	Training & Education	Finance	Other
FINANZIARIE REGIONALI	*Regional organisations financing fixed assets & working capital *See examples below					
FINPIEMONTE SpA Gallana S. Federico 54 10121 Torino Tel: 39.11.5138 61	*Operates in Piedmont and Val D'Aosta					*Minority participation in small and medium sized enterprises *Movable and real estate operations & technical assistance of financial nature
FINANZIARIA LIGURE PER LO VILUPPO ECONOMICO (FI.L.S.E. SpA), Viz Peschiera 16 16122 Genova Tel: 39.10.8188 91	*Liguria financing body for economic development					*Minority participation in SMEs *Promotion of economic and social development - creation of substructure
FRIULIA SpA Via Trento n.2. 34132. Trieste 34100 Tel: 39.40.7631 02/3/4/5/6/7/8/9	*Region: Friuli Venezia Giulia					*Minority participation in production enterprises *Technical assistance of financial nature
ERVET REGIONALE PER LA VALORIZZA-ZIONE ECONOMICA DEL TERITORIO (ERVET), Via Morgagnig 40100 Bologna Tel: 39.51.230567	*Regional body for the economic valorization of the region Emilia Romagna					*Participation in small and medium enterprises *Definition, creation and development of equipped areas
FINANZIANA REGIONALE MARCHE SpA (FIMMARCHE SpA), CS Mazzimi 160 60100 Ancona Tel: 39.71.2015 48	*Region: Marche					*Financial assistance to handicrafts and small enterprises *Assumes participation in capital of small and medium business - guarantees grants *Movable and real estate operations
FINANZIARIA LAZIALE PER LO SVILUPPO (FI.LA.S. SpA), Via Garibaldi 31 00153 Roma Tel: 39.48.9274 1/2/3/4	*Rome area					*Assumes minority participation in small and medium businesses of the region *Constitution and strengthening of equipped areas *Financing of enterprises *Specializes in real estate leasing
SOCIETA REGIONALE PER LO SVILUPPO DELL'UMBRIA SpA Via Don Bosco 11 06100 Perugia Tel: 39.75.258 41/2/3/4	*Regional society for the develop-ment of the Umbrian region					*Minority participation in small and medium enterprises
FIDI TOSCANA SpA Via Ricasoli 21 50122 Firenze Tel: 39.099.2185 57	*Region: Tuscany					*Factoring and leasing of regional enterprises *Short term guarantees and credits

ORGANISATION	NATURE OF ORGANISATION	SOFTWARE			HARDWARE	
		Information/ Advice	Counselling/ Consulting	Training & Education	Finance	Other
VENETO SVILUPPO 2310 S. Marco 30100 Venezia Tel: 39.41.7042 11	*Region: Veneto				*Participation in enterprises promoting new entrepreneurship initiatives *Financial assistance *Pre-arrangements of equipped areas	
E.S.P.I. SpA Via Alfonzo Borrelli 10 90139 Palermo Tel: 39.91.2668 34	*Industrial promotion of Sicily				*Participation in small and medium enterprises	
SOCIETA FINANZIARIA INDUSTRIALE RINASCITA SARDEGNA (S.F.I.R.S. SpA), Via S. Margherita 4 09100 Cagliari Tel: 39.70.6683 71	*Sardegna Industrial re-launch				*Promotion and assistance for economic initiatives in regional enterprises	
FINANZIARIA MERIDIONALE (FIME), Lungotevere Raffaello Sanzio, 15 00153 Roma	*Public financing corporation for Southern Italy				*Channels the savings of south-ern regions into productive indus-trial investment there *Minority par-ticipation in SMEs *Para-banking activities *Intervention in reorganisation of firms	
FINLOMBARDA SpA Piazza Belgioso 2 20100 Milano Tel: 39.2.70585 7/8/9	*Lombardy financing body				*Promotion of activities linked with regional development, particular SMEs	
UNIONE COSTRUTTORI ITALIANI MACCHINE UTENSILE (UCIMU), vIe. F. Testi 128 20092 Cinisello Balsamo (Mi) Tel: 39.2.24971 & MEDIOCREDITO & OTHER BANKS	*National association of manufacturers of tool machines				*Through finan-cial support of Ministry of . Industry & Com-merce provides: -5 year financing of sales to firms manufacturing or buying Italian machine tools whose price ex-ceeds 1 million lire. Maximum assisted amount: 30 billion lire at assisted interest rate Law 28/11/1965 No. 1329	Finance Cont. -Capital grants up to 25% of purchasing value (32% in S. Italy) Law 21/12/1983 n. 696 -Latter limited to craftsman & SMEs employing less than 300 people & with invested capital not ex-ceeding 11.5 billion lire
ARTIGIANCASSA, (CASSA PER IL CREDITO ALLE IMPRESE ARTIGIANE) Lungotevere Michelangelo 6 00192 Roma Tel: 39.6.310093	*Handicraft Bank -- publicly supported 50% from the state & 50% from the Banks				*Credit to Handicraft firms for installation enlargement, & modernisation of laboratories in-cluding machinery & tools & de-velopment of raw material stocks & finished products Law 15/12/1947 n. 1418	

ORGANISATION	NATURE OF ORGANISATION	SOFTWARE			HARDWARE	
		Information/ Advice	Counselling/ Consulting	Training & Education	Finance	Other
CASSE DI RISPARMIO, BANCHE, POPULARI & LOCAL ARTIGIAN- CASSA	*Savings banks people's banks & local artisan banks *local banks (over 600), often the only credit institution at the local level				*Play an important role in SME financing on account of local presence	
GIUNTE REGIONALI	*Regional Governments *Shareholders in: -financial corporations & public venture capital institutions -credit guarantee cooperations -public centres for technological transfer to SMEs (see section, Technological Innovation) *Offer incentives to complement those provided by the Handicrafts bank and other national organisations				Individually, or in association with listed types of organisations are involved in: -financial assistance -minority parti- cipation in the SMEs of the region; -implementation of industrial development areas; -joint guarantees; -real estate -leasing; -factoring	Finance Cont. *Through regional laws, provide grants to the municipalities to establish indus- trial & handi- craft areas; special hardware & software in- centives for handicraft pro- duction; & other supplementary SME incentives
CAMERA DI COMMERCIO, INDUSTRIA, ARTIGIANATO E AGRICULTURE (see List B)

Central Office: UNIONE ITALIANE DELLE CAMERE DI COMMERCIO, INDUSTRIA, ARTIGIANATO E AGRICOLTORA, Piazza Sallustio 21 00187 Roma | *Chambers of Commerce Industry & Agriculture *Independent public bodies *The 95 chambers play an important role through rep- resenting at the local (pro- vincial) level a meeting ground between the state Ministries, the local associates of Industry, Commerce, Handi- crafts & Agricul- ture & the unions of Chamber em- ployees (over 6000 in all) | *Wide range e.g. on local economy; business law, budgetting of joint stock companies, the SME register etc. | *Through the FORMAPER system | *FORMAPER training system (see ASSEFOR below) *Course on: -Foreign Trade -Banking -Insurance -Energy Management -EDP | | |
| COMITATO NATIONALE DELLE PICCOLLO INDUSTRIE, C/O Confindustria vle Astronomia 30, 00144 Roma Tel: 39.6.59031 | *Small Industries Committee within National Confederation of Industry *Has 93 provin- acial gencies | *Advice & consulting, particularly on: labour/union problems; government relations *Some provincial agencies have also organised services in the fields of marketing; exports & training | | | | |
| ASSEFOR, via Faenza, 109 50123 Firenze Tel: 39.55.27731 | *Joint-venture of the Italian Union of Chambers of Commerce, Industry, Agri- culture & Handi- craft, regional & provincial chambers & busi- ness associations with independent by-laws | *Information & advice to SMEs provided through edu- cational pro- grammes for entrepreneurs and managers | *Some counselling also included in educational programmes | *Launched & co- ordinates national and local edu- cational pro- grammes (see above) which include: -Local entre- preneur network building | | |

SMALL FIRMS ASSISTANCE IN ITALY: GENERAL - SUPPLEMENTARY ADDRESSES

LIST A: REGIONAL BRANCHES OF MEDIOCREDITO

        Mediocredito del Lazio - Ple delle belle arti, 2 - 00196 ROMA

        Mediocredito delle Marche - via Minicucci, 4 - 60121 ANCONA

        Mediocredito delle Venezie - calle Ca' d'Oro, 3935 - Cannaregio -
        30121 VENEZIA

        Mediocredito dell'Umbria - Cso Vannucci, 66 - 06100 PERUGIA

        Mediocredito Ligure - via G. D'Annunzio, 23 - 16121 GENOVA

        Mediocredito del Friuli-Venezia Giulia - via Gorghi, 2 - 33100 UDINE

        Mediocredito Piemontese e della Valle d'Aosta - via Solferino, 22 -
        10121 TORINO

        Mediocredito regionale Abruzzese - Cso S. Giorgio - 64100 TERAMO

        Mediocredito regionale Lombardo - Via Broletto 20 - 20100 MILANO

        Mediocredito regionale della Basilicata - via S. Remo, 76 - 85100
        POTENZO

        Mediocredito regionale della Calabria - via D. Assanti, 8 - 88100
        CATANZARO

        Mediocredito regionale della Puglia - via G. Petrone, 120 - 70124 BARI

        Mediocredito regionale della Toscana - via G. Mazzini, 46 0 5032 FIRENZE

        Mediocredito regionale Emilia Romagna - via Marconi, 10 - 40122 BOLOGNA

        Mediocredito Trentino-Alto Adige - via Paradisi, 1 - 38100 TRENTO

LIST B: UNIONS OF THE CHAMBERS OF COMMERCE & INDUSTRY

        Unione delle Camere di Commercio delle Marche - Pza 24 maggio, 1 -
        60100 ANCONA

        Unione delle Camere di Commercio delle Puglie - Cso Cavour, 2 -
        70121 BARI

        Unione delle Camere di Commercio dell'Emilia-Romagna - via U. Bassi, 7
        40121 BOLOGNA

UNIONS OF THE CHAMBERS OF COMMERCE & INDUSTRY - Continued

Unione delle Camere di Commercio del Trentino-Alto Adige - via Garibaldi, 4 - 39100 BOLZANO

Unione delle Camere di Commercio della Sardegna - Cso Vittorio Emanuele, 1 09100 CAGLIARI

Unione delle Camere di Commercio della Calabria - via Calabria, 33 - 87100 COSEN

Unione delle Camere di Commercio della Toscana - via Giusti, 9 - 50121 FIRENZE

Unione delle Camere di Commercio della Liguria - via Garibaldi, 3 - 16124 GENOVA

Unione delle Camere di Commercio della Lombardia - via Cordusio, 2 - 20123 MILAN

Unione delle Camere di Commercio della Campania - Cso Meridionale, 58 - 80143 NAPOLI

Unione delle Camere di Commercio della Sicilia - via E. Amari, 11 - 90139 PALMERO

Unione delle Camere di Commercio della Basilicata - Cso 18 agosto, 34 - 85100 POTENZA

Unione delle Camere di Commercio del Lazio - via de' Burro, 147 - 00186 ROMA

Unione delle Camere di Commercio dell'Abruzzo - via Savini, 50 - 64100 TERAMO

Unione delle Camere di Commercio dell'Umbria - via Don Minzoni, 6 - 05100 TERNI

Unione delle Camere di Commercio del Piemonte - via S. francesco da Paola, 24 - 10123 TORINO

Unione delle Camere di Commercio del Friuli-Venezia Giulia - Pza della Borsa, 14 - 34121 TRIESTE

Unione delle Camere di Commercio del Veneto - San Marco, 2032 - 30124 VENEZIA

LIST C: PRIVATE BUSINESS SCHOOLS AND SELECTED UNIVERSITIES

ISTUD, via Mazzina,121, - 28040 BELGIRATE

CEGOS - Italiana, pza Velasca,7, - 20122 MILANO

IFOA, via G.D'Arezzo,4 - 42100 REGGIO EMILIA

ISDA, via Nazionale,75 - 00184 ROMA

CESA, via Oberdan,7, - 40126 BOLGNA

ISIDA, via Liberta,91, - 90143 PALERMO

FORMEZ, Pal.dei Congressi, Mostra d'Oltramare - 80125 NAPOLI

SDA (Scoula Direzione Aziendale),via Sarfatti,25, - 20136 MILANO

CUOA (Universita degli Studi), via VIII Febbraio,2 - Pal.centrale "IL BO" -
35100 PADOVA

Scuola di Amministrazione Aziendale, Universita degli Studi,via Verdi,8 -
10124 TORINO

The Netherlands

Materials prepared by

Allan Gibb
Durham University Business School, UK

in cooperation with

Pieter Groeneveld
Contactgroep van Werkgevers
in de Metaalindustrie, NV

THE NETHERLANDS

Populations: 14.2 million
Area: 40,844 sq.km.

The Netherlands small firms are defined as enterprises with less than 100 employees. They account for almost 75% of total employment and contribute approximately 28% of the Gross Domestic Product.

There is no formal statement of overall small firms policy. Government policy is directed towards achieving balanced socio-economic development. The policy aims at providing equal opportunities of competition for small and medium business. Specific policies for support of small business aim at improving its efficiency, ensuring adequate access to finance, structural improvements to help particular industry sectors, ensuring fair competition and help in urban renewal and localities. Overall, the philosophy is to seek to re-move disadvantages arising from their limited resource and power position but not to interfere too much with them. The government directly and indirectly supports a variety of consultancy and advisory schemes and organisations which are to be rationalised in future.

Some of the support for small business is organised through public law organisations such as the Chamber of Commerce and the public industrial organisations such as the Central Board for Retail Trade and the Central Board for Craft Trades. These, together with a number of other boards, come under the Social-Economic Council on which both government and industry is represented. Thse organisations are im-portant in regulating activity and training in their sectors under various Acts of Parliament and ensuring qualifications for entrepreneurs in various craft and retail trades. Local authorities also have undertaken a number of small business training and funding ventures to help solve local employment problems. On the finance side, there is a Loan Guarantee Scheme, a variety of "soft" loans available under guarantee from the private banks and a network of equity companies backed by government guarantee.

ORGANISATION	NATURE OF ORGANISATION	SOFTWARE			HARDWARE	
		Information/ Advice	Counselling/ Consulting	Training & Education	Finance	Other
MINISTERIE VAN ECONOMISCHE ZAKEN (MIN. EZ), Bezuidenhout- seweg, 30 post- bus 90490, 2509 LK, Den Haag. Tel: 31.70.7989 11	*Ministry for Economic Affairs *Main Government ministry respon- sible for SMEs *Has directorate of S & M's with staff pf 200. (Small firms defined as up to 100)	*Provides support for a number of advice and counselling schemes including RDK and RND. (see below) *Funds special intensive counselling for innovative scheme with selected small companies. Ten consultants - free service - a limited experiment with relatively few firms. *Transfer point scheme to improve access of small companies to tech- nical know-how. Scheme links demand side (SMEs) with supply side. Started with 5 supply transfer points (TNO, 3 techno- logical & two other universities) and 3 demand transfer points located in RND (see below) Experimental Scheme - rated as successful. Now about 20 transfer points. Subsidized by Ministry (2 1/2 man years each year in each location). Certain other schemes not subsidised			*Loan guarantee scheme for com- panies up to 100 employees. Current lending under the scheme = Loss rate 5- 10%. 100% guarantee - through clearing bank system. Also through Central Bank. Supports equity guarantee scheme (see below)	
RIJKSNIJVER- HEIDSDIENST (RND), Lutherse Burgwal 10 Postbus 20104 2500 EC Den Haag Tel: 31.70.6019 32	*State (Ministry of Economy) funded advice and consultant service for small business. *Three regional offices and 12 others (one for each province). 125 staff (80 advisers)	*Provides technical and economic advice to small firms (up to 200 employees) in manufacturing only. 2 free days a year and then a subsidised charge				
REGIONALE UIENSTVERLENINGS CENTRA KLEIN- BEDRIJF (RDK), Begijlnenhof 27 5611 EK Eindhoven Tel: 31.40.4413 21	*State funded (local and national) advice centres to very small firms (under 10 em- ployees) in 35 locations throughout the country. Each office with three persons	*Provides information/advice to small business mainly on social and legal statutory requirements and benefit schemes (e.g. income assistance for short time working). Not strictly business management advice. Staff rarely go to companies				*Operates scheme with local authorities to provide financial assistance towards reloca- tion or termina- tion of business if caused by renovation of town centres. Also provides assistance to entrepreneurs who close the company down
BUREAU INNOVATIE NU, Postbus 20103 2500 EC Den Haag Tel: 31.70.7988 00	*Information Bureau funded by Ministry of Economy. Not specifically for small business but with aim of providing advice particularly on Government assis- tance. (5 staff plus 2 part time) *80% of enquiries from firms under 100 employees	*Booklets on financial assistance *Deals with 120 telephone en- quiries per week (80% from small companies in manufacturing.)				

ORGANISATION	NATURE OF ORGANISATION	SOFTWARE			HARDWARE	
		Information/ Advice	Counselling/ Consulting	Training & Education	Finance	Other
ONTWIKKELINGS-MAATSCHAPPIJEN (OOM), One such organisation is: Burg van Royensinger 12, 8011 CT Zwolle Tel: 31.52.00147 22	*Autonomous Regional development corporations for specific "problem" areas of the country. *Funded by central government with Municipal and Regional support (5 regions) *Not specifically for small business *Services vary	*Advice on business, financial and locational problems. Limited consultancy. Signposts to government assistance. Free Service			*Can provide low interest loans and equity participation loans in new and innovative firms. Temporary for first few years	
ECONOMISCH - TECHNOLOGISCHE INSTITUTEN (ETI) e.g. Turfsingel 65, 9712 KL Groningen Tel: 31.50.1314 77	*Provincial government funded advice organisations with objective of providing advice on location and planning to business. Not special for small firms *Also aimed at regional promotion (in 13 centres).	*Advice on location and planning. Also regional promotion				
MUNICIPALITIES/ LOCAL AUTHORITIES e.g. Stichting Startfonds Rijnmond (SR) Openbaar Lichaam Rijmond afd. Economische Aangelegenheden Vasteland 96-104, 3011 BP, Rotterdam Tel: 31.01.1113 20	*Local authorities responsible for local development initiatives sometimes in collaboration with banks.	*Varied provision of counselling and advice			*Provide start-up loans and in some cases grants	*Also "managed" workshop centres for small businesses
MINISTRY OF ECONOMY ALONG WITH PRIVATE BANKS OF WHICH MAJOR INCLUDE: ABN AMRO NMB RABO	*Private banks soft loans and guarantees supported by the Ministry of Economy				*All major private banks offer 100% government guaranteed loans scheme as follows: -General purpose loan to 15 years commercial rates of interest for fixed capital -Subordinated loan scheme-maximum 20 years-declining subsidy on interest over years e.g. °Starting companies 1-3 years 50% subsidy. Next 3 years accumulation of 50% of interest due is possible °Existing companies 40% first 3 years. Next 3 years accumulation of 40% of due interest possible °No capital repayment during time of subsidy and accumulation	Finance Cont. -No capital repayment during time of subsidy and accumulation -Technical development loans for new products 5% interest rate up to 78% if the amount needed -Special mortgage loan 40% government guaranteed during maximum of 15 years to make possible higher (up to 85%) of financing of building (normally 50%)

ORGANISATION	NATURE OF ORGANISATION	SOFTWARE			HARDWARE	
		Information/ Advice	Counselling/ Consulting	Training & Education	Finance	Other
NETHERLANDS BANK (CENTRAL BANK), B.P. 98 NL-1000 AB Amsterdam Tel: 31.20.52491 11	*State Central Bank. Official channel for equity guarantee scheme for private participative companies. Has led to a number of equity companies being started by the commercial banks and other organisations *Mainly aimed at assisting small firms *Aimed to improve capital base of small companies. 1984 - about 30 venture companies operating				*Offers to private company (through specialist equity company) up to 4mm guilders. If the company is liquidated the state guarantees 50% of the equity loss. Operating for two years. 50 companies financed in this way to September 1983. 7,000,000 guilders average investment	
DE NATIONALE INVESTERINGS BANK (NIB), Carnegieplein 4, Postbus 380 2501 BH, Den Haag Tel: 31.70.4694 64	*State industry bank specialising in medium-long term loans (5-10 years). Not a specialist small firm bank (only 25% of clients under 100 employees) *Complements clearing bank lending by higher risk				*Medium term loans -5-10 years market rate -Operates loan guarantee scheme -Operates subordinated loan scheme aimed at helping under capitalised companies (with capital repayment delays) -Manages Industrial Guarantee Fund for larger companies	
NEDERLANDSE PARTICIPIE HAATSCHAPPIJI (NPM), Breitmerstraat 3 Postbus 724 1007 JE Amsterdam Tel: 31.20.7607 61	*Netherlands Participation Bank (owned by NIB and private banks) *Is equity capital company for small and medium business				*Operates equity guarantee scheme as described above	
NEDERLANDSE MIDDENSTANDS BANK (NMB), Eduard van Beinumstraat 2, Postbus 1800 1000 BV Amsterdam Tel: 31.20.54391 11	*Partly state owned specialist bank for small and medium business				*Medium/long term lending (5 to 15 years) *Operates subordinated loan scheme for small companies. (Will allow accumulated interest and no capital repayment for first 6 years). See also "Private Banks" above	
EXPORTBEUOR-DERINGS EN VOOR LICHTING-SCHENST (EVD), Bezuidenhou-seweg 151 2594 AG's-Gravenhage Tel: 31.70.7960 39	*Main state organisation for support of exports	*Range of information and advisory services and seminars available to all firms indiscriminately. Arranges trade fairs and exhibitions			*Subsidy scheme for cooperation between small firms to employ an export manager for 3 years *Subsidy scheme for engineers and consultants to help them tender for overseas contracts	

ORGANISATION	NATURE OF ORGANISATION	SOFTWARE			HARDWARE	
		Information/ Advice	Counselling/ Consulting	Training & Education	Finance	Other
KAMERS VAN KOOP HANDEL EN FABRIEKEN KULT (CHAMBERS OF COMMERCE) VERERIGING VAN KAMERS VAN KOOPHANDEL, Watermolenlaan 1, 3447 GT, Woerden Tel: 31.34.80269 11	*Public Law institutions not especially small business. 38 Chambers throughout the country	*Provide standard information (legal, commer- cial, trade). Of importance in export information				
HOOFDBEDRIJF- SCHAP AMBACHTEN (HBA), Bad Huisweg 10R, 2587 CM's - Gravenhage Tel: 31.70.5144 71	*Central Industry Board for the Craft Trades *Is Public Law organisation for the "labour intensive" craft trades *Represents 20,000 small businesses Membership compulsory *21 branches in different industries	*Source of infor- mation and advice to members through branches		*Branches organise management semi- nars as well as technical train- ing. Source of basic training in craft and commercial skills for enterprises		
HOOFDBEDRIF- SCHAP DETAIL- HANDEL (HBD), Nieuwe Parklaan 74 2597 LF's - Gravenhage Tel: 31.70.5142 61	*Central Industry Board for the Retail Trade *Public law organisation (as HBA above) *160,000 enter- prises in retailing, hotels and resta- urants and retail craft shops	*Services as H.B.A. above				
KONINKLIJK NETHERLANDS ONDERNEMERS- VERBANK (KNOV), Broekunolen- weg 20 2289 RE, Rijswiki Tel: 31.15.5693 95	*Privately funded Fmployers organi- sation for small business under 100 employees in crafts, retail and services *24 HO staff and over 60 in the field (advisers) 95000 members	*Provides advice and literature to members on legal questions and planning *Booklets on starting a busi- ness, labour legislation, statutory obli- gations, etc.	*Operates con- sultancy service (bondconsulenten) with over 60 consultants in regions across the country *Covers all aspects of busi- ness/planning. Fees are charged but the bulk of these can be re- claimed under a central guarantee scheme. Deals with 7-8000 enquiries a year			
NETHERLANDS CHRISTELIJK ONDERNEMERS- VERBOND (NCOV), Treubstraat 25 2288 EH Rijswijk Tel: 31.70.9927 22	*Similar organisation to the KNOV for "Christian" employers. Provides similar kinds of services. 11,000 members					
CONTACGROEP VAN WERKGEVERS IN DE METAAL INDUSTRIE, Jonkindstraat, 20 Postbus 1598 3000 BN Rotterdam Tel: 31.10.3600 00	*Trade Associa- tion for companies in the metalluraical industry. 700 members - funded by subscriptions *20 staff *Almost all small firms as members	*Information on legislation, wage agreements, etc. *Circular letters *Advice on finance wage systems (one day a year free then charge)		*Links with other organisations e.a. de Baak for training course including one on subcontracting cooperation		

124

ORGANISATION	NATURE OF ORGANISATION	SOFTWARE			HARDWARE	
		Information/ Advice	Counselling/ Consulting	Training & Education	Finance	Other
CENTRAAL INSTITUT VOOR HET MIDDEN EN KLEINBEDRIJF (CIMK), Dalstindreef 9 12 XC, Dienen Tel: 31.20.9010 71	*State subsidised organisation representing interests of relevant employers and trade associations *Prime role to provide consultancy services for SMEs (mainly retail type firms) *50% funding from Advisory services	*Information/ advice available on design, building, management, planning *Advice on computing and automation of office services	*General management consultancy services for firms up to 100 employees with advisers all over Holland. Has advisers/specialists on industry basis. 190 in all. Fees charged but subsidies available (up to 90%) through 0 and S (see below)	*Runs short seminars and courses often linked with other organisations throughout the country. (1 afternoon to 4 days). Also some programmes for start-ups	*Is main advisory body for credit assessments under the state loan guarantee scheme (2 day assignments for banks, chambers)	
STICHTING ONTWIKKELING EN SANERING VOOR HET MIDDEN EN KLEINBEDIJF (O & S), Gebouw Vijverkof, Dalsteindreef 9, 1112 XC Diemen Tel: 31.20.9010 71	*Government funded foundation with two objectives: -To help small businesses in difficulty and -to help in closure and winding-up.				*Provides subsidy for consultancy advice and training such as turn-round help (for firms in difficulty) or help in winding-up. Provides funding for reports of CIMK on loan guarantee when firm cannot pay for these	
STICHTING KLEINOOD, Princes Beatrixlaan 5 L509 AB's Gravenhage Tel: 31.70.8141 71	*Foundation set up by Netherlands Federation of Industry (VNO)		*Lends experienced retired executives for limited periods free to help small firms			
NEDERLANDSE ORGANISATIVE VOOR TOEGEPOST NATUURWET- ENSCHAPPELIJK ONDERZOEK (TNO), Schoemaker- straat 97 2600 AB Delft Tel: 31.15.5693 50	*Non-profit making research organisation part-funded by government. Staff of 4900 at 35 different locations around the country *Is not a small firm specialist organisation	*Information services for small firms. 5000 enquiries a year. Research for groups of small firms or associations that can be given 100% government grant support *Basic technical research for industries and products (fee paying)				
STICHTING BEDRIJFSKUNDE, Poortweg 6-8, 2612 PF, Delft Tel: 31.15.5692 54	*Public foundation *Institute of Business Administration (Delft) Business School (50 staff)		*Some support for small business through staff and student consulting			
SMALL BUSINESS SCHOOL, Poortweg 6-8, 2612 PF, Delft Tel: 31.15.5692 54	*Part of Institute of Business Administration (see above)			*Small Business Development Programme. (National 20 companies a year) 35 days in one year - action oriented for owner managers or autonomous companies. One third subsidised		

ORGANISATION	NATURE OF ORGANISATION	SOFTWARE			HARDWARE	
		Information/ Advice	Counselling/ Consulting	Training & Education	Finance	Other
TECHNICAL UNIVERSITIES AND TECHNISCHE HOGESCHOOLS For example (TH), Postbus ?, 2600 AA, Delft Tel: 31.15.7819 43	*State funded Universities and Polytechnics in several locations throughout the country	*Operate the "Transfer Point" scheme	*Vary in capability to provide counselling and training. Some school have start-up programmes			
ECONOMISCH INSTITUUT VOOR HET MIDDEN EN KLEINBEDRIJF, Italielaan 33 Postbus 7001 2701 AA Zoetermeer Tel: 31.79.4136 34	*Independent Research Insti- tute with objec- tive of promo- ting fundamental and applied research in small and medium businesses. 150 150 employees (1983) Annual budget 15mn guilders 60% of funds from government - remainder mainly from craft and retail trade organisations	*Interfirm com- parison infor- mation covering 7000 small and medium enter- prises in retail trade and craft *Business economic research in industry sectors *Macro-economic, social and statistical research: as background to policy formation. Includes sector analysis *Library and information service				
BUSINESS TECHNOLOGY CENTRES	*Autonomous centres funded by mix of private and public capital including local government *Liaison with Universities at Enschede, Wageningen and Rotterdam	*Provision of information and advice and common services for the companies in the building *See also special section: Techno- logical Information and R&D				*Managed work- shops for very small companies
CENTRO VOOR MICRO-ELEKTRONICA (CME) e.g. DELFT CENTRE CME TNO, Schoemaker- straat 97 Postbus 67 2600 AB, Delft Also at Eind- hoven & Twente	*Autonomous centres in three locations funded by central government to encourage small firms in micro processor application	*Advice and counselling for small firms in micro-electronic applications *See also special section: Techno- logical Innovation and R&D				

Norway

Materials prepared by

Tor Vangen
Norwegian Productivity Institute, Oslo

NORWAY

Population: 4.1 million
Area: 342,219 sq.km.

The Norwegian definition of small and medium sized manufacturing companies is companies with less than 100 employees. Small industry is defined as companies with less
than 20 employees. Medium sized companies are companies
employing 20 to 99 people. In Norway, some 46% of those
employed in manufacturing work in firms with fewer than 100
employees and, of these, some 31% in firms with fewer than
50 employees.

As elsewhere, attention to small firms has significantly
increased in recent years. A particularly important role is
played by DU, the Regional Development Fund, a state administered body in operation since 1961. Aimed particularly
towards the promotion of employment and industrial development in depressed areas, DU provides information and counselling on finance and loan applications, and grants loans
and loan guarantees particularly for transportation, product
development and training. The STI (National Institute for
Technology), a government sponsored body, also plays an important role at the regional level through its 10 regional
offices offering advice, information, consulting and a range
of training courses.

Industrial support in Norway is generally provided across
the Board without discrimination between large and small
firms. Recently, however, a new public organisation, INKO,
has been created, aimed to promote awareness among firms of
the support and services available to them. At present,
INKO has some 12 regional offices offering free services to
some 2500 clients yearly, particularly to micro companies
(with under five employees).

The Industry and Trade Associations also provide a range of
services, both nationally and locally. Included among these
are: NI (Federation of Norwegian Industry) which has a
special department for advice and counselling to small
firms; NAF (Norwegian Employers' Confederation) offering
advisory services and a range of courses; and credit associations such as A/S Naeringskreditt (Industry, Trade and
Crafts Credit), Norges Hypotekforening for Naeringslivet
(Mortgage Association for Industry) and others at the regional level. In addition, the NPI (Norwegian Productivity
Institute) gives information and advice on productivity improvement and organise training programmes.

The Commercial and Savings Bank offer both advisory services
and loans while various credit institutions (in addition to
those mentioned above) provide various loans and loan guarantees. Included among these are: the Credit Company of
the Norwegian Savings Bank; the Norwegian Bank for Industry;
and the Fund for Handicrafts and Smallscale Industry which
grants guarantees and loans in the regions not covered by
the Regional Development Fund.

ORGANISATION	NATURE OF ORGANISATION	SOFTWARE			HARDWARE	
		Information/ Advice	Counselling/ Consulting	Training & Education	Finance	Other
DISTRIKTENES UTBYGGINGSFOND (DU), Fredrik Selmersvei 4, Helsfyr, Oslo 6 Tel: 47.2.664000	*Regional Develoment Fund *DU is a State administrative body that has been in operation since 1961. It obtains its resources partly by raising loans. Grants are financed in their entirety from the central government budget *DU has 158 employees. In 1983, loans and contributions of 1.299 mill. Nkr. were made	*Advice on financial sources and on business matters in general	*Gives consultative service in conection with application for loans	*Joint start-up program recently launched in cooperation with other agencies	*Grants, loans & guarantees to business which can result in improved, stable and profitable enterprises in low developed areas. Financial support is given as a compensation for disadvantages in establishing business in such areas. Such financial support is given up to 15%, 25%, 35% of the investment depending upon the location. Support is also given to train new local employees *Also provide financial support for transportation of finished and semi-finished products in areas with a poor transportation system. Limit for support is 250-300 km.	Finance Cont. *Loans granted for development of products and processes up to 50% of cost of project *Offers financial support for training new employees as a consequence of relocation of business to less developed regions
INFORMASJON OG KONTAKTFORMIDLING (INKO), Inko-Koordinator Akersgt. 24 C, Oslo 1 Tel: 47.2.204550	*Recently established government information and contact service established throughout the country to help small business find the right information source for solving their problems *INKO offers its service through 12 regional offices. 45 people are employed. The budget is 13 mill. Nkr. INKO had 2060 clients in 1982	*Gives free information on all services available to SMEs including contacts on financing				
STATENS VEILEDNINGSKONTOR FOR OPPFINNERE, Radmann Halmrastsvei 18, 1300 Sandvika Tel: 47.2.542938	*The Norwegian Government Consultative Office for Inventors *Public service office for inventors		*Counsel inventors and acts as a middleman between inventors and industry		*Finances applications for patents	
ARBEIDSDIREKTORATET, Holbergs plass 7 Oslo 1 Tel: 47.2.111070	*Directorate for Labour *Supplies manpower to business through regional offices *Publicly supported	*Publishes weekly job summaries for employers and employees				

ORGANISATION	NATURE OF ORGANISATION	SOFTWARE			HARDWARE	
		Information/ Advice	Counselling/ Consulting	Training & Education	Finance	Other
ARBEIDSTILSYNET, Fr. Nansens vei 14, Oslo 1 Tel: 47.2.459820	*Directorate for Labour *A public body with 12 regional offices, 80 de- partment offices and a budget of 117 mill. Nkr. (1983)	*Gives information about working and environmental laws and how to practise them				
A/S NAERINGS- KREDITT, Munkegt. 21, 7000 Trondheim Tel: 47.75.26105	*Industry, Trade, & Crafts Credit *Industry, Trade, and Crafts Credit works in close cooperation with banks and other credit institutions				*Grants medium and long term loans to indus- try, trade and crafts throughout the country. Amortization is 5 to 20 years	
NORGES HYPOTEK- FOREINING FOR NAERINGSLIVET, Haakon VII's gt. 6, Oslo 1 Tel: 47.2.417830	*Norwegian Mort- gage Associa- tion for Industry *Credit insti- tution				*This private institution offers pri- ority loans against mortgage on real estate and equipment. All loans have to be within 60% of valuation of real estate and within 40% of the valuation of machinery and equipment. Amor- tization period: 18 years	
SPAREBANKENES KREDITTSELSKAP, A/S Akersgt. 11, Oslo 1 Tel: 47.2.202435	*The Credit Company for Norwegian Savings				*Grants medium and longterm loans to small industry and trade. Amorti- zation period: up to 25 years	
A/S DEN NORSKE INDUSTRIBANK, Akersgt. 13, Oslo 1 Tel: 47.2.429180	*Norwegian Bank for Industry				*Grants loans for the purpose of building, modern- izing, business adjustment, ener- gy economizing and environmental protection to small and medium sized industry. Amortization period: 15-20 years	

130

ORGANISATION	NATURE OF ORGANISATION	SOFTWARE			HARDWARE	
		Information/ Advice	Counselling/ Consulting	Training & Education	Finance	Other
HANDVERK OG SMA-INDUSTRI-FONDET A/S DEN NORSKE INDUSTRIBANK, Akersgt. 13, Oslo 1 Tel: 47.2.429180	*Fund for Handi-crafts and Small-scale Industry				*This fund for small industry and crafts grants guarantees and loans in the regions that are not covered by DU. The task is to participate in financing, ra-tionalizing and growth for small industry. The fund offers top financing after other finance possibilities are exhausted. Loans and guarantees usually cover 40-45% of estimated costs. Amorti-zation: 15-18 years	
INDUSTRIFONDET, Skippergt. 31, Oslo 1 Tel: 47.2.426730	*Fund for Indus-trial Growth *Credit Institution				*Gives financial support to the development of Norwegian indus-try and to strengthen its competitivity through a range of specified means	
EKSPORTFINANS, Dronning Maudsgt. 1-3, Oslo 1 Tel: 47.2.425960	*Export Finance *Credit Institution				*See special section: Exports	
GARANTIINSTI-TUTTET FOR EKSPORTKREDITT, Dronning Maudsgt. 1-3, Oslo 1 Tel: 47.2.205140	*Norwegian Guarantee Insti-tute for Export *Credit Institution				*See special section: Exports	
SELSKAPET FOR INDUSTRIVE-KSTANLEGG (SIVA), Eirik Jarlsgt. 6 7000 Trondheim Tel: 47.75.27530	*Industrial Estates Corporation *Builds and runs buildings for local new industry *Government institution.				*Builds and runs buildings for new and local enter-prises at a low rent due to special financing	
COMMERCIAL & SAVINGS BANKS	*Number of commercial banks: 22, savings banks: 308	*Advise on sources of finance. Some have special de-partments for small business service			*The banks supply current account and short and long time loans	

131

ORGANISATION	NATURE OF ORGANISATION	SOFTWARE			HARDWARE	
		Information/ Advice	Counselling/ Consulting	Training & Education	Finance	Other
NORGES INDUS-TRIFORBUND (NI), Drammensvn. 40, Oslo 2 Tel: 47.2.564390	*Federation of Norwegian Industries *Besides being an interest organi-zation, NI pro-vides individual service to its members on legal matters, economy, environmental protection, oil questions, re-sources, educa-tion and exports *NI works through a net of region-al associations which take care of regional interests and service	*NI has a special department for small industry, giving advice and service				
NORSK ARBEIDS-GIVERFORENING, (NAF), Kr. Augustsgt. 23, Oslo 1 Tel: 47.2.202550	*Norwegian Em-poloyers Con-federation *NAF is an organi-zation especially directed to em-ployers negoti-ating with labour unions about wages and working conditions. *NAF gives various service ot its members	*NAF advises its members about production effi-ciency, admini-strative and eco-nomic analysis and planning, organization de-velopment, occu-pational hygiene and medicine, welfare and en-vironmental questions		*NAF offers a wide range of courses		
NORGES HAND-VERKERFORBUND, (NHF), Rosenkrantzgt. 7, Oslo 1 Tel: 47.2.423120	*Norwegian Feder-ation of Craft Enterprise *Promotes local interest for mem-bers and gives service through 120 local craft industry associ-ations in 19 countries *30 branch organi-zations are associated through their own association, giving infor-mation and tech-nical advice	*NHF advises par-ticularly on fi-nance, organi-zation and marketing				

132

ORGANISATION	NATURE OF ORGANISATION	SOFTWARE			HARDWARE	
		Information/ Advice	Counselling/ Consulting	Training & Education	Finance	Other
STATENS TEKNOLO-GISKE INSTITUTT (STI), Akersvn. 24 C, Oslo 1 Tel: 47.2.244550 50	*National Institute of Technology of Norway *A government sponsored institute designed to provide theoretical and practical backup services for Norwegian industry with an emphasis on small and medium-sized firms. These services fall into three main categories: Consulting and advice, specialised courses, research and testing *STI offers its services through 14 regional offices in central and southern Norway	*Gives advice and information	*Provides consulting services	*STI is the largest organiser of technical courses in Norway and in addition, offers a wide range of courses in the fields of management and economics *The institute offers some 600 courses annually: which are attened by about 8000 people. Course for vocational school teachers are also arranged		
NORSK PRODUK-TIVITETS-INSTITUTT (NPI), Akersgt. 64, Oslo 1 Tel: 47.2.209475	*The Norwegian Productivity Institute *The aim of the NPI is to increase productivity in the Norwegian economy to the best advantage of consumers, employees and owners *NPI is an independent institute with 27 employees and a budget of 9 mill. Nkr. (1984). The institute's funds are granted by government	*Gives information about ideas and tools which can improve productivity *Clarifies productivity problems and the need for ventures to promote productivity, record and assess methods and disseminate information from abroad which can assist productivity work in Norway				
SENIOR SERVICE A/S, Rosenkrantzgt. 7 Oslo 1 Tel: 47.2.335720	*Senior Service Ltd. *Retired business leaders available for guidance of small industry.	*Function as discussion partners and advisers for small business on technology and economy. The advisers are recruited among retired business leaders				
STATENS VEILED-NINGS-INSTITUTT FOR INDUSTRIEN I NORD-NORGE (VINN), Lodve Langesgt. 2 8500 Narvik Tel: 47.82.44180	*National Industrial Institute of Northern Norway *Supports industry and economic life in Northern Norway *There are also other special industrial development institutes for the North e.g. The Industry Project Group for Northern Norway & The Association for the Study of North Norwegian Industry			*Offer education with focus on practical problems, undertaking research and development projects		

133

ORGANISATION	NATURE OF ORGANISATION	SOFTWARE			HARDWARE	
		Information/ Advice	Counselling/ Consulting	Training & Education	Finance	Other
UTVIKLINGSSEL- SKAPET FOR NARINGSLIV PA VESTLANDET (UNV), Fantoftvegen 18 5036 Fantoft Tel: 47.5.285405	*Industrial De- velopment Associ- ation for Western Norway. Coordin- ates the INKO service and Senior Service in this part of the country	*Gives infor- mation, advice and makes con- tacts for the members	*Provides consul- tative service			
NAERINGSRAD, Not centralized (can be reached through INKO).	*Local boards for industry and trade *Naeringsrad is a coordinating type of local organi- zation for de- velopment of local industry	*Helps local business to find information sources. Promotes projects of mutual interest within the community				
BRANCH ASSOCIATIONS	*Provide infor- mation mainly to members	*Inform and advise members				
RADET FOR INDUS- TRIAL DESIGN (RID), Uranienborgvn. 2 Oslo 2 Tel: 47.2.566968	*Council for In- dustrial Design *RID is a founda- tion with the aim of encouraging product innova- tion and design		*Judges possi- bilities for new products or product improve- ments			*Offer practical and financial support to companies who wish to explore new product ideas
RADGIVENDE INGENIORERS SERVICE-KONTOR (RIF), Akersgt. 15 Oslo 1 Tel: 47.2.333240	*The Service Bureau of Advis- ory Engineers *Private advisory engineers availa- ble for small industries		*Give technical consultative service			
NORSK FORENING AV RADGIVERE FOR BEDRIFTSLEDELSE, (NFRB), Sandviksvn. 2 B, 1322 Hovik Tel: 47.2.532990	*Norwegian Society of Advisory Engineers *NFRB is an association of private consult- ants consulting to industry		*Advising and if necessary doing jobs the compan- ies do not have competence or capacity to do themselves within the administra- tive and organi- zational field			
NORGES TEKNISK- NATURVITEN- SKAPELIGE FORSK- NINGSRAD (NTNF), Sognsveien 72 0855 Oslo 8 Tel: 47.2.237685	*The Royal Norwegian Council for Scientific and Industrial Research *NTNF is a large scientific organization serving industry				*Giving financial support to research and de- veloping projects in industry	
NORGES EKSPORTRAD, Drammensvn. 40, Oslo 2 Tel: 47.2.114030	*The Export Council of Norway *A service organ- isation promoting Norwegian goods, services and know-how abroad	*For details, see special section: Exports	*Advises and cousels Norwegian exporters. Analyzes export possibilities for different products			

134

ORGANISATION	NATURE OF ORGANISATION	SOFTWARE			HARDWARE	
		Information/ Advice	Counselling/ Consulting	Training & Education	Finance	Other
NORGES EKSPORTSKOLE Drammensvn. 40, Oslo 2 Tel: 47.2.114030	*Norwegian Institute of Export Education *A non-profit organization, whose aim is to cover the need of special education through export courses, seminars, conferences and study groups, as well as creating contact between the exporters	*For details, see special section: Exports				

		Information/ Advice	Counselling/ Consulting	Training & Education	Finance	Other
NORGES EKSPORTSKOLE Drammensvn. 40, Oslo 2	*Norwegian Institute of Export Education *A non-profit					

Portugal

Materials prepared by

Antonio Lopes Paulo and Luis Palma Feria
IAPMEI, Lisbon

PORTUGAL

Population: 9.8 million
Area: 91,632 sq. km.

Of the Portuguese labour force of 4.2 million, 1.6 million is employed in industry (36.3%). The official definition of small and medium sized industries includes those with a labour force of between 6 and 500 workers; within this definition, however, no distinction is made between small firms and medium ones. In 1981, some 520,000 (33.6%) of those working in industry were employed in companies with 5 - 399 employees and a further 20,123 in companies employing less than 5.

An economic policy for small and medium industry was first introduced in Portugal in 1974: since that time it has been updated on approximately an annual basis. Principal objectives of the policy are: restructuring, modernisation and development of SMEs (particularly in view of Portugal's entry into the EEC); promotion of SME support structures (technical assistance, counselling and consulting, sub-contracting centres, etc.); management improvement (training, information, etc.); and on-going economic policy improvement (through the revision and improvement of existing tools).

One important component of the early economic policy was the establishment in 1975, of the Instituto de Apoio as Pequenas e Medias Empresas Industriais - (IAPMEI - the Institute for the Support of Small and Medium Industries), a public institute responsible to the Ministry for Industry and Energy. IAPMEI studies and promotes the execution of measures making up the policy of support to SMEs acting as a catalyst of a national network of SME support including the banks, the Labour Ministry, the Board of Trade, professional associations and other national organisations especially those of the same Ministry. IAPMEI provides both services at a national level (policy review, coordination with other Government agencies and the banks, international representation, etc.) and at a regional and local level. Regionally, IAPMEI has divided the country into three areas each of which has its own autonomous headquarters in line with decentralisation objectives. Through the regional offices, advice, start-up assistance, consulting, and training are offered and, as well, a number of financial measures are made available (guarantees, preferential interest rates, non-repayable loans, etc.).

Additional software services are provided through a number of industry associations and, in addition, IAPMEI sub-contracts a number of its training programmes to organisations such as COPRAI (the Productivity Department of the Portuguese Industrial Association), CIFAG (Centre for Management Training of the IPE Instituto das Participacoes do Estado) and others. Operative training courses are available through a number of local centres of the IEFP (Institute for Training and Employment). Important in the financial support area are two special credit institutions, the Caixa Geral de Depositos and the Banco de Fomento Nacional, Portugal's main development banks.

ORGANISATION	NATURE OF ORGANISATION	SOFTWARE			HARDWARE	
		Information/ Advice	Counselling/ Consulting	Training & Education	Finance	Other
INSTITUTO DE A-POIO AS PEQUE-NAS E MEDIAS EM-PRESAS INDUSTRI-AIS (IAPMEI), Rue Rodrigo da Fonseca, 73 1297 Lisboa Codex Tel: 351.1.5622 11 351.1.561447 351.1.560688	*The Institute for the Support of Small and Medium Industries *Government De-partment depend-ing on the Ministry for Industry and Energy *Founded in 1975, has a staff of 219 members and accounts with a budget of 6.6 million U.S. dollars. 1984 *Has 9 regional branches through the country	*Operates a Ques-tion-and-Answer Service on tech-nical subjects *Searches techni-cal literature on request *Maintains compre-hensive files on Protuguese manufacturers and their products *Publishes a quarterly review *Provides a service for selective dis-semination of technical information	*Offers techni-cal advice on production or-ganization and technology through its own staff, disposing also of a board of private specialists ready to advise firms in different branches, e.g. metallurgy, textiles, plas-tics, chemicals, welding, etc. *Provides an aftercare service to newly and already estab-lished grant aided SMI *Offers technical advice on market-ing both through its own staff and a body of private special-ists ready to advise firms on different matters *Helps SMI in marketing research *Promotes and supports joint export marketing groups of firms *Offers techni-cal advice on several aspects of start-up projects *Analyses start-up projects on a regional basis for smaller projects and at headquarters for larger ones *Promotes start-up contests in cooperation with "Caixa Geral de Depositos" in order to stimu-late the creation of new enter-prises in the Portuguese light industry *Promotes and supports other cooperation schemes among firms, such as mergers, groups for buying, selling, etc. *Gives technical support to the industrial associations	*Promotes the idea of train-into to Indus-trial Profes-sional Associ-ations, assist-ing them in organizing courses and seminars *Has a special programme for the training of fresh graduates to pre-pare them to admission in SMI after a stage of 6 months free-of-charge in the firms *Promotes market-ing courses for SMI managers	*Provides grants towards the cost of management and supervisory training in SMI *Helps the SMI in developing new products and financing the prototypes *Financial aid in the sharing of expenses by means of non-repayable loans, for specific actions in In particular: -Execution of technological research projects -Implementation, modernization & increase of productivity -Vocational training, re-fresher and reconversion courses *Financial aid in the sharing of expenses by means of non-repayable loans for specific actions in particular: -The carrying out of market sur-veys and of feasibility and financial studies -The participation of small and medium sized companies in fairs and exhibitions -The providing of guarantees for financing for working capital, wherever the guarantees given by the small and medium sized companies are considered in-sufficient by the Banks and the operation is recognized as being important -Gives grants towards exports such as market research, sales promotion, cost of product de-sign, etc. -Provides finan-cial help to start-up joint export working groups	*Mobile techno-logical Units prepared for testing raw materials and products in several sectors, such as: -Foundry -Shoeware -Ceramics *Audio-visual centers, located in several re-gions, prepared for training and information activities, available for the Industrial Associ-ations and SMIs (7 units) *Financial Manage-ment Accountancy Centers, located in the "hinter-land," in order to provide low-cost services in this field to SMI (3 centers) to be launched in the short term *Technological research projects *Creation of prototypes and preparation of new products *Energy Savings Mobile Unit - a laboratory prepared to test, on the field, the energy losses of SMI

ORGANISATION	NATURE OF ORGANISATION	SOFTWARE			HARDWARE	
		Information/ Advice	Counselling/ Consulting	Training & Education	Finance	Other
IAPMEI (continued)			*Has technological links with LNETI to help the development of new products		*Provides guarantees for financing investment operations either in fixed assets or in working capital *Preferential interest rates for the financing of prior investments *Financial aid in the form of sharing of expenses by means of non-repayable loans for specific actions such as the short management courses for new entrepreneurs	
LABORATORIO NACIONAL DE ENGENHARIA E TECNOLOGIA INDUSTRIAL (LNETI), Rua de S. Pedro de Alcantara, 79 1200 Lisboa Tel: 351.1.3688 56	*National Laboratory for Industrial Engineering and Technology *LNETI was created in 1977 depending - as a personalized institute - on the Ministry for Industry and Technology. It had regrouped numerous public Laboratories; two main Institutes predomin within LNETI: Energy Institute and Industrial Technology Institute (IE and IT)	*Manages a Center for Technological Information, specially devoted to the dissemination of new technologies	*Assists Industries in technological aspects processes and equipments, through its laboratories *Provides services in the technical design and development of new products equipment and processes *Manages several programs for technological innovation	*Offers a large range of management and technological training the main part of them suited to SMI LNETI runs a specific training Department using its own lecturers either subcontracting courses and seminars to private specialized consultants		*Laboratories, pilot-scale equipment and other machinery (computer-aided design equipment, etc.) are often made available to the SMI staff training *Seminar rooms with support facilities are rented at low rates to industrial associations and other professional bodies
CENTRO PARA O DESENVOLVIMENTO E INOVACAO TECNOLOGICA (CEDINTEC), Rua de S. Pedro de Alcantara 79 1200 Lisboa Tel: 351.1.3688 56	*Government Department depending on the Ministry for Industry and Energy	*Provides a service on development of new products, equipment and processes in some industrial branches and coordinates technological centers				
JUNTA NACIONAL DE INVESTIGACAO CIENTIFICA E TECNICA (JNICT), Av. D. Carlos 1, 126 1200 Lisboa Tel: 351.1.6710 44	*National Organization for Scientific and Technological Research *Government Department depending on the Minister of State	*Coordination of the national R, D&D activities *Department specialized in new products research, in order to produce successful goods to the market *Aid-programmes for innovation				
DIRECCAO-GERAL DA QUALIDADE (DGQ), Rua Jose Estevao 83-a/c 1190 Lisboa Tel: 351.1.5398 91	*General Directorate for Quality *Government Department depending on the Ministry for Industry and Energy	*Promotes the appreciate and application of quality in industries and services through qualifications, standards, and certification *Has a service for design promotion				

140

ORGANISATION	NATURE OF ORGANISATION	SOFTWARE			HARDWARE	
		Information/ Advice	Counselling/ Consulting	Training & Education	Finance	Other
DIRECCAO-GERAL DA ENERGIA (DGE), Rua de Beneficcencia 741 1600 Lisboa Tel: 351.1.7710 13	*General Directorate for Energy *Government Department depending on the Ministry for Industry and Energy head- quarters in Lisbon responsi- ble for the definition of the energy policy in the country. It assures the supplies and promotes the rational utili- zation of energy. It is liable for sectorial legislation	*Provides Infor- mation on energy management *Provides infor- mation through leaflets, book- lets and placards *Advertises on Radio and TV *Promotes direct actions near the customers	*Analyses the conditions of energy utiliza- zation in the firms *Proposes changes aiming the rational consump- tion of energy *Carries out audits and analysis of pro- jects related with the energy savings		*Fiscal and fi- nancial incen- tives for energy conservation and diversification projects *Non-repayable grants for R, D&D projects in the field of re- newable energy	
DIRECCAO-GERAL DA INDUSTRIA (DGI), Av. Conselheiro Fernanco de Sousa, 11 1000 Lisboa Tel: 351.1.5691 61	*General Directorate for Industry *Government Department depending on the Ministry for Industry and Energy	*Proposes the basic orientation about the strategies of industrial growth *Proposes the necessary measures for the promotion of new Industries and for the growth and modernization of the production processes *Participates in the organization and coordination of industrial information *Coordinates the links between the national system of industrial infor- mation and the international ones *Cares about the balance of the intersectorial relationship *Elaborates studies on branches in crisis proposing concrete structural changes				
LABORATORIO NACIONAL DE ENGENHARIA CIVIL (LNEC), Av. do Brasil 101 1700 Lisboa Tel: 351.1.8821 31	*Public Department depending on the Ministry for Housing and Public Works, devoted to research on housing construc- tion materials, as well as dams, bridges, etc. *The Laboratory was created in 1946	*Runs a very developed infor- mation Center on the several matters which constitute the aims of the organization	*Provides infor- mation and counselling on technical speci- fications and standards related with all con- structions and housing materials *Provides tests and analysis on raw and finished materials and runs a special work-shop for the experimentation of prototypes and new products *Certified the quality and ade- quacy for con- struction In- dutry products	*Runs a training department devoted to the realization of courses and semi- nars related to the aims of the Laboratory		

141

ORGANISATION	NATURE OF ORGANISATION	SOFTWARE			HARDWARE	
		Information/ Advice	Counselling/ Consulting	Training & Education	Finance	Other
INSTITUTO DE EMPREGO E FORMACAO PROFISSIONAL (IEFP), Rua das Picoas, 14 1000 Lisboa Tel: 351.1.5638 01	*Institute for the Employment and professional Training - Labour and Social Security Ministry *Created in 1982, succeeding to the former General Direc- torate for Em- ployment and joining together some other insti- tutions of the Secretary of State for Employ- ment and Profes- sional Training	*Information on offer and demand of jobs, at all levels		*Professional training courses at the regional centers dissemi- nated by the country and de- voted to skilled and non-skilled labour *Special programs for training of fresh graduates to prepare them to recruitment by SMI's (six months free of charge to firms and wages paid by IEFP and IAPMEI; the program is con- ducted jointly by the two Institutes	*Provides grants to firms in specific training sections *Provides loans (with no inter- est) for the keeping of jobs in SMI under deep economic difficulties *Provides grants for the creation of new jobs	
INSTITUTO DE COMERCIO EXTERNO DE PORTUGAL (ICEP), Av. 5 de Outubro 101 1000 Lisboa Tel: 351.1.7301 03 351.1.734420 351.1.775498	*Portuguese Board of Trade *Government Department de- pending on the Ministry for Trade and Tourism responsible for the execution of the external trade policies under this name since 1982; 400 staff members	*Provides marketing information and advice on all aspects of overseas markets (e.g. size, prices, quality, distribution, etc.) *Organizes liaison with potential cutomers or agents, display facili- ties, interpreter service, etc. *Produces export market reports and surveys and operates a computerized marketing information service *Provides credit-ratings, size and reports on prospective customers *Advises on product design and selection contracting qualified designers *Promotes joint export marketing groups of firms *Organizes and supports commercial missions to international fairs and exhibitions *Market surveys *Data bank on Portuguese exporting companies *Assists exporting firms in the different domains of inter- national trade *Negociates economic agreements of cooperation with other countries			*Financial sup- port to the participation of companies in ex- hibitions abroad *Grants for export missions abroad and foreign trading missions in Portugal *Guarantees the banking credit to investment pro- jects devoted to exporting goods and equipment	*Delegations in several countries to promote Portuguese exports
INSTITUICOES ESPECIAIS DE CREDITO	*Nationalized Investment Banks *Special Credit Institutions	*General infor- mation about special schemes of credit, new markets, etc.	*May give own counselling or consultancy services in the field or turn- arounds	*Seminars and meetings for managers and staff of SMI	*The main attri- butions of these Institutions are the award of medium and long term industrial credit *Special loan schemes	
CAIXA GERAL DE DEPOSITOS (CGD), Largo do Calhariz, 20 1200 Lisboa Tel: 351.1.3502 46	*The biggest Portuguese Bank specializing in investment operations	*Advice and infor- mation services. Specialized information booklets *Promotion of special schemes of credit for SMI *Promoted start-up contests in cooperation with IAPMEI, in order to stimulate the creation of new enterprises			*Provides loans for financing investment operations *Preferential interest rates for the financing of priority start-up projects namely those of the IAPMEI/CGD projects contests	

ORGANISATION	NATURE OF ORGANISATION	SOFTWARE			HARDWARE	
		Information/ Advice	Counselling/ Consulting	Training & Education	Finance	Other
BANCO DE FOMENTO NACIONAL (BFN), Av. Casal Ribeiro, 59 1000 Lisboa Tel: 351.1.5222 79 351.1.523419	*Development Investment Bank	*Advice and information services. Specialized information booklets *Promotion of special schemes of credit for SMI			*Provides loans for financing investment operations *Preferential interest rates for the financing of Quality Control Invest- ments, in co- operation with CGD and IAPMEI	
BANCOS COMERCIAIS	*Commercial Banks *Nationalized Banks	*Advice and information services. Specialized information booklets *Promotion of special schemes of credit for SMI		*Organization of seminars and meetings for managers and technicians of of small and medium industries	*Short and medium/ long term credit *Some special loan schemes *Operation of loan guarantees schemes with IAPMEI *Bonifications on interest rates for SMI	
CENTRO DE INFORMACAO FORMACAO E APERFEICOAMENTO EM GESTAO (CIFAG), Av. Julio Dinis 11 1000 Lisboa Tel: 351.1.7315 87	*Information and Training Center for Management *Department of IPE (holding of the equity participations from the Govern- ment). This de- partment--CIFAG-- is devoted to training and information in management. It was founded in 1978, has a staff of 25 members, an annual budget of about USD 460,000. Its activity is about 50% devoted to SMI. Covers the all national territory	*Runs and infor- mation Center on Management, pro- viding documen- tation and know- ledge on its particular areas of specialization	*Provides coun- selling and consultancy to the participated companies on management matters	*Offers a wide selection of management train- ing and develop- ment programs, directed to an improvement in the performances of the companies' top and middle management	*The capacity for equity partici- pation in all kinds of indus- trail firms (de- velopment invest- ments) lies at the Institute for Equity Partici- pation--IPE, on which CIFAG depends	
INSTITUTO DE PARTICIPACOES DO ESTADO (IPE), Av. Julio Dinis 11 Tel: 351.1.7315 87	*Institute for Equity Participation *Corporation, mixed capital				*Equity partici- pations (risk capital) in new created companies presenting inno- vative technolo- gies or new products	
INSTITUTO DO INVESTIMENTO ESTRANGEIRO (IIE), Av. da Liberdate 258 1200 Lisboa Tel: 351.1.5580 53	*Foreign Investment Institute *Public Institute reporting to the Ministry for Finance and Planning	*Gives advice and Information to potential foreign entre- preneurs, con- cerning the global fulfill- ment of their investment intentions *Provides full information about the legal re- quests for foreign invest- ment in the country, concern- ing namely the accuracy of technology trans- fers and licencing	*Analysis and appraises the investment pro- jects promoted by foreign investors *After authoriza- tion, gives immediate access to the import of funds and further repatriation of profits or capital *Advises the different part- ners (concerning joint-ventures or licencing) about the risks of the contracts to be signed			

ORGANISATION	NATURE OF ORGANISATION	SOFTWARE			HARDWARE	
		Information/ Advice	Counselling/ Consulting	Training & Education	Finance	Other
INSTITUTO DE SOLDADURA (IS), Rua Tomas Fique- iredo, 16-A-r/c 1500 Lisboa Tel: 351.1.7075 82	*Welding Institute *Industrial Professional Association	*Provides technical assistance and laboratory facilities in welding				
CENTROS DE SUBCONTRATACAO SUBNOR (Norte de Portugal) BSC (Centro de Portugal) BSS (Sul de Portugal), Praca das Industrias 1300 Lisboa	*Subcontracting Centres -SUBNOR (North of Portugal) -BSC (Center of Portugal) -BSS (South of Portugal) *Specific Depart- ments of the Industrial Associations which have the support of the Ministry for Industry and Energy through the Institute for the support of Small and Medium Industries	*The essential aim of these organizations is to make the inventory of the existing means and potentiali- ties, acting as an intermediary in the subcontracting relationships, including export trade *To achieve this purpose, they assist their adherents in the technological and organizational areas in order to help them in offering quality, prompt deliveries and competitive prices				
CENTRO DE APOIO TECNOLOGICO A INDUSTRIA METALOMECANICA (CATIM), Rua do Rio 4200 Porto Tel: 351.1.4819 49	*Center for Technological Support of Metallic Industry *Industrial Professional Association	*Provides technical assistance and offers laboratory facilities to metallic industry				
CENTRO NACIONAL DE EMBALAGEM (CNE), Rua do Telhal.37 Matinha 1900 Lisboa Tel: 351.1.38599 12	*National Center of Packing *Industrial Professional Association	*Provides technical assistance and laboratory facilities in packing				
CENTRO DE FORMACAO PROFISSIONAL DA INDUSTRIA DO CALCADO (CFPIC), Apartado 13 3701 S. Joao da Madeira Tel: 351.1.26151 2/3/4	*Professional Training Center of Shoe Industry *Industrial Professional Association	*Provides technological assistance and offers laboratory facilities in shoe industry				
CENTRO TECNOLOGICO DA CERAMICA E DO VIDRO (CTCV), Rua da Ceramica Lusitania 3000 Coimbra Tel: 351.1.34347	*Technological Center of Ceramics and Glass *Industrial Professional Association	*Provides technological assistance and offers laboratory facilities to Ceramics Industry				
CENTROS TECNICOS DE UNIVERSIDADES PORTUGUESAS	*Technical Centers of Portuguese Universities *Universities depending on the Ministry for Education	*Development of prototypes and making of tests with new products				

ORGANISATION	NATURE OF ORGANISATION	SOFTWARE			HARDWARE	
		Information/ Advice	Counselling/ Consulting	Training & Education	Finance	Other
COMPANHIA DE SEGUROS DE CREDITO, EP (COSEC), Av. da Republica 58 1000 Lisboa Tel: 351.1.7601 31	*Company of the Credit Insurance *Public Enter- prise devoted to all kinds of credit insurance, mainly for the export markets	*Promotion of the Credit Insurance concept and procedures, its advantages and difficulties in order to optimize the effects of ex- ports, minimizing the respective risks	*Advice on the clients of the SMI in order to avoid the unsuccess of business in the home market and abroad	*Training and information activities (meetings) for industrialists and exporters in order to spread the concept of credit insurance	*Credit insurance either for internal opera- tions, either for export ones	

145

Spain

Materials prepared by

Manuel Ludevid and Montse Olle
Escuela Superior de
Administracion, y
Direccion de Empresas
Esade, Barcelona

SPAIN

Population: 37.5 million
Area: 504,783 sq.km.

In Spain, some 38% of the labour force employed in manufacturing in small firms with fewer than 50 employees and a further 37% in firms with between 50 and 499 employees.

While a formal small business policy has yet to be articulated, the Minister of Industry and Energy recently stated that "the definition and application of a small and medium business policy...is one of the main pillows upon which we shall rest the reindustrialisation process....". Towards this end, the Government appears to be laying particular stress on: priority SME financing; an improved range of software services to be administered by the 18 autonomous communities within Spain - these have been gradually restored since 1978, but with varying degrees of administrative and political responsibility: start-ups; better service coordination among the various service deliverers - coordination between IMPI (see below), the Employers Association and others is apparently in need of some improvement; and, an improved coordination of the Ministry of Industry's own small and medium business agencies.

As indicated above, the Ministry of Industry and Energy plays a major role in SME support at the national and regional level. Its small business institute, IMPI (a self governing state agency) offers information and advisory services; training and education (through the subsidization of management courses organised by trade and industry associations and the Chambers of Commerce and the running of its own TAGE - Applied Management Techniques - courses); and various forms of financial assistance including interest rate reduction on certain types of investment/innovation projects, participation in mutual fund societies and technical innovation project participation. In addition, the CDTI (Centre for Industrial and Technological Development) which specialises in technological information, international trade fair representation and the financing of R&D and venture capital companies and the Industrial Credit Bank which offers special credit schemes for small firms are both responsible to the Ministry of Industry. The Ministry of Economics, Treasury and Commerce also plays a role particularly through IRESCO (Institute for the Reform of Business Structures) which offers information and advice and credit cost subsidies and INFE (The National Export Promotion Institute). In addition, the National Employment Office (INEM) offers assistance through schemes to promote job creation and the employment of temporary help.

148

Other financial support is provided at offices of the Ministry of Treasury, the Branch offices of Espana (a primarily public bank), the commercial banks and the mutual fund societies. Additional support is provided by the Spanish Employers' Association, CEOE, and CEPYME, a member organisation of CEOE, but especially serving a SME membership. Some of the private management schools are also playing an increasing role in specialist small firm training.

Regional level support is provided through various institutions of the autonomous communities (support is particularly of a financial nature and varies from one community to another); the provincial offices of IMPI, CDTI, BCI, INFI and IRESCO; the industry associations and the Chambers of Commerce.

...ATION		SOFTWARE			HARDWARE	
		Information/ Advice	Counselling/ Consulting	Training & Education	Finance	Other
INSTITUTO DE LA MEDIANA Y PEQUENA EMPRESA INDUSTRIAL (IMPI), Balmes 89-91, 5°, 7°, Barcelona Tel: 34.93.254160 04 & P° de la Castellana, 141 Madrid 28046 Tel: 34.91.27967 23	*Institute of Small & Medium Enterprise *Self-governing state agency. Dependency of the Ministry of Industry	*Information and advice on finan- cial, techno- logical and training assis- tance available to small business firms	*Participates in joint marketing action abroad (advice, techni- cal assistance, minority partici- pation in company capital up to 45% for 3 years, re- newable for 3 additional years	*Subsidizes management courses organ- ized by trade associations, em- ployers' associa- tions and the Chamber of Commerce -TAGE (Tecnicas Aplicadas a la Gestion Empresarial) -Courses on specific subjects -Seminars -Roundtable discussions	*Reduction of up to 3 interest points on cer- tain small business investments *Participates in capital by means of collective shares *Participates in mutual fund societies *Reduction of up to 3 points interest on loans destined for technological innovation *Participates in projects with technological innovation firms	
INSTITUTO DE REFORMA DE LAS ESTRUCTURAS COMERCIALES (IRESCO), Orene 4, 4° Madrid 28020 Tel: 34.91.45596 23	*Institute for the reform of Commercial Structures *Self-governing state agency. Dependency of the Ministry of Economy and the Treasury	*Information and advice on fi- nancial, tech- nological and training assis- tance available to small business firms			*Subsidies de- signed to reduce the cost of credits re- quired to im- prove produc- tivity and rationalize oper- ations. Destined for commercial operations	
CENTRO PARA EL DESARROLLO TECNOLOGICO E INDUSTRIAL (CDTI), R. Avellano, s/n Madrid 28043 Tel: 34.91.41314 59	*Centre for Technological & Industrial Development *Public agency, dependency of the Ministry of Industry	*Technological information	*Organizes employers pre- sence in inter- national trade & technological fairs		*Finances research and development projects. Offers financing to capital venture companies *Participates in projects de- veloped by tech- nological inno- vation associ- ations. The amount of assis- tance is usually between 45-60% of the cost of the project, which must be of technological and commercial interest. The assistance is repaid with a percentage of the	Finance cont: sales of the new product. If the project is a failure, CDTI recovers only those costs spent on pur- chasing equipment. The remainder is then considered a non-refundable subsidy
PROGRAMA DE ORGANIZACION Y GESTION DE LA INVESTIGACION (OGEIN) Plaza de Salamanca 8 28020 Madrid Tel: 34.91.40233 99	*The Public Cor- poration Foun- dation. Depen- pendency of the National Insti- tute of Industry			*Organizes courses courses to im- prove the opera- tions of business research units and assist in devising business strategy and technological policy		

ORGANISATION	NATURE OF ORGANISATION	SOFTWARE			HARDWARE	
		Information/ Advice	Counselling/ Consulting	Training & Education	Finance	Other
COMISION ASESORA DE INVESTIGACION CIENTIFICA Y TECNICA (CAICYT), Rosario Pino 14-16, Madrid 28021 Tel: 34.91.45005 02	*Commission for scientific & technical investigation *Consultant to public administration on matters of research *Dependency of the Office of the President of the Government	*Information and advice on establishing Agreed Research Plans with business firms			*Agreed basic and applied research plans with business firms. The amount of assistance may be up to 50% of the funds budgeted for the research project by the company. Interest-free loans, generally to be repaid in 5 years. If the research proves commercially unfeasible, the subsidy is considered a non-refundable grant	Finance Cont. *Should an Official Research Center provide 60% of the project's financing, CAICYT assistance can be as high as 80% and will take the form of an interest-free loan to be repaid in 8 years
INSTITUTO NACIONAL DE EMPLEO (INEM), Breton de los Herreros 41, Madrid 28003 Tel: 34.91.44115 00	*National employment office *Dependency of the Ministry of Labor			*45% reduction in Social Security costs per worker for companies employing apprentices and trainees. 38.52% of the reduction is on the company's quota and the reduction is on the company's quota and the remaining 6.75% is on the amount paid by the employee for Social Security		*A number of special programmes to stimulate temporary employment e.g. -Apprenticeship contracts: 45% reduction in Social Security payments for employees under the age of 28 who are contracted for between 3 and 12 months -Hiring of workers ineligible for unemployment benefits or with family responsibilities: °Length of the contract: Up to one year; °Exemption: 50% from the employer's fees for Social Security; °Length of the contract: Up to two years; °Exemption: 50% the first year and 75% the second year *The smaller the company staff, the better the chances to employ temporary help (contract ranging from 6 months to 2 years) For example: -Companies with 251-500 employees: may employ temporary help up to an equivalent of 15% of the permanent staff -Companies with 26-50 employees: may employ temporary help up to an equivalent of 40% of the permanent staff

151

ORGANISATION	NATURE OF ORGANISATION	SOFTWARE			HARDWARE	
		Information/ Advice	Counselling/ Consulting	Training & Education	Finance	Other
SOCIEDADES DE DESARROLLO INDUSTRIAL (SODI)	*Public societies for business development (particularly in the depressed areas of Spain)				*Guarantees credits made to member firms *Up to 45% capital participation	
DELEGACION PROVINCIAL DEL MINISTERIO DE HACIENDA	*Branch offices of the Ministry of Treasury *Range of financial support measures				*Reductions on corporate taxes: -12-15% tax deduction on investments in new fixed assets (up to a limit equal to 30% of the taxes due) -10% deduction for foreign investments (up to a limit equal to 20% of the taxes due). *Corporate tax reliefs: 15% tax deduction on investments in R. & D. programs, up to a limit of 25% of total investment *10% reduction in corporate taxes in the event of: -opening new establishments or branches (minimum participation: 25%) or participation in foreign companies -Cost of advertising, promotion and exhibition at trade fairs: up to 20% of the cost *Assistance for industrial reconversion -99% reduction on Property Transfer Taxes and Legalized Contracts involving taxes on loans, and capital increases destined for investments in new fixes assets. -99% reduction on General Sales Tax, customs duties and import taxes on first-time import of investment goods not manufactured in Spain -Flexible pay-off times in accordance with special plans: Law on Personal Income Taxes (44/1978) and the Law on Corporate Taxes (61/1978)	Finance Cont. -15% deduction on corporate taxes (up to a maximum of 40% of taxable income, with the rest deductible over a period of 4 years) on: °investments in new fixed assets °research costs °costs of promoting exports -Tax benefits in the event of merger (Law 76/1980 - Corporate Merger Taxation Bill) -Installment payment or deferred payment of outstanding taxes -Exemption from Operating Tax on activities covered by the Law 82/80 on energy conservation measures during a period of 5 years -Subsidy of up to 30% of research investments. -Preferential access to official credits -Expropriation of the property and right necessary to install or enlarge solar energy installations -95% reduction in sales tax, customs duties and import taxes on goods not manufactured in Spain

152

ORGANISATION	NATURE OF ORGANISATION	SOFTWARE			HARDWARE	
		Information/ Advice	Counselling/ Consulting	Training & Education	Finance	Other
GENERALITAT DE CATALUNYA Palau de la Generalitat Departament de Presidencia Plca Sant Jaume 08002 Barcelona Tel: 34.93.31719 32	*Catalan Government				*Promotes Mutual Guarantee Funds by providing up to 50 million pts. in its capa- city as Sponsor- ing Member. Terms that the Mutual be active in Catalonia, have a minimum of 200 participating members, that the Generalitat's do- nation not exceed 25% of the total membership fees paid by the participating members and the other sponsoring members	
COMISSIO INTER DEPARTAMENTAL D'INVESTIGACIO I INNOVACIO TECNOLOGICA (CIRIT), Urgell 240, 7e Barcelona 08036 Tel: 34.93.32126 46	*Interdepartmental commission for technological innovation *Catalan version of the CDTI Dependency of the Department of Industry and Energy of the Generalitat de Catalunya				*Total and partial subsidies for technological innovation projects: -That increase or help increase the technological level and equipment in Catalonia -That create infrastructures for services to facilitate technological innovation	Finance Cont. *CIRIT collabora- tion is governed by specific cooperation agreements established for each particular case
DEPARTAMENT DE COMERC I TURISME DE LA GENERALITAT DE CATALUNYA, Valencia 279 Barcelona 08009 Tel: 34.93.21597 00	*Catalan Ministry of Commerce and Tourism				*Finances invest- ments for small Commercial Business Firms (FIEC): subsidies to reduce inter- est on loans re- quested for in- vestments to im- prove produc- tivity and rationality of businesses and cooperative association (of producers and consumers), re- tailers associa- tions and busi- ness firms in- cluded in a business recon- version plan of a specific district	Finance Cont. *Also offers credits to new businesses. Loans may be for as much as 70% of the investment and up to 25 million Pts. (except in exceptional cases: loans for larger amounts must be negoti- ated through the Banco Hipotecario de Espana)
CENTRE D'INFORMACIO I DESENVOLUPAMENT EMPRESARIAL (CATALONIA) (CIDEM), Paseo de Gracia 55, Barcelona 08007 Tel: 34.93.21571 78	*Business Information & Development Centre *Dependency of the Department of Industry & Energy of the Generalitat de Catalunya	*Information on existing systems and assistance in developing new products and processes, patents, etc. *Information and advice on finan- cial techno- logical and training assis- tance available to small business firms	*Counselling			

ORGANISATION	NATURE OF ORGANISATION	SOFTWARE			HARDWARE	
		Information/ Advice	Counselling/ Consulting	Training & Education	Finance	Other
COMISSIO INTERDEPARTA- MENTAL D'AJUDA PER A LA RECONVERSIO INDUSTRIAL A CATALUNYA (CARIC), Paseo de Gracia 55, bajos, Barcelona 08007 Tel: 34.93.21554 08 215-58-14	*Interdepartmental Commission for Industrial Development *Agency of the Department of Industry and Energy of the Catalan regional government (Generalitat de Catalunya)				*Guarantees the first loans re- quested by companies in order to carry out the recon- version plans sponsored by CARIC Guarantees loans of up to 70% of the fi- nancing require- ments for the re- conversion Plan. *Credit guarantees of up to 110 million Pts. Cost: 0.5% of amount guaranteed	Finance Cont. -Terms: presen- tation of a medium and long- term feasibility plan; the credit may not exceed 70% of the plan or 60% of the company's own resources
GOBIERNO AUTONOMO VASCO Paladio Ajuria- Enea, Vitoria 01010 Tel: 34.945.231 616	*Basque Country autonomous government				*Subsidizes in- dustrial in- vestments in fixed assets de- signed to create new jobs, or, in cases of techno- logical inno- vation, maintain existing ones. The amount of the subsidy is a per- centage of the new investment and varies in accordance with the number of jobs created	
DEPARTAMENTO DE INDUSTRIA Y ENERGIA DEL GOBERNO VASCO, Duque de Welling- ton, s/w Vitoria 01010 Tel: 34.945.24. 99.00	*Basque Ministry of Industry & Energy				*Subsidizes research & development *Creates R. & D. departments for individual companies or groups of com- panies. Finances up to 40% of the R. & D. depart- ment's annual costs, up to a maximum of 12 million ptas. per company per year	
SOCIEDAD PARA LA PROMOCION Y RECONVERSION INDUSTRIAL, S.A. (BASQUE COUNTRY) Duque de Wellington s/n Vitoria 01010 Tel: 34.945.24. 99.00	*Society for Industrial Development *Agency of the Department of Industry and Energy of the Basque government				*Credits destined to create or de- velop firms, in- vest in fixed assets or in operating funds. Advantageous credit terms on up to 33% of the total investment	
OTRAS ORGANIZACIONES REGIONALES DE LAS COMMUNIDADES AUTONOMAS	*Other public organizations depending on the various autono- mous governments				*Regional policy instruments: subsidized in- vestments for up to 10-20% of their total, preference on official credits, tax reliefs	

ORGANISATION	NATURE OF ORGANISATION	SOFTWARE			HARDWARE	
		Information/ Advice	Counselling/ Consulting	Training & Education	Finance	Other
BANCO DE CREDITO INDUSTRIAL (BCI), Manila 56-58 Barcelona 08034 Tel: 34.93.20413 66	*Industrial Credit Bank *Public·bank. Dependency of the Ministry of Industry				*Special credit for small in- dustrial and commercial busi- ness with no more than 200 million Pts. in equity and not more than 20% owned by a larger firm. -Financing of up to 75% (max. 30 million Pts.) for new investments in fixed assets designed to create, remodel and modernize company instal- lations. 12.5% interest for up to 6 years	Finance Cont. -Finances rotating capital in amounts of up to 25% and budget invest- ments in fixed assets (max. 15 million Pts.) on condition the investment is in fixed assets. 13.5% annual interest for up to 2 years
BANCO EXTERIOR DE ESPANA COMMERCIAL AND SAVINGS BANKS (by means of compulsory coefficient) Carrera de San Jeronimo 36 Madrid 28014 Tel: 34.91.45005 02	*Bank, the majority of the capital of which is public.				*Rotating capi- tal credit: 10% interest at 1 year. Amount to be financed: de- pending upon specific customs tariffs. (This credit will finish in 1985 in accordance with the EEC standards *Pre-financing credits for in- vestment and consumer goods. 10% interest. Amount: 80% of FOB value (85% with Export Letter) *Short-term credits for exports. (See export section)	Finance Cont. *Medium and long- term credits for export purposes: (see export secion) *Purchasers' Credits: depend- ing on duration and country: 10-11% interest at 2-5 years Amount: 85% FOB value (mini- mum contract 14 million Pts.); 10-11, 25% 5-8, 5 yrs. Developing countries: 10% interest for 8.5- 10 years
CAJAS DE AHORROS, Caballero.de Gracia 28 Madrid 28013 Tel: 34.91.23105 71	*Spanish confed- eration of savings banks *Public and private firms				*Special credit terms: finances up to 70% of in- vestment at 12% annual interest *Credits for in- vestment goods: finances up to 80% of the in- vestment at 12% annual interest	
VENTURE CAPITAL COMPANIES (SEFINNOVA, FIISA, BANCAYA, AND EMPRESA NACIONAL DE INNOVACION, S.A.)	*Public and private firms				*Minority share- holder in companies with original and advanced technology *Provide conven- tional financing opportunities, management and administrative assistance to participating companies	

155

ORGANISATION	NATURE OF ORGANISATION	SOFTWARE			HARDWARE	
		Information/ Advice	Counselling/ Consulting	Training & Education	Finance	Other
CONFEDERACION ESPANOLA DE ORGANIZACIONES EMPRESARIALES (CEOE), Paseo de la Castellona 83 Madrid 28046 Tel: 34.91.44599 00	*Leading Spanish employers' association	*Information and advice on finan- cial techno- logical and training assis- tance available to small business companies		*Runs training courses with subsidies from IMPE		
CONFEDERACION ESPANOLA DE LA PEQUENA Y MEDIANA EMPRESA (CEPYME), Diego Leon 50 Madrid 28006 Tel: 34.91.26125 87	*National small business organi- zation. Member of CEOE	*Advice on the terms and requi- sites for receiv- ing this assistance				
UNION DE LA PEQUENA Y MEDIANA EMPRESA ESPANOLA (UNIPYME), Gran Via 32, 5° Madrid 28013 Tel: 34.91.27420 06	*Represents owners of small businesses throughout Spain. Independent of CEOE	*Advice on the terms and requi- sites for receiv- ing this assistance				
PETITA I MITJANA EMPRESA DE CATALUNYA (PIMEC), Mallorca 279, 1°.3°, Barcelona 08037 Tel: 34.93.21588 31	*Organization of small business owners in Catalonia. Inde- pendentof CEOE	*Advice on the terms and requi- site for re- ceiving this assistance				
CAMARA OFICIAL DE COMERCIO, INDUSTRIA Y NAVEGACION DE BARCELONA, Ample 11 Barcelona 08002 Tel: 34.93.39233 66 34.93.3184682	*Chambers of Commerce & Industry *Public associations	*Information & advice	*Export promotion, trade fairs, international relations, certificates of origin, arbi- tration in trade conflicts			
UNIVERSIDADES ESTATALES (Departamentos de Administracion de Empresas)	*State Universities			*University degree programs in business administration		
ESCUELAS DE FORMACION OCUPACIONAL	*Public occu- pational train- ing schools			*Short training courses to pro- vide workers with broader training, specialization or training in a new occupation -Free of charge to company -Pay 70% of mini- mum wage through- out course to un- employed young people from families in reduced financial circumstances		

156

ORGANISATION	NATURE OF ORGANISATION	SOFTWARE			HARDWARE	
		Information/ Advice	Counselling/ Consulting	Training & Education	Finance	Other
FORMACION DE PERSONAL CUALIFICADO	*Vocational training schools			*Courses designed to train young people as skilled and specialized laborers		
ESCUELAS PRIVADAS DE DIRECCION DE EMPRESAS	*Private manage- ment schools			*Courses and training activi- ties on various levels: a) university de- gree programs. b) executive de- velopment pro- grams: either devoted to particular functional areas or to general management		

Sweden

Materials prepared by

Magnus Hult
University of Vaxyo

SWEDEN

Population: 8.3 million
Area: 449,751 sq. km.

In Sweden, approximately one-third of the labour force is
employed in small and medium sized firms with fewer than 200
employees and, of these, some 18% is in firms employing less
than 50 people. The number of companies with just one employee has increased sharply in recent years, particularly
in the fast growing service sector.

Over the last decade, the Swedish Government has taken a
number of steps to reduce the difficulties confronting SMEs,
both through increased credit availability and through increases in training and other software services. At the
national level, the principal organisations involved in
assisting SMEs are: SIND (the National Board of Industry
under the Ministry of Industry), the lead government agency
for small firms, providing both software and hardware support; the STU (National Board for Technical Development),
also under the Ministry of Industry and providing technical
advice and counselling as well as grants for R&D; the
State-owned Investment Bank (loans and risk capital); the
State Business Capital Agency (financing); the State Industry Credit Agency Limited (finance for buildings); and
the Export Council.

A particularly important role in SME support is provided
through 24 Regional Development Funds (RDs), financed by
SIND. The RDs offer free information and counselling services, export assistance, start-up training, loans, guarantees and product development loans specifically for small
firms. Some software support is also provided through the
education sector and the Local Authority Industrial Development Agencies.

The major business and local savings banks provide a variety
of loan schemes, leasing and factoring services, advisory
and counselling services and occasional seminars; the Swedish Employers' Confederation (SAF), provides information
services and consulting and training through its subsidiary,
The Swedish Management Group; the Company Management Institute (IFL) provides training; and various Small Business
Clubs provide useful mechanisms for contact between small
businessmen at the local level.

ORGANISATION	NATURE OF ORGANISATION	SOFTWARE			HARDWARE	
		Information/ Advice	Counselling/ Consulting	Training & Education	Finance	Other
STATENS INDUSTRIWERK Liljeholmysvagen 30 117 86 Stockholm Tel: 46.8.74490 00	*The National Swedish Indus- trial Board *Organisation under Depart- ment of Industry *Lead government organisation for small firms	*Branch - programmes in order to support changes in the industry structure			*Loan guarantee *Special grant schemes for some branches of industry, e.g. firms in tex- tiles, furs, casting, furni- ture, wood, glass	
REGIONAL DEVELOPMENT FUNDS Further information from: UTVECKLINGS- FONDEN 1 STOCKHOLMS LAN, Dalagatan 100, Box 23135, 10435 Stockholm Tel: 46.8.151400	*24 agencies across Sweden *Financed by SIND & the county councils, each with a board of directors appointed by the county council *Established in 1978, they took over the role of the existing regional develop- ment associations with increased regional develop- ment funds 600 employees *Target group industrial firms and service enterprises servicing industrial firms	*Free services offered	*Consulting experts provide free services for between 2 & 5 days *Export counselling including: Export Manager for hire programs (see special section: Exports)	*Start-up Programmes: -informational (1-2 days, fee 500 SEK, 2000 participants pa) -longer (5-10 days over 6 month period, 5000 - 10000 SEK but frequently sponsored, 400 - 600 participants pa)	*For firms employ- ing up to 200 people provide loan guarantees & loans (up to 50% of cost) for product development	
DEPARTMENT OF LABOR					*Can give grants and loans for firms in support areas (mainly in the north)	*Up to 70% of costs for buildings
ARBETSMARKNADS- STYRELSEN, Sundbyberasvagen 9 171 99 Solna. Tel: 46.8.73060 00	*State industry credit agency, Ltd. *Owned by commercial banks and state				*Buy shares or convertible loans *Finances buildings for small and medium-sized companies	*Help financing firms
SVERIGES INVESTERINGS BANK AB Malmskillnads- gatan 32 Box 16051 103 22 Stockholm Tel: 46.8.221440	*State-owned bank				*Gives loans to- gether with RDA: risk capital up to 1 mkr	
PRIVATE BANKS	*Both major business banks and local saving banks	*Provide variety of specialists information booklets and ongoing digests	*Banks normally have specialists advisory/coun- selling services for small firm customers. These services have expanded	*Occasional seminars	*Variety of special loan schemes including equity provision. The Banks have special companies for leasing, factoring and other services *Operation of loan guarantee schemes with the Department of Industry	

ORGANISATION	NATURE OF ORGANISATION	SOFTWARE			HARDWARE	
		Information/ Advice	Counselling/ Consulting	Training & Education	Finance	Other
SVENSKA ARBETSGIVARE- FORENINGEN Sodra Blasieholm- shammen 4A 103 30 Stockholm Tel: 46.8.76261 19	*Swedish Em- ployers' con- federation (SAF) & Swedish Management Group (part of SAF)	*Through SAF Regional Offices which employ secretaries representing different trade organizations	*The Management group offers consultancy and an educational program for small firms			
LOCAL AUTHORITY INDUSTRIAL DEVELOPMENT AGENCIES	*Recently started in some regions. Varying in struc- ture and powers and degree to which they work with small busi- ness support. Normally working as coordinators of the local authorities (RD , manpower agencies, com- munes, commercial banks, etc.)		*Use of pro- fessional consul- tants and advisers as well as voluntary service		*Give, in some cases, support for market research	
EDUCATION SECTOR BUSINESS SCHOOLS, ETC.			*Occasional provision of specialists	*A variety of short and long full-time and part-time pro- grammes but not mainly for the small firms		
INNOVATION CENTERS	*Departments at 3-4 universities	*Varying in struc- ture and extent				
SMALL BUSINESS CLUBS	*An old, informal way for small business owners to get in con- tact with other entrepreneurs in the local area	*In some cases the Clubs have built export houses for products produced by the members	*Informal coun- selling by Club members	*Guest speakers *Seminars *Regular discussion meetings		

Since finalization of the charts shown on the previous
pages, the following organisations have been suggested for
inclusion:

* FORETAGSKAPITAL AB
Klara s Kyrkogatu 1
Box 1646
111 86 Stockholm
Tel : 46.8.235075
State Business Capital Agency.   Provides venture capital.

*SVENSKA MANAGEMENTGRUPPEN AB
103 30 Stockholm
Tel : 46 8 235410
Swedish Management Group.   See previous page under Swedish
Employers' Confederation.

* SVERIGES INDUSTRIFORBUND
Box 5501
114 85 Stockholm
Tel : 46.8.7838000
The Federation of Swedish Industries.   Provides advice on
e.g. taxation, finance.

* FORETAGERFORBUNDET
Odengatan 87
113 22 Stockholm
Tel : 46.8.150950
The Swedish Association of Free Enterprises.   Provides
information, publications and advice on trends in government
policy regarding SMEs.

* SHIO - FAMILJRFORETAGEN
Nyforgsgaten 17
11622 Stockholm
Tel : 46.8.7430600
Provides information, publications and advice on trends in
government policy regarding SMEs and also promotes
cooperation between firms at the local level.

Switzerland

Materials prepared by

Hans Pleitner and Margrit Habersaat
Swiss Research Institute of Small Business,
St. Gallen

SWITZERLAND

Population: 6.3 million
Area: 41,288 sq. km.

In Switzerland, of the 2.1 million people employed in firms
(both manufacturing, trade and service), approximately 46%
are employed in establishments with fewer than 50 employees
and 31% in medium-sized firms (50 - 499 employees, 1975
figures). Small firms are currently estimated to account
for some 45% of value-added.

Although Switzerland has no specific small firms' policy, it
has a long tradition of support for SME development based,
similar to Germany, on a dictum of "help for self help".
Indeed, the Swiss Association of SMEs frequently urges the
Government not to loose its way in complicated systems of
selective support measures but to continue to cultivate and
improve the overall climate for selfemployment and entrepreneurial management. Typically, emphasis has been placed
upon: vocational training; fair competition; and appro-
priate financial support. For instance, some selectivity in
support has been introduced by the government since 1974
through special, investment aid schemes for mountain areas
and other economically depressed regions. Twelve regional
credit guarantee cooperatives and the Swiss Credit Cooperative for small firms, all private cooperatives, support
the middle and long term loans for SMEs provided by the commercial and savings banks.

The independent cantons and local authorities also provide
development aid, financial information and financial assistance such as low interest loans, different tax schemes,
etc. (This is often of a competitive nature between the
various cantons). Recently, an increased interest in
start-ups and job maintenance or creation has been evidenced
in certain cantons.

As intimated above, the Swiss Association of SMEs
(Schweizerischer Gewerbeverband) plays an important role in
the provision of information and advice, the founding of
special pension and insurance institutions, and through
specialized training activities by the affiliated Swiss
Institute for Training of Managers in Small Firms
(Schweizerisches Institut fur Unternehmerschulung im
Gewerbe). In addition, some 25 local SME associations en-
gage in information, advice, and counselling, selective
financial support and continuation training. Twenty Chambers of Commerce, all private, provide further information
and management assistance and over 190 professional associations also play a significant role in software support.

Of particular importance in the provision of consulting,
training and research is the only university institute in
Switerzland dealing exclusively with SMEs, the Swiss Re-
search Institute of Small Business at the St. Gall Graduate
School of Economics, Law, Business and Public Administration
(Schweizerisches Institut fuer Gewerbliche Wirtschaft). A
few issues in this field are also covered by the Institute
of Management and Industrial Engineering of the Federal
Institute of Technology (Betriebswissenschaftlisches
Institut der Eidg. Technischen Hochschule Zuerich).

ORGANISATION	NATURE OF ORGANISATION	SOFTWARE			HARDWARE	
		Information/ Advice	Counselling/ Consulting	Training & Education	Finance	Other
BUNDESAMT FUER INDUSTRIE, GEWERBE UND ARBEIT, Bundesgasse 8 CH-3003 Bern Tel: 41.31.6129 44	*Federal Office for Industry and Labour *Government agency *National coverage				*Credit guarantee and interest subsidies in regions or branches of in- dustry with poor economic outlook	
BUERGSCHAFTSGE- NOSSENSCHAFTEN (BG), e.g. OBTG Rorschacher- strasse 63 CH-9000 St. Gallen Tel: 41.71.2631 31	*Regional Credit guarantee cooperatives *Private Insti- tutions with Government support *Specialized SMEs *Regional cover- age: 12 coopera- tives operate across the country	*Provide Infor- mation on credit guarantee for loans (startups and existing firms)	*Provide manage- ment consulting		*Provide guaran- tee for pur- chasing firms, extension and rebuilding of business premi- ses, transfer of firms from father to son and in- vestment in via- ble firms. Limit Fr. 80000.	
SCHWEIZERISCHE BUERGSCHAFTS- GENOSSENSCHAFT FUER DAS GEWERBE GBG, Merkurstrasse 4 CH-9001 St. Gallen Tel: 41.71.2334 36	*Swiss Credit Guarantee Co- operative for Small Firms *Private coopera- tive with govern- ment support *National coverage *Specialized SMEs				*The Swiss credit guarantee cooper- ative for small firms may enhance the regular amount of the credit guarantee by Swiss Fr. 100000 up to Fr. 180000. In addition they guarantee credits for firms located in mountain areas up to Fr. 500000	
KANTONALE AEMTER FUER WIRTSCHAFTS- FOERDERUNG, eg. Delegierter fur Wirtschafts- forderung Gerechtigkeits- gasse 81 CH-3001 Bern Tel: 41.31.6448 38	*Cantonal Agen- cies for Eco- nomic Development *Regional coverage	*Advice on subsi- dies, loans and risk capital			*Grant loans *Offer subsidies aiming at job creation *Subsidize inter- est completely or in part *Subsidize the development of building areas *Subsidize part of of insurance premiums for export risk guarantee or risk exchange rate guarantee	Finance Cont. *Guarantee in- vestment loans *Guarantee credits for small firms located in regions coping with econo- mic difficulties. The federal guarantee may be enhanced by an additional can- tonal guarantee. Projects, however, have to promise diversification or innovation
INDELEC FINANZ AG, Talstrasse 70 CH-8001 Zurich Tel: 41.12.1156 56 Arnold-Boecklin- Str. 11 CH-4002 Basel Tel: 41.61.5433 55	*Financing Corporation				*Provide venture capital and development capital	
INAS AG FOERDER- UNGSGESELLSCHAFT FUR INTEGRALE SYSTEME ANGE- PASSTER TECHNO- LOGIE UND SICHERHEIT, Zollikerstrasse 228 CH-8008 Zurich Tel: 41.12.4138 64	*Society for the Promotion of Integral Systems of Adequate Technology and Security *Private companies associated to main merchant banks *National coverage				*Provide venture and development capital	

167

ORGANISATION	NATURE OF ORGANISATION	SOFTWARE			HARDWARE	
		Information/ Advice	Counselling/ Consulting	Training & Education	Finance	Other
ZENTRALE VOR-SORGEKASSE SCHWEIZ. GEWER-BEVERBAND, Schwarztorstrasse 26 CH-3000 Bern Tel: 41.31.2527 91	*Central Provision Fund of the Swiss Association of SMEs in Manu-facturing, Retail Trade and Services *Foundation of the Swiss Association of SMEs *National coverage *Specialized SMEs					*The Central Pro-vision Fund of the Swiss Associ-ation of SMEs in manufacturing re-tail trade and services provides an old age and survivors' pension plan for members of small firms to whom their profes-sional association does not offer any insurance
ERG GESCHAEFTSSTELLE FUER DIE EXPORT-RISIKOGARANTIE, Kirchweg 4 CH-8008 Zurich Tel: 41.14.766 56	*Office for Guarantee of Export Risks *Private Insti-tution with public support affiliated to Swiss Association of Machinery Manufacturer *National coverage				*Credit quarantee for risks of ex-port (political, transfer, manu-facturing, mone-tary risk and contingency for public insti-tutions and utilities)	
BANKS e.q. Gewerbekasse in Bern (Bank for SMEs in Bern), Bahnhofplatz 7 CH-3011 Bern Tel: 41.31.2245 11	*Private	*Offer information and advice in the field of business manage-ment			*Local and re-gional banks provide short and long term loans	
CHAMBERS OF COMMERCE/ INNOVATIVE CON-SULTING CENTRES e.q. Kaufmaen-nisches Directorium, Gallusstrasse 16 CH-9000 St. Gallen Tel: 41.71.2315 15	*Private associ-ations *Regional cover-age: 20 chambers of commerce	*Provide infor-mation especially on sources of risk capital *Offer information and industrial directories	*Several chambers of commerce have established special inno-vation centres providing also management assistance		*Subsidies for management con-sulting may be obtained	
PROFESSIONAL ASSOCIATIONS e.q. Schweiz. Metall-Union, Seestrasse 105 CH-8002 Zurich Tel: 41.12.0173 76	*Private associations *Specialized SMEs *National cover-age: 191 associations	*Publish in their periodicals papers on manage-ment development *Establish bidding lists & coordin-ate bidding among member firms	*Numerous Pro-fessional Asso-ciations of small firms offer management assis-tance to their members *Various profes-sional associ-ations help member firms to identify export opportunities	*General training programmes, often in-house training *Numerous associa-tions provide technical con-tinuation training		*A series of professional associations provide social security plans and bookkeeping service
LOCAL ASSOCIA-TIONS OF SMEs e.q. Kantonaler Gewerbeverband Zurich Raemistrasse 35 CH-8001 Zurich Tel: 41.12.5223 72	*Private associations *Specialized SMEs *Regional coverage: 25 associations	*Publish manage-ment information in their periodicals *Numerous associ-ations provide information and advice	*Numerous local associations of small firms pro-vide accounting services		*Various local associations of small firms pro-vide credit quarantees	

168

ORGANISATION	NATURE OF ORGANISATION	SOFTWARE			HARDWARE	
		Information/ Advice	Counselling/ Consulting	Training & Education	Finance	Other
SCHWEIZERISCHER GEWERBEVERBAND, Schwarztorstrasse 26 CH-3007 Bern Tel: 41.31.2577 85	*Swiss Associa- tion of SMEs in Manufacturing, Retail Trade and Services *Private associ- ation *National coverage *Specialized SMEs	*Publishes management infor- mation in their weekly newspaper *Offers infor- mation and advice to professional and local associations	*Foundation of a specific institute (SIU) for training and consultancy		*Foundation of several insti- tutions providing old age pension plans, insurance plans, etc.	
SCHWEIZ. HANDELS UND INDUSTRIE VEREIN/PME ARBEITSGRUPPE, Boersenstrasse 26 CH-8001 Zurich Tel: 41.12.2127 07	*Swiss Associa- tion for Industry and Trade/SME Work Group *Private association *National coverage	*Publication of manuals and research findings in a special series				
SCHWEIZ. ARBEITS- GEMEINSCHAFT GESTALTENDES HANDWERK, Vordere Haupt- gasse 29 CH-4800 Zofingen Tel: 41.62.5220 45	*Swiss Work Group of Handicraft Firms for the Development of Design and Exhibition *Private association *National coverage *Specialized SMEs		*Promotes design through expert judging of members' products and exhibitions			
CENTRE POUR L' INNOVATION DU GROUPEMENT DES JEUNES DIRIGEANTS D'ENTREPRISES, rue Cornavin 11 CH-1201 Geneva Tel: 41.22.3148 58	*Innovation Centre of the Association of Young Managers *Private association *Regional coverage	*Collection of data and infor- mation on new products				
PURCHASING COOPERATIVES e.g. Handels- genossenschaft des Schweiz. Baumeisterver- bandes, Postfach CH-8039 Zurich Tel: 41.12.4243 11	*Private coopera- tives often affiliated to professional associations *National coverage *Specialized SMEs					*Purchasing co- operatives in various branches of manufacturing (e.g. construc- tion, painting, garages, con- fectioners, electricians)
ASSOCIATIONS OR FOUNDATIONS FOR THE DEVELOPMENT/PRO- MOTION OF TRADE & INDUSTRY e.g. Office pour la Promotion de L'Industrie Genevoise (Geneva) and others in e.g. Lausanne	*Private associ- ations/founda- tions with public support *Regional Coverage		*Varying services e.g. carrying out market studies, helping local firms with mar- keting, mounting exhibitions, pro- viding assistance in getting guar- antees, advising on where to locate, etc.			

ORGANISATION	NATURE OF ORGANISATION	SOFTWARE			HARDWARE	
		Information/ Advice	Counselling/ Consulting	Training & Education	Finance	Other
SCHWEIZ. INSTITUT FUER GEWERBLICHE WIRTSCHAFT AN DER HOCHSCHULE ST. GALLEN IGW, Dufourstrasse 48 CH-9000 St. Gallen Tel: 41.71.2334 61	*Swiss Research Institute of Small Business at the St. Gall Graduate School of Economics, Law, Business & Public Administration *Semi-public university institute *National coverage *Specialized SMEs	*Within its range of services, the Institute offers advice in the sector of business development	*Consults SMEs in the field of business management	*Contributes to management development through linking consulting, interfirm comparison, exex-groups for owner-managers in various branches *As part of management development programmes, member firms of exex-groups start cooperation, often sub-contracting		
SCHWEIZ. INSTITUT FUER UNTERNEHMERSCHULUNG IN GEWERBE SIU, Schwarztorstrasse 26 CH-3007 Bern Tel: 41.31.2577 85	*Swiss Institute for Training of Managers in Small Firms *Private cooperative society *Specialized SMEs *National coverage	*Offers various publications, a news service and a quarterly periodical compiling management advice	*Acts as intermediary for management advice	*Offers training programme for various sectors (manufacturing, trade, services, catering)		
BETRIEBSWISSENSCHAFTLICHES INSTITUT DER EIDG. TECHNISCHEN HOCHSCHULE ZURICH (BWI), Zurichbergstrasse 18 CH-8028 Zurich Tel: 41.14.70800	*Institute of Management and Industrial Engineering of the Federal Institute of Technology *Semi-public university institute *National coverage		*Consulting for planning, organization, management, manufacturing, logistics, data processing, etc.	*Provides continuation training, especially in the field of management		
SWISSEXPORT, c/o Exim-index AG Hauptgasse 9 Postfach 212 CH-4880 Zofingen Tel: 41.63.5192 82	*Association for export development *Private association *National coverage	*Range of software services: see special section: Exports				
SCHWEIZ. ZENTRALE FUER HANDELSFOERDERUNG Stampfenbachstrasse 84 CH-8035 Zurich Tel: 41.16.02250	*Swiss Office for the Development of Trade *Private association with public subsidies *National coverage *See special sections: Exports	*Publications for member firms				*Organises export promotion through fairs & exhibitions
EXPORTGEMEINSCHAFT FUER INDUSTRIE UND GEWERBE, Irchelstrasse 18 CH-8057 Zurich Tel: 41.13.6266 10	*Export Association for Trade and Industry *Private cooperative society *Specialized SMEs *National coverage	*See special section: Exports				
DATRON AG DATENVERARBEITUNG UND ORGANISATION, Fuerstenlandstrasse 35 CH-9001 St. Gallen Tel: 41.71.2911 41	*Data Processing and Organisation *Private joint-stock company *Regional coverage *Specialized SMEs		*This data center develops standardized software for small firms			

ORGANISATION	NATURE OF ORGANISATION	SOFTWARE			HARDWARE	
		Information/ Advice	Counselling/ Consulting	Training & Education	Finance	Other
SCHWEIZERISCHES INSTITUT FUER TECHNISCHE INFORMATION (SITI), Waldheim- strasse 18 CH-3000 Bern 9 Tel: 41.31.2403 33	*Swiss Institute for Technical Information *Semi-public institute affili- ated to the Swiss Associ- ation for the promotion of research *National Coverage	*See special section: Techno- logical Innovation & R&D				
CENTRE SUISSE D' ESSAIS DES COMPOSANTS ELECTRONIQUES, ruelle Vaucher 22 CH-2000 Neuchatel Tel: 41.38.2418 00	*Swiss Centre for Testing Elec- tronic Components *Semi-public institute sup- ported by Swiss Electrotechnical Association *National coverage	*See special section: Technological Innovation and R&D				
FONDATION DES TERRAINS INDUS- TRIELS PRAILLE ET ACACIAS, av. Vibert 10 CH-1227 Geneva Tel: 41.22.4221 60	*Foundation for Industrial Real Estate *Private Foun- dation *Regional coverage					*Purchase and de- velopment of real estate or build- ings for facili- tating the estab- lishment of firms
SWISS INDUS- TRIAL DEVELOP- MENT INSTITUTE (SIDI), Postfach 671 CH-8201 Schaff- hausen Tel: 41.53.82031	*Private Institute *National coverage	*Informs members on development projects in the Third World and respective export oppor- tunities. *See special section: Exports	*Telephone con- sulting service	*Assists member firms in training employees and managers from co- operating firms in developing countries		
EIDGENOESSISCHE MATERIALPRUE- FUNGSUND VER SUCHSANSTALT, Unterstrasse CH-9001 St. Gallen Tel: 41.71.20911 41 Ueberlandstrasse 129 CH-8600 Dubendorf Tel: 41.18.2355 11	*Swiss Federal Laboratory for Materials Testing and Research *Public Insti- tution *National coverage		*Tests on demand material and supplies for firms and authorities			
SCHULZORGANI- SATION DER PRIVATENS AKTI- ONGESELLSCHAFTEN St. Jakobs- Strasse 71 CH-4052 Basel Tel: 41.61.22.20 91	*Swiss Associ- ation of privately need companies limited by shares *Private association	*Periodical information on tax and company law *Representation in legal matters	*General assis- tance to member firms namely in company law and tax matters			*Assistance to member firms in arranging stock capital
AKTIONGESELL- SCHAFT FEUR BETEILIGUNGEN AN PRIVATEN UNTERNEHMEN St. Jakobs- Strasse 71 CH-4052 Basel Tel: 41.61.22.52 00	*Private company					*Provide venture and development company

171

ORGANISATION	NATURE OF ORGANISATION	SOFTWARE			HARDWARE	
		Information/ Advice	Counselling/ Consulting	Training & Education	Finance	Other
UNION SCHWEIZE- RISCHER HANDELS- KAMMERN IM AUSLAND c/o Sandoz Lichtstrasse 35 CH-4002 Basel Tel: 41.61.242236	*Union of Swiss Chambers of Commerce abroad *Private associations *National coverage	*Informs members on market opportunities and cooperation	*Carries out market analyses			
UNION OF SWISS CHAMBERS OF COMMERCE ABROAD (Union Schweiz Handeerskammern in Ausland)	*Private Association	*Informs members on market opportunities and cooperation	*Provides market analyses	*Organises conventions		*Organises fairs and exhibitions

172

United Kingdom

Materials prepared by

Allan Gibb
*Durham University
Business School, UK*

UNITED KINGDOM

Population: 57.5 million
Area: 244,045 sq.km.

The U.K. has a working population of 26.5 million. Small
firms are usually defined as those having less than 200 employees in manufacturing although different thresholds have
been suggested for different sectors to provide a relative
measure for the sector: for example, small firms in the
building and construction industry are defined as having
under 25 employees. And in some sectors turnover figures
are used, for example retailing. In all, there were over
2.1 million self-employed persons in 1981, almost one in ten
of the labour force. In 1979, firms with under 200 employees contributed to 19.5% of manufacturing output.

There is no formal published statement of overall small
firms policy. But there are clear indications of the present conservative government's commitment to small firms.
This commitment is primarily oriented towards removing areas
of disadvantage and discrimination against the smaller business. The present government has introduced over 100 measures in support of small business, many of them related to
easing taxation burdens, encouraging investment in small
businesses and removing some of the bureaucractic burdens.

In England, much of public support of small business is
channelled through regional Small Firms Centres which provide an information and telephone enquiry service for local
small firms in the region. They also act as the area base
for a counselling scheme using retired or semi-retired executives. In Scotland, Wales and Northern Ireland, much of
public support for small firms is organised through semi-
autonomous agencies such as the Scottish and Welsh Development Agencies. Local authorities are now, however, also
substantially supporting small businesses with their own
counselling and advisory schemes. In addition, many of
these authorities are in partnership with Local Enterprise
Agencies. These Agencies are the newest and perhaps most
important institutions to emerge in the U.K., linking together national government blessing, companies and local
government support for local economic development operating
under the umbrella of a company limited by guarantee. The
main thrust of this support is in providing counselling information and advice services in the local area. In mid-
1984 there were almost 200 of these Agencies in operation.

Support for training at the national level is organised by a
semi-autonomous public body, the Manpower Services Commission, which supports a variety of programmes for would-be
or existing small business managers throughout the country.
These courses are mainly located in the education sector
including Business Schools, Polytechnics, Colleges of Further and Higher Education, etc. A variety of other programmes are provided at the local level by Colleges, Chambers of
Commerce and Small Business Associations. It should be
noted, however, that the Chambers of Commerce are of relatively less importance compared with several other European
countries.

There are no special soft loan or grant schemes for small business per se outside of those provided by courtesy of the European Economic Community and a scheme to encourage the unemployed to set up in business, the Enterprise Allowance Scheme. There are, however, ranges of special loans and grants offered by the Development Agencies and under regional assistance policy though these are open to large as well as small firms. The banks have a variety of term loans aimed particularly at small business and the government in the last few years has introduced a Loan Guarantee Scheme.

The small firm support scenario in the United Kingdom is changing rapidly. Since Autumn 1984, a number of changes hae been introduced. These have been mainly aimed, from the official viewpoint, as reducing the number of "entry-points" into small firms' assistance, particularly those related to support for technical innovation.

ORGANISATION	NATURE OF ORGANISATION	SOFTWARE			HARDWARE	
		Information/ Advice	Counselling/ Consulting	Training & Education	Finance	Other
DEPARTMENT OF TRADE AND INDUSTRY Ashdown House 123 Victoria Street London SW1 Tel: 44.1.21230 00	*Government De- partment with Small Firms Division *Lead government organisation for small firms *Small Firms Division (HQ staff 47) (Field staff 130)	*Through regional system of Small Firm Information Centres (SFIC's) Telephone en- quiry "free- phone" service. Wide range of information booklets	*Based on re- gional SFIC's. Counselling Ser- vice using re- tired or semi- retired personnel *Subsidised Specialist Tech- nical Counselling Service also. 275 counsellors. 18000 coun- sellings 1983	*Short sessions (usually on start-ups)	*Loan Guarantee Scheme (70% guarantee). Lending guaran- teed 175 m in 1983. Special grant schemes for engineering and higher tech- nology industry *Business Expan- sion Scheme Tax Relief System to encourage inves- tors in small business - up to 30% of the equi- ty. Money must be invested for 5 years to get relief	*Provision through national company, English Indus- trial Estates, of small size fac- tories/workshops at low rent.
DEPARTMENT OF ENVIRONMENT 2 Marsham Street, London SW1P3EB Tel: 44.1.21234 34	*Government De- partment with prime reponsi- bility for Urban Areas and Rural Development	*Has links with the private sector through "Business in the Community" (see below) to support small enterprise and supervises work of COSIRA (see below) in rural areas			*Support for lo- cal government loans and premi- ses schemes through the Urban Aid Pro- gramme. This is a special pro- gramme to provide particular finan- cial support to inner urban areas *Also involved in designation of special Enterprise Zones throughout the U.K. where special tax and other exemptions are offered to firms. Not particularly "small firms" however.	*Provides support for cheap premises of local govern- ment through Urban Aid Programme
MANPOWER SERVICES COMMISSION Moorfoot, Sheffield S1 4PQ Tel: 44.1.74270 4995	*State financed semi-autonomous organisation charged with pro- vision and direc- tion of training and employment services nationally		*Support for experimental "pilot" or "rent an executive" programmes de- signed to place a senior execu- tive in a small company at no or low cost to help development	*Various "managed" workshops for training/retraining unemployed parlicularly young people: based on producing a marketable product. Some degree of financial subsidy. Involved also in special "community enterprise" schemes		

ORGANISATION	NATURE OF ORGANISATION	SOFTWARE			HARDWARE	
		Information/ Advice	Counselling/ Consulting	Training & Education	Finance	Other
TRAINING DIVISION Moorfoot, Sheffield S1 4PQ Tel: 44.1.74270 4995	*Division of above organisation concerned with national pro- vision of man- power training at all levels (organised regionally) *Has a small firms division (8 staff)		*Only linked with training	*Provision through links with education and consultancy sector of wide variety of pro- grammes divided as follows: -Start-ups. A range of "action oriented" pro- grammes, 8 weeks to 4 months, for those with a business idea, aiming to get into business -Programmes for those wishing merely to ex- plore the small business option as a career alternative (Skills into Business) -Existing compan- ies. Management Extension Pro- gramme aimed at providing support for the develop- ment of the small company by the retraining - placement (free of charge) in a small firm of an unemployed large company manager for periods vary- ing from 13 weeks to 1 year. Variants of this scheme are being attempted as pilot experiments linked with specialist de- velopment of small firm activity -Action learning programmes for groups of small firms -Growth pro- grammes to help small business exploit an idea -Export programmes	*In start-up programmes will pay programme costs and sub- sistence as well as certain costs involved in the development of the business proposal *Operates Enter- prise Allowance Schemes under which unemployed starters prepared to commit 1,000 pounds of their own resources to a business venture receive payment of 40 pounds per week from the State for one year. Some counselling compulsory under under the Scheme. 1000 places a week	
COUNCIL FOR SMALL INDUSTRY IN RURAL AREAS 141 Castle Street, Salisbury, Wiltshire SP1 3TP Tel: 44.772.6255	*Semi-autonomous organisation responsible ultimately to the Department of Environment for the development of rural areas (defined as localities of under 10000 population). In existence for over 50 years *Operates from regional offices with organisers for each area backed up by specialist advisers	*Provision of information (reactive) through regional offices and organisers	*General Advisory Service and back up Specialist Adviser Services in Marketing, Production, Finance, at sub- sidised rates	*Organises short management and craft courses. Also has central workshops for training in traditional craft skills	*Provides "last resort" loans at modest interest	*Premises provision

177

ORGANISATION	NATURE OF ORGANISATION	SOFTWARE			HARDWARE	
		Information/ Advice	Counselling/ Consulting	Training & Education	Finance	Other
EDUCATION SECTOR BUSINESS SCHOOLS, POLYTECHNICS COLLEGES OF FURTHER AND HIGHER EDUCATION e.g. CENTRAL LONDON POLYTECHNIC 309 Regent Street London W1 Tel: 44.1.48658 11 DURHAM UNI-VERSITY BUSINESS SCHOOL Mill Hill Lane Durham Tel: 44.385.41919 MANCHESTER BUSINESS SCHOOL Booth Street West Manchester Tel: 44.61.27382 28	*Supported by a mixture of local authority and national funds. Represent the main thrust of small business education and training in the U.K.	*Occasional provision of "Advice Centres"	*Occasional provision of specialist counselling and consultancy services	*Wide variety of short and long full-time and part-time pro-grammes mainly for start-ups and often sponsored by Manpower Services Commission or local authorities		
SPECIAL REGIONAL DEVELOPMENT AGENCIES e.g. WELSH DEVELOP-MENT AGENCY Glontaf House Trebrest Indus-trial Estate Pontypridd Mid Glamorgan Tel: 44.44385. 2666	*Industrial De-velopment Boards for N. Ireland, Welsh & Scottish Development Agencies. High-land and Islands Development Board in Scotland. Quasi - indepen-dent organi-sations in Wales and Scotland who act as "comprehen-sive" providers of a range of facilities in particular link-ing in provision with the Depart-ment of Industry. Are not special-ist small firm agencies but have specialist divisions	*Advice and Information Services	*Use of own professional consultants and advisers as well as voluntary counselling service	*Operate own training schemes or link with colleges	*Provide range of specialist finance services. Equity, loans guarantees	*Provide range of premises/work-shops
LOCAL AUTHORITY INDUSTRIAL DEVELOPMENT OFFICES ---------------- LOCAL AUTHORITY DEVELOPMENT AGENCIES ---------------- LOCAL ENTER-PRISE BOARDS -------------- NEW TOWNS DEVELOPMENT AGENCIES e.g. WASHINGTON DEVELOPMENT CORPORATION Usworth Hall Stephenson District 11 Washington, Tyne and Wear Tel: Washington 463591	*Varying in structure and powers and area and degree to which they "specialise" in small business support. Examples include "Mersey-side Industrial Development Authority," "London Enter-prise Board," "Washington (new town) Development Corporation	*Can provide specialist infor-mation services to attract new small firms or "common services"	*May have own counselling or consultancy service	*Occasional work-shop or seminar	*May provide range of specialist finance (grants, loans)	*Usually provide small factories and workshops

178

ORGANISATION	NATURE OF ORGANISATION	SOFTWARE			HARDWARE	
		Information/ Advice	Counselling/ Consulting	Training & Education	Finance	Other
COOPERATIVE DEVELOPMENT AGENCY Broadmead House, 21 Panton Street London SW1Y4DR Tel: 44.1.83929 88	*Government financed agency to assist development of cooperatives. Has local branches *There are a variety of Local Cooperative Development Agencies which may be affiliated to the national organisation	*Provides information, advice and counselling on cooperative ventures (mainly small)		*Developments and links with specialist train- ing programmes	*Has associated financial provision	
BUSINESS IN THE COMMUNITY (Local Enter- prise Agencies) Tel: 44.1.25337 16	*Private organi- sation sponsored by government set up by group of large compan- ies with the aim of expansion and development of Local Enterprise Agencies. These agencies of which there are now over 200 in the U.K. seek to combine the re- sources of local large companies and local govern- ment to help local indigenous company develop- ment. Services vary from one locality to another but can include:	*Provision of information and advice. Local advisory offi- cers. Market research and information schemes.	*Counselling and consultancy and occasional oper- ation of "common services" schemes for small firms	*Linkages with local colleges in variety of training schemes/ conferences	*Occasional in- volvement with local authority loan and govern-	*Occasional provi- sion of premises and workshops
LARGE COMPANIES direct or through Business in the Community e.g. BRITISH STEEL CORPORATION (INDUSTRY) Ltd, N.L.A. Tower 12 Addiscombe Rd. Croydon CR9 3JH Tel: 44.1.6860366 --------------- SHELL U.K. ICI BANKS Small Business Unit, Shell Mex House The Strand London SC2R RODX Tel: 44.1.25731 85	*Support mainly through secondees to Local Initiatives but can be compre- hensive as in the case of British Steel Corporation (Industries) Ltd. which provides comprehensive support to local steel closure areas	*Through secondees to local initiatives	*Through secondees to act as counsellors or by making available "in company" facilities		*Can assist in operation of special EEC loan schemes in high unemployment areas. May also provide own grant and loan schemes (e.g. British Steel Corporation (In- dustry) Ltd. in steel closure areas)	*Provision of premises at times inde- pendently or in joint venture with local authority
PRIVATE BANKS e.g. NATIONAL WESTMINSTER BANK, PLC Small Business Section, Domestic Banking Division 116 Fenchurch St. London EC3M 5AN Tel: 44.1.72610 00	*Major clearing banks in the U.K. Barclays Lloyds Midland National Westminster	*Provision of variety of specialist information booklets and on-going digests	*Certain banks operate spe- cialist advis- ory/counselling services for small firm customers	*Occasional support of specialist training programmes	*Variety of "special" loan schemes in- cluding equity provision *Operation of loan guarantee scheme with the Department of Trade and Industry *Certain "joint" schemes with the Department of Industry using EEC money in "special areas"	*Occasional local involvement in "special small firm" premises/ workshop provision

179

ORGANISATION	NATURE OF ORGANISATION	SOFTWARE			HARDWARE	
		Information/ Advice	Counselling/ Consulting	Training & Education	Finance	Other
BUSINESS CLUBS e.g. TEESIDE SMALL BUSINESS CLUB 52, Corporation Road Middlesborough Cleveland 7412RN Tel: 44.642.2234 21	*A recent phenomenon in the U.K. but growing *The Clubs are private organi- sations of small firms based on a local area. "Services" will vary but can include:	*Club newspaper and information sheets	*Informal counselling by Club members	*Guest speakers *Seminars *Regular discussion meetings		

		Information/ Advice	Counselling/ Consulting	Training & Education	Finance	Other
BUSINESS CLUBS e.g. TEESIDE SMALL BUSINESS CLUB 52, Corporation Road	*A recent phenomenon in the U.K. but growing *The Clubs are	*Club newspaper and information sheets	*Informal counselling by Club members	*Guest speakers *Seminars *Regular discussion		

Part III

Assistance in Key Areas

Exports

ORGANISATION	NATURE OF ORGANISATION	SOFTWARE			HARDWARE	
		Information Advice	Counselling/ Consulting	Training & Education	Finance	Other
AUSTRIAN FEDERAL ECONOMIC CHAMBER	*Independent body under public law	*Regular publications on matters of foreign trade, market opportunities, customs regulations, fairs, exhibitions and trade missions abroad *Advice concerning product marketing abroad and contacts with possible business partners *Advice concerning participation at fairs, exhibitions and trade missions abroad	*Regular and continuing export counselling, free of charge	*Courses in export administration *Foreign language courses *Cooperation with Economic Universities and organisation of export-management courses *Organisation of group exhibits at fairs and exhibitions abroad *Organisation of special exhibitions, fashion and other presentations *Organisation of business opportunity meetings and trade missions	*Partial refunds for individual participation at fairs and exhibitions abroad *Partial refunds of travelling expenses in connection with above and for participation at trade missions and business opportunity meetings *Partial refunds of cost of export-publications *Partial refunds for advertising abroad *Financial support towards cost off foreign language courses and for foreign language correspondence *Financial support for training of mechanics from developing countries	
KONTROLLBANK	*Subsidized by Federal Ministry of Finance to support exports			*Export credits refinanced by Osterreichische Kontrollbank AG: -To finance the export of goods and services with medium and long term payment periods		
WIFI-INSTITUTES FOR ECONOMIC DEVELOPMENT OF THE AUSTRIAN FEDERAL ECONOMIC CHAMBER			*Export promotion activities include: -Close cooperation with the Department of foreign trade and policy of the Federal Economic Chamber -Trade fairs, technical symposia WIFI's trade fairs abroad (1983/ events) promote and support enterprises by financial information and advisory services which include the provision of documents in foreign languages -Consulting Within the framework of the various focal points for consultancy such as innovation, marketing and cooperation, an attempt is made to create the "infrastructure" which is sometimes missing for export activities -Export academy and training programmes The area of primary and further training is also of special importance in this respect. In addition to specialised seminars and courses at universities of economics, a special export academy was established			

ORGANISATION	NATURE OF ORGANISATION	SOFTWARE			HARDWARE	
		Information Advice	Counselling/ Consulting	Training & Education	Finance	Other
OFFICE BELGE DU COMMERCE EXTERIEUR/BELGISCHE DIENST VOOR DE BUITERLANDSE HANDEL, 162 BLD. E. JACQMAIN 1000 BRUXELLES TEL: 32.2.219.45. 50	*Belgian Office for Foreign Trade	*Statistical information on imports-exports *Commercial, economic, and financial information *Tenders *Technical norms and all practical information *Compendium of exporters, combining all relevant information and advice sent to all exporting companies			*Financial support for training costs of foreign trainees with the purpose to promote Belgian exports in the trainee's country. This intervention amounts to 15.000 to 22.000 BF per month and is available to all companies provided the training is of a technological nature *Provides subsidies to finance 50% of expertise costs of SB willing to create an export service and which need the assistance of an outside consultant *Assistance of up to 50% of various expenses of companies showing a special effort for prospecting difficult markets and which incur exceptional financial costs *Financial participation in commercial events such as fairs, exhibitions, etc. *Free market studies to detect distribution channels	
INTERNATIONAL TRADE INVESTMENT INSTITUTE (ITI), 2, Ave. de Broqueville 1150 Bruxelles Tel: 32.2.7119880	*Founded in 1977 by specialist professors & experts in foreign trade *Pursues promotion policy for Belgian exports & international investment			*Trains graduates in foreign trade and makes enterprises aware of market abroad *Certified training programme "specialists in Foreign Trade" *Other export oriented courses		
INSTITUT DE REESCOMPTE ET DE GUARANTIE, 78 Rue du Commerce, 1040 Bruxelles Tel: 32.2.5117330	*Institute of Rediscount and Guarantees				*Short term financing of exports through rediscount of bills presented by banks - credit export medium term financing for companies exporting equipment goods	

185

ORGANISATION	NATURE OF ORGANISATION	SOFTWARE			HARDWARE	
		Information Advice	Counselling/ Consulting	Training & Education	Finance	Other
COMITE POUR LA PROMOTION DU COMMERCE EXTERIEUR DU MINISTERE DU COMMERCE EXTERIEUR, 4, RUE DES QUATRE BRAS, 1000 BRUXELLES TEL: 32.2.5136240	*Committee for the promotion of exports of equipment goods				*Aims at reducing interest credit rates for exports outside the EEC for companies exporting equipment goods of an economic and social interest for Belgium	
TECHNICAL COMMITTEE FOR THE PROMOTION OF FOREIGN TRADE	*Dependent on the Ministry of Foreign Trade				*Grants to companies to support the training of personnel for foreign trade	
OFFICE NATIONAL DU DUCROIRE (OND)/ NATIONAL DELCREDERE DIENST, 40 Square de Meeus, 1040 Bruxelles Tel: 32.2.5123800	*National insurance body providing guarantee against risks linked to exports in countries outside the EEC				*Provides through insurance policies guarantees against various risks linked to export outside the EEC and in communist countries (risks of credit, production, exchanges, etc.)	
SERVICE OF ECONOMIC EXPANSION OF SB MINISTRY OF THE WALLOON REGION	*Regional authority implementing the legislation concerning economic expansion				*Extension of the benefit period for interest rate subsidy (see general matrix) for companies which increase their exports by 20% during a period of 12 consecutive months after obtaining credit	
MINISTRY OF THE BRUSSELS REGION	*Idem for Brussels					
MINISTRY OF THE FLEMISH REGION	*Idem for Flanders					
UME, 42, Rue Capitaine Crespel, 1050 Bruxelles Tel: 32.2.5134534	*Walloon union of enterprises *Private union		*Temporary assistance of up to 3 years by an expert in export problems of SME's *Promotion of the creation of exporting groupings. Presently 6 such clubs are in existence in Wallonia			

186

ORGANISATION	NATURE OF ORGANISATION	SOFTWARE			HARDWARE	
		Information Advice	Counselling/ Consulting	Training & Education	Finance	Other
DANISH COUNCIL FOR CRAFTS, TRADES & SMALL INDUSTRY	*National trade organisation (see general matrix)		*Marketing and Export Consultants *"Hire an Export Manager Scheme" The consultant assesses the firm's possibility for export. The work tasks may include: -collecting market information at home and abroad -compiling market analyses -establishing contacts and starting transactions -following-up on customer contacts -training the sales staff in the area of exports Up to 20, no more than 60 days of work, often divided into intervals Fees: per consultant day: Dkr. 1,410, including domestic travel and travel abroad according to agreement. Possibility of reduction of fees, depending on the actual project *Manages a number of consultants partly financed by the "Productivity and Consultancy Scheme"			
DANISH TRADE FUND Codanhus GE. Kongevej 60 DK 1850 Copenhagen V Tel: 45.1.313825	*Directorate of Ministry of Industry administering Danish Export Credit Council & Export Promotion Council (see below)					

ORGANISATION	NATURE OF ORGANISATION	SOFTWARE			HARDWARE	
		Information Advice	Counselling/ Consulting	Training & Education	Finance	Other
DANISH EXPORT CREDIT COUNCIL Codanhus GE Kongevej 60 DK 1850 Copenhagen V Tel: 45.1.37.3825						*Export Credit Scheme: -Guarantees against loss on out- standing foreign debts. Security for financial institutions for loans for an operational financing export scheme (not for initial financing) -For firms that export Danish products and services. Not to be used for starting a new business -The most common securities cover up to 90% of the required loan. The terms of the loans and the rates of interest vary according to the conditions of the individual guarantee/security arrangement *Financing of Long-Credit: -Financing the export of Danish-produced capital assets, factory works, etc. plus know-how, projects, etc. Financing of at least 2 years connected with export. -Present interest rate: from 10-12.5%. In case of export to the EEC countries current market rates apply. Term of loan: at least 2 years, normally limited to 5 years. Normally at least Dkr 500,000. At least 15% paid in advance. Series loans
EKSPORTFREMMERADET Prinseese Maries alle 2 DK-1908 Copenhagen V Tel: 45.1.231444	*Export promotion council					*Grants in support of collective exports e.g. for: -cultivation of new markets of introduction of new methods of export -hiring an export consultant -participation in fairs, exhibitions, conferences abroad -preparation of quotation materials only available for groups of firms (at least 3 participants) -advertising publications -export cooperation 40$ of the direct expenses are subsidized, more when consultant arrangements are involved (55% of maximum salary of Dkr 180,000). Support is granted no more than 3 times for the same activity. Support for consultancy up to 3 years (4 years in very special cases). "No cure no pay" may be arranged in some individual cases
FINANCING INSTITUTE FOR INDUSTRY & CRAFT (DANISH EXPORT FINANCE CORPORATION)	*Private National Purpose to effect advantageous long-term investment funds *Details in general matrix					*EM loan for export, environment & energy purposes: for exporting firms who can compete with imported products, loans for starting new production, expanding production, etc. are offered (details in general matrix)
TRADE DIVISION OF MINISTRY OF FOREIGN AFFAIRS		*Offers market research, contact arrangement, data bank service through which: -If a company wants to export its products, the Trade Department of the Ministry of Foreign Affairs may assist in finding the right markets, in establishing a contact to potential cutomers and in solving other export problems -The assistance is confidential and free of charge (only for definite, ordered services the cost price is paid). However, the assistance is individual and adapted to solving the problems of the individual compay				

188

ORGANISATION	NATURE OF ORGANISATION	SOFTWARE			HARDWARE	
		Information Advice	Counselling/ Consulting	Training & Education	Finance	Other
FEDERATION OF DANISH INDUSTRIES		*Information and services and credit facilities, international and Danish work on standards and standardization, export possibilities and technical impediments to trade, etc. *Operates Export Bureau to assist industrial companies in solving their marketing problems both on the home market and abroad *The Export Bureau collects, evaluates, registers and communicates knowledge on export markets, partly directly to the individual member firms, partly as a link in collective activities directed towards promoting exports *The export promoting tasks are handled by four departments: -the Project Department -the Marketing Department -the Data Department -the Consultancy Department				

ORGANISATION	NATURE OF ORGANISATION	SOFTWARE			HARDWARE	
		Information Advice	Counselling/ Consulting	Training & Education	Finance	Other
MINISTRY OF TRADE AND INDUSTRY						*Supports the improvement of exports (extension, new products) *Finances the expenses for exhibitions
	*The Export Guarantee Board					*Gives the financial institutions, customers, etc. security for financing
	*The Customs Administration Board	*Information about customs and statistics - imported and exported articles classified by trade-marks				
SUOMEN ULKOMAANKA UPPALITTO Arkadiankatu 4-6B 00100 Helsinki Tel: 358.0.69591	*The Finnish Foreign Trade Association *Promotes Finland's foreign trade *Is Maintained by the Confederation of Finnish Industries and its suborganisations, about 800 member companies, the State of Finland and the Finnish Furniture Exporters' Association and serves all Finnish companies engaged in export trade *Employs about 150 people, 12 at regional offices outside Helsinki	*Makes export advisory services available to Finnish companies, provides information on markets and trade opportunities, arranges promotional and PR campaigns, issues publications presenting Finland's export supply, and offers services related to import trade *Is also the operational liaison centre for the Commercial Secretaries stationed in the Commercial Sections of the 58 Finnish diplomatic missions abroad *Clients outside Finland are furnished with information on Finland's industry and market as well as on prospects for doing business. On request they are also put in touch with Finnish exporters and importers. The computerized register of Finnish exporters and their products and services is available to clients in and outside Finland.				
COMMERCIAL SECRETARIES (Can be contacted through Foreign Trade Association, above)	*The Commercial Secretaries form the Finnish Foreign Trade Association's operational network abroad. The Association coordinates their work, but administratively they are subordinate to the Finnish Ministry for Foreign Affairs *The Commercial Secretaries are recruited from the private sector and posted to Finland's diplomatic missions for five-year periods	*Provide clients with information on Finnish industry, the range of Finnish exports and trade opportunities. *Finish companies are furnished with information on markets and sales opportunities, and they can request advice and assistance in their marketings efforts				

190

ORGANISATION	NATURE OF ORGANISATION	SOFTWARE			HARDWARE	
		Information Advice	Counselling/ Consulting	Training & Education	Finance	Other
SUOMEN VIENTILUOTTO OY Etelaesplanadi 8 P.O. Box 123 00131 Helsinki Tel: 358.1.177171	*Finnish Export Credit Ltd. *FEC is a joint-stock company that promotes the export of Finnish goods, services and know-how by granting medium and long-term credits *FEC finances its operations by issuing long-term subordinated debentures and by borrowing on the domestic and international capital markets		*Project study and advisory services at different stages of product exports		*Finances the export of capital goods, of contstruction and of consulting services including projects exports in the form of medium and long-term credits *Credits are also available for setting up consignment stocks abroad and to finance foreign leases of Finnish equipment as well as certain equity investments abroad	
VIEXPO EXPORT CENTER	*Co-operation owned by 300 members *Government and local municipalities *Promote exports of small and medium sized industry in Ostrobothnia (Province of Vaasa plus adjacent regions) *Employees: 10 Budget: FIM 2.7 Mill. (1984) *Mainly working with companies employing 10-100 *Regional *Is one of a number of regional organisations established to develop SME export activity	*Business contacts, market information (partly through databanks), information on practical matters in exports (e.g. customs papers, requirements, transport, agreements, etc.), technical information (standards, requirements), etc. Trade office in the Mid-Nordic (Mittnorden) co-operation	*Market surveys, marketing plans, export projects, technical checkups, representative "hunting" translation and interpreting service *Fees paid according to subsidised price list (approx. 50%) *C. 700 consulting hours	*Export marketing, export papers, export financing *1/2 - 2 days *Subsidized *c. 250		*Export projects -exhibitions -sales missions in groups of 6-8 companies *Exhibition equipment -complete equipment for erection of c.500 sq.m *Computer service -register of all producers with more than 5 emp. in the region -databank services *Video equipment
SUOMEN MESSUT P.O. Box 21 00521 Helsinki Tel: 358.0.141400 (Helsinki Exhibition and Congress Centre, HECC)	*The Finnish Fair Corporation *Founded in 1919 *Owned by Finnish industry and commerce *Arranges trade fairs and exhibitions in Finland and abroad	*Congress activities (facilities and services)				
THE CHAMBERS OF COMMERCE		*Inform and gets information about articles of commerce by using connections around the world				
	*The Finnish Institute of Export	*Provides special knowledge and training for persons engaged in export activity				

ORGANISATION	NATURE OF ORGANISATION	SOFTWARE			HARDWARE	
		Information Advice	Counselling/ Consulting	Training & Education	Finance	Other
CENTRE FRANCAIS DU COMMERCE EXTERIEUR (CFCE), 10 avenue d'Iena 75116 Paris Tel: 33.1.7236123	*French Center for Foreign Trade	*Edits information booklets and magazines (e.g. MOCI and "Actualites reglementations"), surveys and research on foreign markets *Edits guides for exporters *Facilitates contacts with marketing officials abroad (P.E.E.) *Organizes conferences, etc. *Is preparing a foreign trade data bank *Has set up an agency to deal with info and advice on foreign trade to S.B. (SOFREDEX)				
REGIONAL COUNCILS (Conseils Regionaux)	*Public decentralized bodies having broad powers. Intervene in economic, social and administrative matters. Some has set up development agencies (e.g. Agence Regionale de Developpement in the Nord-Pas-de-Calais Region) with research field activities	*Edit information documents, including exports *Support selected operations broad (e.g. negotiations of a contract between a group of French exporters in the North Region and Algeria); help create and develop contacts with foreign firms and organisations *Participate in fairs and missions abroad, develop contacts with marketing officials abroad (PEE), support collective activities (e.g. promotion of new techniques for which foreign outlets are sought, etc.)		*Supports business schools, training centers for activities related to foreign operations	*Subsidies or financing of operations relating to selected foreign operations *Participate in procedures of low-cost financing by special bodies or committees (e.g. CORRI, CODEFI, CIRI)	

192

ORGANISATION	NATURE OF ORGANISATION	SOFTWARE			HARDWARE	
		Information Advice	Counselling/ Consulting	Training & Education	Finance	Other
BANQUE FRANCAISE DU COMMERCE EXTERIEUR (BFCE), 21 Blvd. Haussmann 75009 Paris Tel: 33.1.2474747	*French Bank for Foreign Trade *A public bank specialized in the financing of exports				*Grants special loans to exporters in cooperation with such institutions as Credit National, CEPME, SDR, CIDISE. A special procedure is the so-called "Pret IX",to an annual amount of 3-5 billion FF, most of which goes to S.B.	
COMPAGNIE FRANCAISE D'ASSURANCE POUR LE COMMERCE EXTERIEUR (COFACE), 32 rue Marbeuf 75008 Paris Tel: 33.1.2566020	*French Foreign Trade Company *A public organisation granting guarantees for all types of operations on foreign markets. Has set up ten regaional agencies to be in close touch with SB				*Some procedures, e.g. "Assurance-Foire" (Foreign Fairs), "Assurance Credit simplifiee", "Assurance Prospection" and "Assurance Prospection simplifiee" "Assurance Credit" (sales interruption, defaults, exchange risks, global policies) are in particular suited to S.B. needs	
CREDIT NATIONAL 45 rue Saint-Dominique 75007 Paris Tel: 33.1.7833470	*Public bank for medium and long term credit. Very large scope of operations. May assist S.B. in supplying finance for operations tied to exports or investment abroad				*A special type of financing (DIE procedure) is especially designed for exporters, including S.B.	
SOFININDEX (SOFINNOVA) 51 rue Saint-Georges 75009 Paris Tel: 33.1.2806870	*Semi-public finance company designed to finance equity especially for S.B. engaged in foreign trade				*Subscribes to new shares, for a limited period of time. It has a capital of 20 M FF (1980)	
GUARANTEE FUNDS	*Some organisations (COFACE, SOFRESCAU, Credit National, UFINEX) have set up guarantee funds to cover banks and firms against foreign operations risks				*Provide guarantees, cautions or counterguarantees	

ORGANISATION	NATURE OF ORGANISATION	SOFTWARE			HARDWARE	
		Information Advice	Counselling/ Consulting	Training & Education	Finance	Other
CHAMBERS OF COMMERCE		*Have generally info. offices to give information to S.B. involved in - or envisaging foreign operations		*Organises training, seminars, etc. for S.B. involved in - or envisaging - foreign operations		
ASSOCIATIONS OF S.B. AND ORGANISATIONS DEALING WITH FOREIGN OPERATIONS	*There is a wide variety of associations and networks between exporters, chambers of commerce, etc. Examples of such associations are "export clubs", export management groups, associations organising group activities such as missions board, pilot projects and "piggy-back" operations					
INSTITUT DU COMMERCE EXTERIEUR (ICI), 5 avenue Pierre 1er de Serbie 75116 paris Tel: 33.1.7236123				*A specialized school and training centre for persons or staff working or preparing to work in foreign trade and related activities		
CONSEIL PERMANENT DE LA FORMATION A L'EXPORTATION (Council for Training in Foreign Trade)	*Is, designed to survey, coordinate and improve training activities in the field of foreign trade					

194

		Information Advice	Counselling/ Consulting	Training & Education	Finance	Other

ORGANISATION	NATURE OF ORGANISATION	SOFTWARE			HARDWARE	
		Information Advice	Counselling/ Consulting	Training & Education	Finance	Other
BUNDESSTELLE FUR AUSSENHANDELS INFORMATION (BFAI), Blaubach 13, D-5000 Koln 1 Tel: 49.221.205 71	*Government agency for foreign trade information and assistance	*Specialized trade information and advice offered				
LANDER GOVERNMENTS						*Promotion of cooperative export measures Subsidies for market research and consultancy *Subsidies for trade fair/exhibition participation
BUNDESVERBAND DES DEUTSCHEN GROSS-UND AUSSENHANDELS (BGA), Kaiser-Friedrich Str. 13 D-5300 Bonn 1 Tel: 49.228.2180 57	*Particularly specialized national federations experienced in export business					
BUNDESVERBAND DES DEUTSCHEN EXPOSTHANDELS Gotenstr. 21 D-2000 Hamburg 1 Tel: 49.40.236016 25						
BUNDESAMT FUR GEWERBLICHE WIRTSCHAFT (BAW), Frankfurter Str. 29-31 D-6236 Eschborn Tel: 49.6.196.4041						
AUSSTELLUNGSUND MESSAUSSCHUSS DER DEUTSCHEN WIRTSCHAFT (AUMA) Lindenstr. 8 D-5000 Koln 1 Tel: 49.221.219091	*Exhibitions and Fairs Committee for German Industry					
CHAMBERS OF COMMERCE AND INDUSTRY & CHAMBERS OF CRAFTS, BUSINESS ASSOCIATIONS, TRADE AGENTS, BANKS, RKW	*See general matrix	*Major partners in informing and advising SMEs about Chambers of Commerce and Industry abroad, about financing, public or private, assurance facilities and contract conditions				

195

ORGANISATION	NATURE OF ORGANISATION	SOFTWARE			HARDWARE	
		Information Advice	Counselling/ Consulting	Training & Education	Finance	Other
IRISH EXPORT BOARD (CTT)	*A state owned sponsored limited liability company with major responsibility of promoting export services to firms. Is not small firms specialist but 70% of enquiries are from firms under 100 employees. Staff of 330, 1/3 overseas. Have small firms export department	*Information and research on markets from published sources and network of 25 overseas offices. *Special advisory service with 40 staff and some regional officers proactively concerned with plant visiting and advice on exports (1,000 firms interviewed in 1982) *Special advisory service on design and product development for overseas markets -Support for exhibitions	*Is encouraging development of export groups. Seven group schemes at present. Fund salary for limited period of "group" export salesman		*General available financial support for exhibitions, promotions as per standard service	
INDUSTRIAL TRAINING AUTHORITY (ANCO)	*State supported "autonomous" agency charged with the development of training throughout Ireland. Staff 2,000. Budget IR 67m in 1982. Operates levy grant system to raise small amount of revenue. Funded by the European Social Fund and Youth Employment Agency and Irish government *Has now special Small Firms Division			*Overseas Marketing Programme to place trained personnel in small company. For personnel over 25. Company pays a fee but tutorial costs and personal allowances of trainee are paid. -Export Marketing Programme matching company and trained personnel over 6 months. 13 Workshops of 3 days each. Company pays fee but all allowances and tutorial costs of trainee are met		

ORGANISATION	NATURE OF ORGANISATION	SOFTWARE			HARDWARE	
		Information Advice	Counselling/ Consulting	Training & Education	Finance	Other
CENTRAL MEDIOCREDITO THROUGH REGIONAL MEDIOCREDITO -IRI -EFIBANCA -MEDIOBANCA -CONTROLBANCA -INTERBANCA AND WITH THE AUTHORISATION OF MINISTRY OF FOREIGN TRADE OF OF SACE	*National public medium term financing corporation *Public insurance company				*Credit to supplier (export of goods supply of services, feasibility studies, construction in foreign countries) 5 year loans, maximum assisted amount: 30 billion lire. Interest rate varies according to the time space and the reference currency. Law 24/5/1977 n. 227 *Credit to the "buyer" Financing to the foreign banks who let the buyers pay cash to the Italian supplier. Same law advance upon or discount against shipping documents and letters of credit *Above financing limited to SMEs	
ITALIAN SOCIETY FOR CREDIT INSURANCE (SIAC)	*Insurance company					*Insurance plans specialised for small business, maximum 100 million exports and two clients only
NATIONAL INSURANCE INSTITUTE (INA)	*Independent public company					*Credit insurance
FOREIGN TRADE INSTITUTE (ICE)	*Public body *Ministry of foreign trade network of representatives abroad	*Bank data *Information concerning foreign trade *Promotion of Italian exports and assistance in introductions to foreign markets	*Operative technical assistance *Assistance for contracts with foreign firms *Marketing organisation *Assistance in cases of commercial controversies *Advertising in the official magazine (English language)	*Courses on foreign trade (8 months) for young men with degrees and candidate for the foreign department of Italian firms		*Incentives for participation of Italian firms in foreign exhibitions *Delegations of Italian entrepreneurs and managers in foreign countries
INSTITUTE FOR ASSISTANCE AND DEVELOPMENT OF THE SOUTH (IASM)	*Public		*Assistance and market promotion to SMEs in Southern Italy			
CERVED	*Owned by Italian Chambers of Commerce, Industry, Agriculture and Handicraft *Not specific SME	*Comprehensive information by data-bank on markets, production, distribution structures of many foreign countries				

ORGANISATION	NATURE OF ORGANISATION	SOFTWARE			HARDWARE	
		Information Advice	Counselling/ Consulting	Training & Education	Finance	Other
CHAMBERS OF COMMERCE, INDUSTRY, AGRICULTURE AND HANDICRAFT	*Act directly and through regional centers for foreign trade	*Information on foreign markets, world custom laws, treaties and agreements, schedule of local importers and exporters		*Courses similar to ICE's (see above) at local level		*Arbitral chamber *Promotion of Italian participation in foreign exhibitions
FEDEREXPORT	*Agency of Confindustria *Not specific SME		*Undertakes promotional activities			
ITALIAN CHAMBERS OF COMMERCE IN FOREIGN COUNTRIES	*Private *Not specific SME		*Assistance to Italian exporters			
CAPAC	*Private, but assisted by public funds - Agency of Unione Commercianti (Commerce Employers' Federation)			*Courses similar to those of ICE (see above) at local level		
INTERCOOP, ESTEUROPA, ITALIMPEX, RESTITAL, COOPIMPORT-EXPORT, RARUM, COMMIMPEX	*Companies owned by Lega delle Cooperative (Cooperatives Association)		*Promote, in the eastern communist countries and in the Republic of China, the export of different products of Italian cooperatives even by counter trade agreements *Assistance to exporting cooperatives			
INTEREXPO	*Private		*Assistance to SMEs in foreign exhibitions			

198

| | | | Information Advice | Counselling/ Consulting | Training & Education | Finance | Other |

ORGANISATION	NATURE OF ORGANISATION	SOFTWARE			HARDWARE	
		Information Advice	Counselling/ Consulting	Training & Education	Finance	Other
EXPORTBEUOR- DERINGS EN VOOR LICHTINGSCHENST (EVD)	*Main state organisation for support of exports	*Range of information and advisory services and seminars available to all firms indiscriminately *Arranges trade fairs and exhibitions			*Subsidy scheme for cooperation between small firms to employ an expert manager for 3 years. Subsidy scheme for engineers and consultants to help them tender for overseas contracts	
CHAMBERS OF COMMERCE	*Public Law institutions not especially small business. 38 Chambers throughout country	*Provide standard information (legal, commercial, trade) Of importance in export information				
FEDERATION FOR THE NETHERLANDS EXPORT (FENEDEX) The Hague	*Private non-profit organisation which promotes Dutch exports - not specifically small firm. (800 members)	*Provides advice, experience exchange, promotions and advice on partners and overseas cooperation agreements		*Organises seminars		

There are few special services exclusive to small firms. In addition to the above, the private banks have trade promotion departments and produce export credit and insurance through links with the Nederlandische Credietverzekering Maatschappij NV. (Netherland Credit Insurance Company)

199

ORGANISATION	NATURE OF ORGANISATION	SOFTWARE			HARDWARE	
		Information Advice	Counselling/ Consulting	Training & Education	Finance	Other
THE EXPORT COUNCIL OF NORWAY	*The Export Council of Norway assists Norwegian companies with the marketing of their goods and services abroad. In addition to the head office in Oslo, its 32 stations around the world are at the service of Norwegian firms *The Export Council collaborates closely with the Norwegian foreign service. Its representatives are attached to Norway's diplomatic and consular stations in the relevant country	*Important aspects of the Council's activities include provision of information and the making of useful contacts abroad. The demand for specialised assistance is on the increase and the Export Council's services are being constantly adapted to meet such requirements. The services available are: market analysis and marketing plans, market entry, promotional activities and special services		*As a result of the Export More Campaign, local export clubs have been established in several counties. They serve as a local forum for exchange of experiences on export matters	*Direct state aid is available for export promotion activities	
THE NORWEGIAN INSTITUTE OF EXPORT EDUCATION	*The Norwegian Institute of Export Education is a non-profit organization, whose aim is to cover the need of special education through export courses, seminars, conferences and study groups, as well as creating contact between the exporters *The Institute is also responsible for the training of personnel employed by the Export Council of Norway and the Royal Ministry of Foreign Affairs *The Institute is the only institute in the field of export marketing in Norway			*The Institute has a close cooperation with a number of Norwegian organizations and associations in various fields, and undertakes special training programmes, seminars, etc. for organizations and industrial companies, in Norway and abroad. The Institute offers short term programmes: one day - three weeks	*Grants available for students according to special rules	

ORGANISATION	NATURE OF ORGANISATION	SOFTWARE			HARDWARE	
		Information Advice	Counselling/ Consulting	Training & Education	Finance	Other
INSTITUTE FOR THE SUPPORT OF SMALL AND MEDIUM INDUSTRIES (IAPMEI)	*Government Deparment depending on the Ministry for Industry and Energy	*Offers technical and marketing, both through its own staff and a body of private specialists ready to advise firms in different matters *Helps SMEs in marketing research *Promotes and supports joint export marketing groups of firms *Helps to prepare market studies for presentations to banks		*Promotes marketing courses for SME Managers	*Financial support in the sharing of expenses by means of non-repayable loans for specific actions in particular: -the carrying out of market surveys and of feasibility and financial studies -the participation of small and medium sized companies in fairs and exhibitions -the provision of guarantees for financing for working capital, wherever the guarantees given by the small and medium sized companies are considered insufficient by the Banks and the operation is recognized as being important -grants towards exports such as market research, sales promotion, cost of product design, etc. -financial help to establish joint export working groups	
PORTUGUESE BOARD OF TRADE (ICEP)	*Government Department depending on the Ministry for Trade and Tourism	*Provides marketing information and advice on all aspects of overseas markets (e.g. size, prices, quality, distribution, etc.) *Organizes liaison with potential customers or agents, display facilities, interpreter service, etc. *Produces export market reports and surveys and operates a computerised marketing information service *Provides credit-ratings, size and reports on prospective customers *Advises on design or choice of designers *Promotes joint-export marketing groups of firms *Organizes and supports commercial missions to international fairs and exhibitions				
COMMERCIAL BANKS	*Nationalized banks				*Realize short term credit operations for exports	

ORGANISATION	NATURE OF ORGANISATION	SOFTWARE			HARDWARE	
		Information Advice	Counselling/ Consulting	Training & Education	Finance	Other
COMPANY OF CREDIT INSURANCE (COSEC)	*Public enterprise devoted to all kinds of credit insurance, mainly for export markets	*Promotion of the Credit Insurance concepts and procedures, its advantages and difficulties, in order to optimize the effects of exports, minimizing the respective risks	*Advice on the clients of the SME in order to avoid the failure of business, in the home market and abroad	*Training and information activities (meetings) for industrialists and exporters, in order to spread the concept of credit insurance	*Credit insurance either for internal operations, or for export ones	
INDUSTRIAL ASSOCIATIONS	*Sectoral Associations	*Publish sectoral industrial periodic bulletins and reviews				

ORGANISATION	NATURE OF ORGANISATION	SOFTWARE			HARDWARE	
		Information Advice	Counselling/ Consulting	Training & Education	Finance	Other
INSTITUTE OF SMALL & MEDIUM ENTERPRISES (IMPI)	*Self-governing state agency . *Dependency of the Ministry of Industry	*Participates in joint marketing action abroad (advice, technical assistance)		*Subsidizes managment courses organized by trade associations, employers' associations and the Chamber of Commerce -TAGE (Technicas Aplicadas a la Gestion Empresarial) -Courses on specific subjects -Seminars -Roundtable discussions	*Minority participation in company capital up to 45% for 3 years, renewable for 3 additional years	
CONSEJO SUPERIOR DE CAMARAS DE COMERCIO; INDUSTRIA Y NAVEGACION Claudio Coello 19 28001 Madrid Tel: 91.275.3400	*Public associations of Chambers of Commerce, Industry and Shipping	*Promotion of exports *Advice, trade missions, organize trade fairs, international relations. Certificates of origin, arbitration in trade conflicts				
INSTITUTO NACIONAL DE FOMENTO A LA EXPORTACION (INFE)	*Dependency of the Ministry of Economy and the Treasury	*Information, market studies and sectoral planning		*Individual trips to study market opportunities. Subsides to attend trade fairs		
COMPANIA ESPANOLA DE SEGUROS DE CREDITO A LA EXPORTACION (CESCE) Paseo Castellana 147 28046 Madrid Tel: 34.91.2795900	*Insures risks on foreign trade operations				*Covers foreign trade risks (manufacturing period, loan payment period, special coverage)	
BRANCH OFFICES OF THE MINISTRY OF TREASURY					*Subsidize cost of advertising, promotion and exhibition at trade fairs: up to 20% of the cost *"Export Letter" issued for 4 years; reduced interest on different types of credit (5-10% interest); preference in using promotion measures; reduced insurance premiums (5%), higher percentage (10%) in temporary compensation for damages	

SMALL FIRM ASSISTANCE IN SPAIN: EXPORTS

ORGANISATION	NATURE OF ORGANISATION	SOFTWARE			HARDWARE	
		Information Advice	Counselling/ Consulting	Training & Education	Finance	Other
BANCO EXTERIOR DE ESPANA & COMMERCIAL AND SAVINGS BANKS					*Short-term credit for exports: 10% interest. Amount:80% FOB value (85% with Export Letter) *Medium and long-term credits for export purposes: Interest 10-12%. Amount: 80% FOB value (85% with Export Letter)	

ORGANISATION	NATURE OF ORGANISATION	SOFTWARE			HARDWARE	
		Information Advice	Counselling/ Consulting	Training & Education	Finance	Other
REGIONAL DEVELOPMENT FUNDS	*24 regional agencies financed by SIND and the communities *RD s are the operating organizations for both the Export-Council and for SIND (see below)	*RD s can give information about business opportunities and technical advice on marketing. Normally each RD agency has 2-3 consultants working in the export area. Together with the "Export-manager-for-hire" (formally employed by Export-Council). RD s promote joint export/marketing groups of firms. They also organize commercial missions to international fairs and exhibitions			*Provide financial help for joint export-marketing groups. Can also provide grants toward experts such as market research, sales promotion within special limits	
SVERIGES EXPORTRAD, Storgaten 19 Box 5513 114 85 Stockholm Tel: 46.8.7838500	*Swedish export council *Government Department within the Ministry of Trade	*Provides marketing, information and advice on all aspects of export markets (e.g. size, prices, quality) *Organizes liaison with potential customers or agents, display facilities, interpreter services, custom question services, etc. *Produces export market reports and surveys *Promotes joint export marketing groups of firms *Organizes and supports commercial missions to international fairs and exhibitors *Promotes "export-seminars for SMEs", "action-programmes", "market-introduction services", and "Export-manager-for-hire"			*Gives financial help within the programme: -Small Business Export Package -Action Programme up to 40% of costs -Market-introduction services up to 40.000 SEK *5000 crown-grants	
AB SVENSK EXPORTKREDIT Biblioteksgatan 11 Box 7353 103 93 Tel:468.14.4800	*The Swedish Export Credit Corporation *A limited company under Ministry of Trade				*Provides state guarantee financial support to companies exporting to developing countries where trade is regulated by state *Also provides guarantee credits for trade with countries with instability in banks and/or commercial life	
SWEDISH NATIONAL INDUSTRIAL BOARD (SIND)		*Market research within the so called branch program (for some special branches) *Promotion of export cooperation and training				
SVENSKA HANDELS- KAMMARFORBUNDET Tradgardsgatan 9 Box 16050 103 22 Stockholm Tel:468.23.12.00	*The Association of Swedish Chambers of Commerce and Industry	*Inform and get information about articles of commerce by using connections around the world. Give services in export technical questions. Also promote export cooperation between SMEs				
INDUSTRIAL ASSOCIATIONS		*Publish periodic sectorial industrial bulletins and reviews				

ORGANISATION	NATURE OF ORGANISATION	SOFTWARE			HARDWARE	
		Information Advice	Counselling/ Consulting	Training & Education	Finance	Other
CHAMBERS OF COMMERCE/ INNOVATION CONSULTING CENTRES	*Private associations	*Offer information and industrial directories				*Assistance in export procedures
EXPORT ASSOCIATION FOR TRADE AND INDUSTRY (EXPORT GEMEINSCHAFT FUER INDUSTRIE UND GEWERBE)	*Private cooperative society	*Provide member firms data on export markets	*Help member firms to identify export opportunities			*Handle export procedures for member firms
OFFICE FOR GUARANTEE OF EXPORT RISKS GESCHAEFTS- STELLE FUR DIE EXPORTRISI- KOGARANTIE -ERG	*Private institution with public support affiliated to Swiss Association of Machinery Manufacturers					*Credit guarantee for risks of export (political transfer, manufacturing, monetary risk and contingency for public institutions and utilities)
PROFESSIONAL ASSOCIATIONS	*Private associations		*Various professional associations help member firms to identify export opportunities			
SWISS INDUSTRIAL DEVELOPMENT INSTITUTE (SIDI)	*Private institute	*Inform members on development projects in the Third World and respective export opportunities *Provide export opportunities for manufacturing and contracting companies	*Telephone consulting service			
SWISS EXPORT EXIM-INDEX (ASSOCIATION FOR EXPORT DEVELOPMENT)	*Private association	*Handle library, inform on export opportunities, offer telephone consulting service	*Assist member firms by consulting in matters of export	*Organise seminars and in-house training		*Search of export partners
SWISS OFFICE FOR THE DEVELOPMENT OF TRADE (SCHWEIZ ZENTRALE FUER HANDELS- FOERDERUNG)	*Private association with public subsidies					*Organises export promotion through fairs and exhibitions
CANTONAL AGENCIES FOR ECONOMIC DEVELOPMENT (KANTONALE AEMTER FUR WIRTSCHAFTS- FOERDERUNG)	*Agencies of Cantonal Governments				*Subsidize part of insurance premiums for export risk guarantee or risk of exchange rate guarantee	

206

ORGANISATION	NATURE OF ORGANISATION	SOFTWARE			HARDWARE	
		Information Advice	Counselling/ Consulting	Training & Education	Finance	Other
BRITISH OVERSEAS TRADE BOARD, 1 Victoria St. London, SW1 Tel: 44.1.2155751	*Department of government specialising in services to exporters with business involvement on the Board *General Services not specific to the small firm although available to it include: -Computerised daily Export Intelligence Service to subscribers (associations and companies) - specific information on eight market areas				*Market entry Guarantee Scheme. Funding of 50% of certain overhead costs of new market entry including: overseas office accommodation staff costs; training; travel and expenses; warehousing; sales promotion. Department takes levy on sales in return. Minimum expenditure 20,000 maximum 150,000	
	*Export Intelligence Market Branches	*Free Advice				
	*Export Market Research Scheme				*Grants for consultation; travel costs; in-house expenses; salary and costs of researchers. (Betweeen 33% and 50% of the costs)	
	*Export Representative Service	*Information and advice on finding agents and representatives. (free if acted upon - 100 pounds otherwise)				
	*Inward Mission Scheme				*50% of costs of bringing to the U.K. visitors who can influence exports	
	*Market Prospects Service	*Advice on prospects for selling goods abroad - includes detailed analysis. 150 pounds refund- able if acted upon				
	*Outward Mission Support				*Financial assistance towards the cost of overseas trade missions for selected markets	
		Other services include: Support for Trade Fairs; Statistics and Market Intelligence; Aid and Trade provision Support Schemes: support for bidding for overseas contracts; overseas seminars				
DEPARTMENT OF TRADE AND INDUSTRY, EXPORT CREDITS GUARANTEE DEPARTMENT, P.O. Box 46, Clements House 14-18 Gresham Street, London, EO2V 7JE Tel: 44.1.7264050	*Government department with nine regional offices. Responsible to Secretary of State, Department of Trade and Industry				*Insures exporters against risks of non-payment and gives guarantees to banks to assist granting of finance to exporters often at favourable rates of interest	

ORGANISATION	NATURE OF ORGANISATION	SOFTWARE			HARDWARE	
		Information Advice	Counselling/ Consulting	Training & Education	Finance	Other
MANPOWER SERVICES COMMISSION	*State financed·semi-autonomous organisation charged with provision and direction of training and employment services nationally			*Special programmes for small exporters providing short workshops linked with in-company activity to help implementation. Linked also with a scheme to provide special support through use of trained manager (formely unemployed) and loaned to the company for a period to help implementation		

208

		Information Advice	Counselling/ Consulting	Training & Education	Finance	Other
MANPOWER SERVICES COMMISSION	*State financed·semi-autonomous					

Start-Ups

ORGANISATION	NATURE OF ORGANISATION	SOFTWARE			HARDWARE	
		Information Advice	Counselling/ Consulting	Training & Education	Finance	Other
ECONOMIC AND SOCIAL INSTI- TUTE OF MIDDLE CLASSES (IESCM)	*Within the Ministry of Middle Classes	*Publishes a brochure "How to start a business"	*Advice and assistance on the creation of firms, location, perspectives of the sector, financing			
MINISTRY OF EMPLOYMENT & LABOR	*National Ministry	*Provision of information to unemployed people or others willing to start a business		*When an unem- ployed worker follows manage- ment training provided in an institute recognized by the Ministry of Middle Classes he is dispensed from daily registration during one year	*An unemployed person willing to start an independent job in given activities may get a loan of up to 500.000 Bf with a favourable interest rate (4% or 5%) for a period between 10 and 15 years *No contribution to the social security fund is due during 2 years for inde- pendent workers hiring their first worker	
PARTICIPATION FUND OF THE CNCP	*Set up within the National Bank for Professional Credit				*Since the revision of its statutes, can grant credits to unemployed workers benefiting from unemployment allowances in order to help them start their own business	
MINISTRY OF THE FLEMISH REGION MINISTRY OF THE WALLOON REGION	*Regional authority *Regional authority				*Premiums foreseen by the Recovery Laws for young workers starting their own busi- ness have been suppressed since June 1, 1982	
IFSCM & RTBF &	*Institute de- pending on the Ministry of Middle Class & Belgian French speaking television	*Series of 6 programmes in- tended for inde- pendent workers on how to create a company. Pro- vides informa- tion on rights and duties. Management and marketing problems and the keys to success				
BRT	*Flemish television	*Idem, but in Flemish language				
GOM, Baron Ruzettelaan 33 8320 Brugge Tel: 32.50.358131	*The Regional Development Society of West Flanders					*In 1984, created the Bedrijven Centrum with the assistance of a private bank. This centre provides premises to about 25 companies

ORGANISATION	NATURE OF ORGANISATION	SOFTWARE			HARDWARE	
		Information Advice	Counselling/ Consulting	Training & Education	Finance	Other
NATIONAL AGENCY OF TECHNOLOGY	*Directorate of *Ministry of Industry, administering: -Council of Technology which administers technological information centres and other services	*Free information to SMEs and would-be entrepreneurs through technological information centres (see general matrix)	*Financial support for the schemes and courses operated by technological institutes and ATV institutes		*Financial support for: *Consultancy service for entrepreneurs starting new production -300-500 projects a year. For persons interested in starting their own business or who have just started a business within the past year. The service includes: *public restrictions/requirements *marketing *financing *product development -The first hours of service are free of charge. The subsequent hourly rate is Dkr 68 (not incl. VAT). Travel time is free, but travel expenses must be paid by the client. Grants usually 75% of consulting expenses *Bursary for entrepreneurs starting new science-based production/firms -To further the establishing of new "science-based" production firms, persons who have prospective ideas are given bursaries under certain conditions. Support is given as salary for the bursary-holders work with various aspects in developing his own ideas, such as technological marketing and financing. Amounts and durations are individually allocated. The framework maintains maximum of contribution to Dkr 15.000 monthly, in 12 months *Programme for promotion of product ideas from private inventors. Provision of technical and marketing advice and risk financing of new inventions and product ideas at the critical stage, i.e. investigation of the technical, commercial viability of the product. Also available for licensing. The idea must have a marketing perspective. The grant is to be repaid only if the invention becomes a source of income. Up to 100% of the expenses associated with experimentation, functional investigation testing, etc. As a rule, the maximum sum is Dkr 80,000-100,000 per projects	
TECHNOLOGICAL INSTITUTES & ATV INSTITUTES	*See general matrix		*Run counsultancy service for entrepreneurs starting new productions (see finance column above)			
DANISH INVEN-TION CENTRE	*Department at Jutland and Taastrup Technological Institutes		*Provide assistance for private Danish inventors/ entrepreneurs with regard to: -product management, coordi-nation, and follow-up including: *prototype production *functional investigation *advisory service on licencing and contract negotiations *The above is part of the programme for promotion of product ideas from private inventors and the bursary for entrepreneurs starting new science-based productions/firms as shown in National Agency of Technology finance column			

SMALL FIRM ASSISTANCE IN FINLAND: START-UPS

ORGANISATION	NATURE OF ORGANISATION	SOFTWARE			HARDWARE	
		Information Advice	Counselling/ Consulting	Training & Education	Finance	Other
MINISTRY OF TRADE & INDUSTRY	*Government Industry	*Arranges start-up days			*Helps companies starting their activity to get support and loans (investment, start-ups)	
THE REGIONAL DEVELOPMENT FUND OF FINLAND Ltd (IKERA)	*Promotion of regional economic development	*Gives advice and counselling			*Grants loans and cash grants to firms starting their activity in developing regions. Furnishes security	
FINNISH NATIONAL FUND FOR R&D (SITRA)	*Foundation emphasising technical and product development				*Finances product development (see general matrix)	
SPONSOR OY	*Venture Capital Corporation				*Equity investment in SMEs (see general matrix)	
THE INDUSTRI- ALIZATION FUND OF FINLAND Ltd (IFF)	*Development financing	*Information, advice and consultancy to start-ups (see general matrix)			*Investment loans & equity investment (see general matrix)	
MINISTRY OF LABOUR	*Government ministry	*Arranges training for new companies starting up				
SME - FOUNDATION	*Foundation for small & medium industry	*Arranges help for firms to get information about their possi- bilities and to realize them			*Supports research work and subsidizes consulting costs	
FINNISH EM- PLOYEES MANAGE- MENT DEVELOP- MENT INSTITUTE (FEMDI)	*Backed by Finnish Employers Association & The Federation of Finnish Government Employers	*Provides seminars and consultancy services *Full details in general matrix				
HELSINKI SCHOOL OF ECONOMICS	*University *Mikkeli & Helsinki campuses		*Development schemes and consultancy services are being planned for the participants	*Start up your business programmes. About 400 hours in about 20 periods within 2 years time		
CHAMBERS OF COMMERCE		*Information about different forms of entrepreneur- ship and start-ups				

ORGANISATION	NATURE OF ORGANISATION	SOFTWARE			HARDWARE	
		Information Advice	Counselling/ Consulting	Training & Education	Finance	Other
AGENCE NATIONALE POUR LA CREATION ET LA REPRISE D'ENTREPRISES NOUVELLES (ANCE) 42, Rue du Bac F - 75007 PARIS Tel: 33.1.544.38. 25	*National Start-up Agency *Public organisation created in 1979 with the two fold tasks: -of facilitating start-ups through information and initiatives -of contributing to the emergence of new small entrepreneurs by appropriate actions *1983 budget was 25 million FF			*Joint actions/programmes with such bodies as Chambers of Commerce, Regional Councils		
REGIONAL COUNCILS (CONSEILS REGIONAUX)	*Among their various activities, intervene to evaluate applications for financial help granted by public authorities for start-ups (see "Finance" column)	*Have taken many initiatives - e.g. jointly with ANCE -to supply information, develop associations, clubs or networks of new entrepreneurs, to collect data and create data banks, to help potential entrepreneurs in administrative procedures, etc. *In some cases, have created agencies (such as Agence Regionale de Developpement in Nord-Pas-de-Calais Region) or development institutes, e.g. ARD Lille has given technical assistance to 45 new entrepreneurs from Sep. 82 to Sep. 83 (380 new jobs created) *Assist unemployed persons seeking to create a new enterprise (e.g. ARD Lille supplies a consultant free to make the feasibility analysis)			*Grant "regulated" subsidies for regional development (PAT), regional employment (PRE), and for start-ups (PRCE). For example, the Regional Council of Nord-Pas-de-Calais has granted (1981-1983) 60 PAT's (35.8 millions FF), 36 PRE's (5.4 millions FF), 66 PRCE's (6 millions FF) May grant subsidies to associations, etc. concerned with start-ups (e.g. SCOP's, Boutiques de Gestion, etc.)	
AGENCY FOR APPLIED RESEARCH (ANVAR)					*Grants to small companies (not branches of, not affiliated to another firm). This consists of giving 50 per cent of the cost of the project up to 150000 FF. The procedure is decentralized (regional agencies)	

213

ORGANISATION	NATURE OF ORGANISATION	SOFTWARE			HARDWARE	
		Information Advice	Counselling/ Consulting	Training & Education	Finance	Other
REGIONAL AGENCIES OF THE MINISTRY OF LABOR AND EMPLOYMENT (DDTE)					*Persons who lose their jobs and then decide to create a new enterprise may obtain prepayment of their social security indemnities covering (a maximum of 114000 FF in 1983)	
ASSOCIATIONS, NETWORKS, CLUBS OF NEW ENTRE-PRENEURS, BOUTIQUES DE GESTION AFaCE, ESPACE EGEE, N'L COMMITTEE OF ASSOCIA-TIONS OF NEW ENTREPRENEURS, SCOP's, "CENTRES DE PARRAINAGE"	*There is a great variety of such organisations, some public, some private. An illustrative, not complete, list is given below: -Ass'n FAIRE (1 avenue de la Liberation, 78350 Jouy-en-Josas) -Club Createurs Yvelines/Val d'Oise (21 avenue de Paris, 78000 Versailles) -Mouvement ETHIC (Les Mercuriales, 40 rue Jean Jaures, 93170 Bagnolet)	*Supply information and/or advice to potential new entrepreneurs *Facilitate contact with "experienced" businessmen, e.g. Allo Creation, Tel: 362.11.17 (ETHIC group) *Some initiatives have some originality e.g. "hotels d'entreprise" which provide temporary collective industrial or office facilities e.g. at EVRY (Relais de l'entreprise, du commerce et de Partisanat, EVRY/Essonnes) -France-Initiative 10 rue Falguiere, 75015 Paris -Comite National des Createurs, 8 Boulevard du Roi Rene, 49000 ANGERS -Agence pour l'Industrialisation de l'Ardeche (AIDA) -Fondation Claude Bourg, 41 Blvd des Capucines, 75002 PARIS -Association pour la Promotion Industrielle du Languedoc Roussillon (APRIL), (Allee Jules Milhaux, 34000 MONTPELLIER)			*A few organisations (such as AFaCE, Fondation Claude Bourg, Groupe des Banques Populaires) grant loans at moderated rates (e.g. AFaCE, about 25 loans of about 110000 FF each per year; Fondation Claude Bourg 5 loans of about 60000 FF per year, etc.)	
CHAMBERS OF COMMERCE	*A total of 152	*Are - or will gradually become - the "unique office for procedures", thus facilitating the accomplishment of the many formalities (at present some 100) to be made at various public offices and ministerial departments		*Have wide activities in this field		

214

ORGANISATION	NATURE OF ORGANISATION	SOFTWARE			HARDWARE	
		Information Advice	Counselling/ Consulting	Training & Education	Finance	Other
NEWSPAPERS & MAGAZINES FOR NEW ENTRE- PRENEURS	*The most important are: -Les Nouvelles de la Creation d'Entreprises (AFaCE) -"CREEZ" -"CRENEAUX ET OPPORTUNITIES"					
CENTER FOR THE RAPPROCHE- MENT OF ENTERPRISES	*An association created in 1980 by some professional organisations and private consultants	*Have established data bank on supply of and demand for acquisitions				
OPPORTUNITY AND ACQUISI- TION NETWORK (RIO)	*Association promoted by the Ministry of Industry and by ANCE	*Has a data bank on patents, acquisitions (supply/demand), and various commercial activities				
UNIVERSITIES, BUSINESS SCHOOLS, TRAINING CENTERS				*Diversified and growing activity in this field		

ORGANISATION	NATURE OF ORGANISATION	SOFTWARE			HARDWARE	
		Information Advice	Counselling/ Consulting	Training & Education	Finance	Other
MINISTRY OF ECONOMICS (BMWI)	*Federal ministry housing small business secretariat	*Guidebook "Start-hilfe" *Guidebook "The financial aids from the ERP-fonds" *Brochure: "Financial and Non-Financial Aids from the Federal Government for the Small Business Sector *Brochure: "More successful through management assistance"	*Financial assistance to support freelance consulting available -75% of daily fee + travel contribution refunded for 5 days before and 15 days after starting the business		*Risk capital in form of long-term low-interest (without securities but complete liability), up to 28% starting from minimum investment amount of 40.000 DM. The "starter" must contribute 12% and the rest has to come from other resources. Conditions: maximum DM 300.000; 20 year time period, first 10 years without redemption; 2 years interest free; 3rd year 2%; 4th year 3%; 5th year 5%; then common interest rates *Also ERP (European Recovery Plan) loans for start-up, acquisition, shareholdership, acquisition of fittings to people aged between 21 and 50. Conditions: maximum DM 300.000. Interest 7% over 10-15 years depending on reason for loan; max. 2 years interest redemption. Collaterals have to be furnished as usual	
MINISTRY OF RESEARCH AND TECHNOLOGY	*Federal ministry	*Brochures: -"Informations about public aids from the BMFT" -"TOU-Program Public Assistance for Technology - oriented start-ups"	*Operates pilot programme specialised in technology oriented (innovative) start-ups. Existing firms using the programme must be less than three years old with fewer than ten employees. This programme is divided in three phases and will be operated in six regions until 1986. According to the product-life-cycle-concept different instruments are applied in each phase: -Phase 1: The business founder primarily gets consultant aids in order to develop a proper business plan; during this phase he can also ask for technical aids. -Phase 2: In the second phase up to 75% of the total develoment costs are subsidized by an unrepayable grant from the BMFT -Phase 3: In the third phase the BMFT takes an 80% risk share in each specific case for bank loans which are needed for machinery and marketing start-ups -Further conditions: -Phase 1: The business founder can apply for a not repayable grant up to 90% of the occurring costs during this phase (max. amount DM 54.000) -Phase 2: Max. amount DM 900.000 -Phase 3: Max. amount DM 1,6 Mio. These bank loans have to be given with two years free of redemption	*Training and consultancy is given by 10 technological consultant agencies in regions selected		
LANDER (STATE) GOVERNMENT MINISTRIES, DEPARTMENTS AND AGENCIES e.g.	Assistance provided varies from state to state					
MINISTERIUM FUR WIRTSCHAFT, MITTELSTAND UND BADENWURTTEMBERG H. TECHNOLOGIE Theodor-Heuss Str. 1 7000 Stuttgart 1	*Land ministry. Public authority	*The Land has a special institution (Landesgewer- beamt, Stuttgart) and a bank (Karlsruhe) which provide all information brochures requested	*Funding of the RKW *Funding of the Landesgewerbeamt Baden-Wurttemberg	*Financial support for seminars with the topic of business start-ups	*Loans for start-ups, acqui- sition, shareholdership and acquisition of a first warehouse in all business sectors with the exception of catering service. Conditions: If the investment costs are lower then DM 30.000 these loans can amount up to 50%, else 33% (maximum amount DM 200.000), interest 5% over 12 years with max. 4 years without redemption	

ORGANISATION	NATURE OF ORGANISATION	SOFTWARE			HARDWARE	
		Information Advice	Counselling/ Consulting	Training & Education	Finance	Other
LANDER (STATE) GOVERNMENT MINISTRIES, DEPARTMENTS AND AGENCIES e.g. continued						
SENATOR FUR WIRTSCHAFT UND AUBENHANDEL BERLIN Martin-Luther Str. 105 1000 Berlin 62	*Land ministry. Public authority	*Brochure: "Public aids for small business in Berlin"	*Financial assistance to support freelance business start-up consulting. DM 1.360 for a two-day consultancy	*Financial support for seminars with the topic of business start-ups		*"Business start-up savings premium": A 25% premium (max. DM 12.500) is granted for savings which have been made for the purpose of a business start-up. This savings plan has to last at least three years *"Business start-up premium": The equity base of a business start-up will be granted by a 20% premium on the private equity capital which is used to finance the start-up *There is furthermore a so called "Innovation funds" where the founder of a high technology company can apply for loans or equity capital. The conditions will be determined in each specific case
DEUTSCHE AUSGLEICHSBANK (DLAB)	*Public institution					*Administers government provision of longterm low-interest loans *Also administers loans via start-up scheme of European Recovery Programme (ERP) *Also offers additional investment loans for start-ups Conditions: maximum 300.000 - DM, interest 6.75% over 10 years *Guarantees for business founders in the sector of independent professions
KREDITANSTALT FUR WIEDERAUFBAU	*Public institution					*Loans for business start-ups. Conditions: up to 50% of the investment costs (max. DM 5 Mio.) interest 6.75% over a period up to 10 years, max. two years without redemption, collaterals have to be furnished as usual
REGIONAL BANKS e.g. **LANDESKREDIT BANK BADEN-WURTTEMBERG** **NORDWESTDEUTSCHE BURGSCHAFTSBANK**	*Public institutions				*Various start-up loans	

ORGANISATION	NATURE OF ORGANISATION	SOFTWARE			HARDWARE	
		Information Advice	Counselling/ Consulting	Training & Education	Finance	Other
CHAMBERS OF COMMERCE AND INDUSTRY	*69 Chambers across Germany *Membership compulsory	*Advisory services, particularly with regard to finding business partners and the purchase of existing firms. Also on patents, licensing, franchising *Support in preparation of credit applications *Series of start-up planning leaflets *Information on the general economic situation of a region *A couple of chambers of commerce and industry offer a "Retired-executive" programme. The business founder can apply for the assistance of a retired executive at a free-of-charge basic *Information and brochures on the public aids of federal government and the government of the land	*Keep lists of consultants and/or own Consultancy Departments	*Organise so-called "start-up seminars" for business founders; topic: "How to start and run a small business"; fee: DM 100,- (average)		
CHAMBERS OF CRAFT INDUSTRIES	*42 across Germany, representing not only traditional crafts industries but also various types of engineering and electrical activities Membership compulsory *52 Technical Associations	*Information on business for sale in particular industry sectors for the attention of relevant "masters" *Support in preparation of credit applications *Information on the general economic situation of a region *Information on federal and land-programmes	*Consulting scheme similar to RKW also government financed and usually undertaken by the Chambers' own consultants or from Landesgewerbeamt list	*Organise one-week course for recently qualified "masters". Course covers the various functional areas of business. Some courses designed for specific industries. Sometimes followed up by a further weeks course one year later. Financial support from Federal & Land Goverments, marginal costs covered by HWKS. *Organise start-up seminars		

218

ORGANISATION	NATURE OF ORGANISATION	SOFTWARE			HARDWARE	
		Information Advice	Counselling/ Consulting	Training & Education	Finance	Other
GERMAN PRODUCTIVITY ASSOCIATION (RKW)	*Non-profit working closely with Chambers of Industry and Commerce, Trade Associations and scientific institutes *74 centres across Germany	*Operates innovation, licenses and patents clearing house *Information on possible co-ventures in region served *Counselling support *Publishes monthly magazine	*Consulting services supported by Federal and Land Governments., and also administers public funds for subsidized consultancy services. Consultants are selected from RKW approved list	*One-week course with 2 x 3 days follow-up over next 3-6 months run by free-market consultants but organised by RKW. Six courses yearly, 12 participants per course. Direct costs paid by land (Model of Baden Wurttemberg)		

ORGANISATION	NATURE OF ORGANISATION	SOFTWARE			HARDWARE	
		Information Advice	Counselling/ Consulting	Training & Education	Finance	Other
INDUSTRIAL DEVELOPMENT AUTHORITY (IDA)	*State supported 'autonomous' development agency responsible for all aspects of Irish industrial development. Has Small Industries Division with 70 staff (10% of total) Eight offices through- out Ireland. 200m budget		*Special advice and consultancy assistance under Enterprise Development Programme provided by link with Irish Productivity Centre		*Enterprise Development Programme for suitably qualified people to set up in manufacturing industry for the first time. Support includes: -Loan guarantees -Internal subsidies -Equity investment -Cash grants (as outlined in main chart) *Since 1978-82 129 projects approved - 85 in operation	
SHANNON DEVELOPMENT CORPORATION	*Limited liability company with shares held by three ministries. Has responsibility for promoting indigenous industry (under 50 employees) in area surrounding Shannon Airport Community *Cooperative Support Programme	*Checklists and guides to starting a small business, patenting, marketing, etc. *Advisory services for forming new cooperatives *Matchmaker service to link products and service requirements with large industry in midwest			*Feasibility study grants of up to 50% *Grants to support all or part of salary of manager during first three years *Various grants for site and buildings (45%-60%) Machinery (45%-60%) worker training (100%) *Cash grants for: -Site and site development (45%-60%) -New buildings and reconstruction (45%-60%) -Factory rent reductions (45%-60%) -New machinery and equipment (45%-60%) -Research and development (up to 50%) -Worker training (up to 100%) -Feasibility studies (up to 50%) for companies under 50 or with assets of less than 500,000 pounds	*Workspace in small units of 350 sq. ft. with common services *Maximum tax rate of 10% up to year 2000

ORGANISATION	NATURE OF ORGANISATION	SOFTWARE			HARDWARE	
		Information Advice	Counselling/ Consulting	Training & Education	Finance	Other
INDUSTRIAL TRAINING AUTHORITY (ANCO)	*State supported 'autonomous' agency charged with the development of training throughout Ireland. Staff 2,000 Budget IR 67m in 1982. *Operates levy grant system to raise small amount of revenue. Funded by the European Social Fund and Youth Employment Agency and Irish government (see below) *Has now special Small Firms Division	*Small Business Hotline - training advisory and information service		*Starting Your Own Successful Business. 20 week programme for those with business idea. Organised at Centres throughout the country. Allowances and training costs paid *Community based training programme (LINK) to help unemployed and those who wish to be self-employed. 26 weeks. Links with local community committee. Youth Enterprise Programme. 15 week programme for young people wishing to explore starting a business		
YOUTH EMPLOYMENT AGENCY	*Autonomous state owned company funded by special 1% levy on all declared income. Aims to provide training and work experience for young people and to develop new aproaches to job creation. (120m budget 1983) *Community and Youth Enterprise Programme	*Advice to groups who want to take a community initiative	*Provision of Enterprise Workers funded for up to 12 months to help with the project (up to£16,000 grant)		*Planning grants to groups who wish to investigate goods and services for industry locally. Financial aid for capital and revenue requirements and project management costs	
BANK OF IRELAND & YOUTH EMPLOYMENT AGENCY					*Youth Self-Employment Programme. Loans of up to 3,000 per person for new business idea of those 15 - 25 years and unemployed	

ORGANISATION	NATURE OF ORGANISATION	SOFTWARE			HARDWARE	
		Information Advice	Counselling/ Consulting	Training & Education	Finance	Other
ASSEFOR	*Association for training backed by Italian Union of Chambers of Commerce, Industry, Agriculture and Handicraft and some Chambers			*"Build your workplace": four day programme, check-up of candidate entrepreneurs and a lot of start-up information		
SDA (BOCCONI) (UNIVERSITY)	*Business School *Not SME specific but now introducing some small firm training		*To develop innovation within the firm	*Gemina Project: in depth courses of 15 new firms with innovation projects		

222

		Information Advice	Counselling/ Consulting	Training & Education	Finance	Other
ASSEFOR	*Association for training backed			*"Build your workplace": four		

ORGANISATION	NATURE OF ORGANISATION	SOFTWARE			HARDWARE	
		Information Advice	Counselling/ Consulting	Training & Education	Finance	Other

The support network as described in the general matrix is available to all start-ups. The schemes special to, or solely for start-ups are:

ORGANISATION	NATURE OF ORGANISATION	Information Advice	Counselling/ Consulting	Training & Education	Finance	Other
MINISTRY FOR ECONOMIC AFFAIRS	*Has directorate of SME's with staff of 200. Small firms defined as up to 100. Main Government ministry responsible for SME's	*Support for advisory services and general booklets such as RND and RDK (see general matrix). Much of the work of these institutions is start-ups			*With banks, operates loan guarantee and some soft loans in particular: subordinated loan scheme - maximum 20 years - declining subsidy on interest. Starting companies for first three years get 50% subsidy and on next three years can accumulate up to 50% of the interest due	
REGIONAL DEVELOPMENT CORPS (OOM)	*Autonomous Regional development corporations for specific 'problem' areas of the country. Funded by central government with Municipal and Regional support. (5 regions). Are not specifically for small business	*Advice on business, financial and locational problems. Limited consultancy. Signposts to government assistance. Free Service. Special information packs for start-ups			*Can provide low interest loans and equity participation loans in new and innovative firms. Temporary for first few years. Can provide low interst loans for start-ups	
MUNICIPALITIES LOCAL AUTHORITIES	*Services vary *Local authorities responsible for local development initiatives sometimes in collaboration with banks. Example: Stichting Startfonds Rijnmond (SR) Openbaar Lichaam Rijmond afd. Economische Aangelegenheden Vasteland 96-104, 3011 BP, Rotterdam	*Varied provision of counselling and advice			*In some cases provide start-up loans and grants	*Managed workshops for starters and small business combining low rents with access to services and advisers
NMB BANKS CIMK KNOV NCOV plus others	*Small firm bank and support organisation	*Joint publication of manual on starting a business containing 54 points including regulations				
FOUNDATION FOR SMALL & MEDIUM FIRMS (O&S)	*Government funded foundation with two objectives: -To help small businesses in difficulty and -To help in closure and winding-up				*Provides subsidy for consultancy advice and training as turn-round help for firms in difficulty or help in winding-up. Provides funding for reports of CIMK on loan guarantee when firm cannot pay for these	

ORGANISATION	NATURE OF ORGANISATION	SOFTWARE			HARDWARE	
		Information Advice	Counselling/ Consulting	Training & Education	Finance	Other
CENTRAL INSTITUTE FOR SMALL & MEDIUM FIRMS	*State subsidised organisation representing interests of relevant employers and trade associations. With prime role of providing consultancy services for SME's (mainly retail type firms). 50% funding from Advisory services	*Booklets/handouts published	*60% of its credit assessment counselling under the loan guarantee scheme is for start-ups. Of 3,300 advisory services in 1982 over 2,000 were concerned with credit assessments	*Some start-up programmes at locations throughout the country often in collaboration with other organisations (universities, colleges)		
CENTRAL IN- DUSTRY BOARD FOR CRAFT TRADES (HBA) CENTRAL IN- DUSTRY BOARD FOR RETAIL TRADE (HBD)	*Are Public Law organisations for the 'labour intensive' craft trades. *Represents 20,000 small businesses. Membership compulsory. 21 branches in different industries	*Source of information and advice to members through branches		*Provide basic training in technical and commercial skills for a wide variety of crafts and trades necessary for obtaining a licence to operate		
TECHNICAL UNIVERSITIES & TECHNISCHE HOGESCHOOLS	*State funded Universities and Polytechnics in several locations throughout the country		*Vary in capability to provide counselling and training. Some schools have start-up programmes			
BUSINESS TECHNOLOGY CENTRES	*Autonomous centres funded by mix of private and public capital including local government. Liaison with Universities at Enschede, Wageningen and Rotterdam	*Provision of information and advice and common services for the companies in the building				
STICHTING KLEINWOOD	*Foundation set up by Netherlands Federation of Industry (VND)		*Lends experienced retired executives for limited periods free to help small firms. Much of the work is for start-ups			
KONINKLIJK NETHERLANDS ONDERNEMERS- VERBAND (KNOV)	*Privately funded. Employers organisation for small business under 100 employees in crafts, retail and services. 24 HQ staff and over 60 in the field (advisers) 95000 members	*Basic booklets on start-ups		*Of consultant enquiries almost 60% are start-ups (see general matrix)		

ORGANISATION	NATURE OF ORGANISATION	SOFTWARE			HARDWARE	
		Information Advice	Counselling/ Consulting	Training & Education	Finance	Other
NATIONAL INSTITUTE OF TECHNOLOGY NORWAY (STI)	*A government sponsored institution designed to provide theoretical and practical backup services for Norwegian industry, with the emphasis on small and medium sized firms			*Start-up courses. 2 days courses up to 6 months programmes. Organised as "start-up school"	*The school has been supported by DU with approximately 400.000 Nkr	
THE REGIONAL DEVELOPMENT FUND (DU)	*The Regional Development Fund is a State body that has been in operation since 1961. Grants are financed in their entirety from the central government budget *The aim of the Regional Development Fund is to promote measures which will ensure increased, permanent and profitable employment in districts with special employment problems or where underdeveloped industrial conditions prevail		*DU has, in cooperation with INDEVO, Norway and private consultants, launched a "lift yourself by the hair" programme for starting new business especially in Northern Norway. 1100 applied for the programme, 520 were selected. Results 100 new enterprises and 200 new jobs (1983)		*Cost of projects approximately 5 mill. Nkr. From 1984 grants are available amounting to 10000 Nkr per month per person limited to a total of 100000 Nkr. Grants also available for educating personnel	

ORGANISATION	NATURE OF ORGANISATION	SOFTWARE			HARDWARE	
		Information Advice	Counselling/ Consulting	Training & Education	Finance	Other
INSTITUTE FOR THE SUPPORT OF SMALL & MEDIUM INDUSTRIES	*Government Department depending on the Ministry for Industry and Energy	*Provides a service for selective diffusion of technical, market, financial and legal information. Several booklets and guides *Offers technical advice on start-up projects *Analyses start-up projects on a regional basis for smaller projects and in the headquarters for bigger ones (within a specific service) *Promotes start-up contests together with "Caixa Geral de Depositos", in order to stiumlate the creation of new enterprises in Portuguese light industry		*Short management courses for new entrepreneurs	*Provides guarantees for financing investment operations either in fixed assets or in working capital *Preferential interest rates for financing of prior start-up projects *Financial support in the form of sharing of expenses by means of non-repayable loans for specific actions such as the short management courses for new entrepreneurs	
CAIXA GERAL DE DEPOSITOS (CGD)	*The biggest Portuguese Bank specializing in investment operations	*Advice and information services. Specialized information booklets *Promotion of special schemes of credit for SMEs *Promotes start-up contests in cooperation with IAPMEI (see above)			*Provides loans for financing investment operations *Preferential interest rates for the financing of priority start-up projects namely those of the IAPMEI/CGD project contests	
SPECIAL CREDIT INSTITUTIONS	*National Investment banks				*Award medium and long term industrial credit	
INSTITUTE FOR EQUITY PARTICIPATION (IPE)	*Corporation, mixed capital				*Equity participations (risk capital in newly created companies presenting innovative technologies or new products	
COMMERCIAL BANKS	*Nationalized Banks				*May collaborate in start-up with the investment banks e.g. to make the main loan for fixed assets	
PUBLIC ENTER- PRISE OF INDUSTRIAL ESTATES (EPPI)	*Public Company depending on the Ministry for Industry and Energy					*Provides industrial estates in excellent conditions in the "hinterland"
NATIONAL LABORATORY FOR INDUSTRIAL ENGINEERING & TECHNOLOGY	*Government Department depending on the Ministry for Industry and Energy	*Has a center for technical and technological information *Aids programmes for innovation *Provides a service in the technical design and development of new products, equipment and processes		*Offers a broad range of management and technological training often suited to the needs of SMI		
INSTITUTE FOR EMPLOYMENT & PROFESSIONAL TRAINING (IEFP)	*Government Department depending on the Labour and Social Security Ministry			*Offers a broad range of courses to skilled workers throughout the country	*Grants assistance or loans with no interests for the creation of new jobs in SMEs	

226

ORGANISATION	NATURE OF ORGANISATION	SOFTWARE			HARDWARE	
		Information Advice	Counselling/ Consulting	Training & Education	Finance	Other
BRANCH OFFICES OF THE MINISTRY OF TREASURY	*Government bodies				*Opening new establishments or branches (minimum participation: 25%) or participation in foreign companies *10% reduction in corporate taxes	
BASQUE COUNTRY AUTONOMOUS GOVERNMENT	*Government				*Subsidize industrial investments in fixed assets designed to create new jobs or, in cases of technological innovation, maintain existing ones. The amount of the subsidy is a percentage of the new investment and varies in accordance with the number of jobs created	
SOCIETY FOR INDUSTRIAL DEVELOPMENT (BASQUE COUNTRY)	*Agency of Department of Industry and Energy of the Basque Government				*Credits destined to create or develop firms, invest in fixed assets or in operating funds. Advantage as credit terms on up to 33% of the total investment	
CATALAN MINISTRY OF COMMERCE & TOURISM	*Government Ministry				*Also offers credits to new businesses. Loans may be for as much as 70% of the investment and up to 25 million m (except in exceptional cases: loans for larger amounts must be negotiated through the Banco Hipotecario de Espana)	

227

ORGANISATION	NATURE OF ORGANISATION	SOFTWARE			HARDWARE	
		Information Advice	Counselling/ Consulting	Training & Education	Finance	Other
REGIONAL DEVELOPMENT FUNDS	*The aim of the RDss is to promote measures which will ensure increased, permanent and profitable employment	*Give information and advice to entrepreneurs. Help the entrepreneur to write their business plans.		*Start-up courses 2-day courses	*Offer risk capital loans (Royalty loans)	
SWEDISH NATIONAL INDUSTRY BOARD (SIND)		*In cooperation with RDs, SIND has launched "start your own company" programmes for starting new businesses				
BANKS		*Give information through their business consultants			*Some banks offer a lower interest (-5%) for companies start-up	
LANSSTYRELSEN I STOCKHOLMS LAN Hantverkargatan 29 Box 22067 104 22 Stockholm Tel: 08.785.40.00	*Local government	*Have developed and financed several community programs mainly in districts with special employment problems				
TRYGGHETSRADET SAF-PTK Jakobsgatan 6 Box 16291 101 23 Stockholm Tel: 08.24.50.90	*Private body financed by a fee on all salaries paid to all clerks in private companies	*This fund has supported about 2000 persons for whom the alternative often is to be unemployed			*The fund can give 6 months salary and pay consultancy needed by the entrepreneur	
BOARD OF LABOUR	*Under the Ministry of Labour	*9+9 weeks courses on "start your own company"			*Pays salaries for the participants	
Private Firmse.g **INDEVO** Vasagatan 40 Box 262 101 23 Stockholm Tel: 08.24.50.90	*Private organisation	*Private companies offering special "start your own company" programmes				
UNIVERSITIES		*Some offer 5-10 weeks courses in entrepreneurship				

ORGANISATION	NATURE OF ORGANISATION	SOFTWARE			HARDWARE	
		Information Advice	Counselling/ Consulting	Training & Education	Finance	Other
BANKS	*Private				*Local and regional banks provide short and long term loans	
REGIONAL CREDIT GUARANTEE COOPERATIVES	*Private institutions with Government support		*Provide management consulting			*Regional credit guarantee cooperatives provide credit guarantee for loans
FOUNDATION FOR INDUSTRIAL REAL ESTATE (FONDATION DES TERRAINS INDUSTRIELS PRAILLE ET ACACIAS FIPA)	*Private foundation					*Purchase and development of real estate or buildings for facilitating the establishment of firms
INAS, INDELEC HOLDING AG, (FINANCING CORPORATIONS)	*Private companies associated with main merchant banks				*Provide venture and development capital	
CHAMBERS OF COMMERCE/ INNOVATION CONSULTING	*Private associations	*Provide information especially on sources of risk capital				
LOCAL ASSOCIATIONS OF SMES	*Private associations	*Numerous associations provide information and advice				*Various local associations of small firms provide credit guarantee
OFFICE FOR THE DEVELOP- MENT OF COMMERCE & INDUSTRY IN THE CANTON OF VAUD	*Private association with public support		*Provides assistance in getting and guaranteeing credits			
SWISS RESEARCH INSTITUTE OF SMALL BUSINESS AT THE ST. GALL GRADUATE SCHOOL OF ECONOMICS, LAW, BUSINESS AND PUBLIC ADMINISTRATION	*Semi-public university institute			*Contributes to management development through consulting, interfirm comparison, exex-groups for owner-managers in various branches		
PROFESSIONAL ASSOCIATIONS	*Private assocations	*Professional associations of small firms provide information on sources of finance	*Numerous professional associations of small firms offer to their members management assistance	*General training programmes often in-house training		*A series of professional associations of small firms provide social security plans and bookkeeping service
SWISS INSTI- TUTE FOR TRAINING OF MANAGERS IN SMALL FIRMS	*Private cooperative society		*Acts as intermediary for management advice	*Offer training programme for various economic sectors		

229

ORGANISATION	NATURE OF ORGANISATION	SOFTWARE			HARDWARE	
		Information Advice	Counselling/ Consulting	Training & Education	Finance	Other
TISSOT FOUNDATION FOR ECONOMIC DEVELOPMENT	*Private foundation		*Consults enterprises willing to set up a business in the Canton of Neuchatel			
ASSOCIATION OF THE PROMOTION OF INDUSTRIAL JOBS IN THE CANTON OF THE GRISONS	*Private association				*Helps establishing small manufacturing units in the Canton of the Grisons	
CANTONAL AGENCIES FOR ECONOMIC DEVELPOMENT	*Agencies of Cantonal Governments		*Cantonal agencies for the development of industry and trade advise on subsidies, loans and risk capital		*Grant loans offer subsidies aiming at job creation subsidize interests completely or in part	*Guarantee investment loans

230

		Information Advice	Counselling/ Consulting	Training & Education	Finance	Other

ORGANISATION	NATURE OF ORGANISATION	SOFTWARE			HARDWARE	
		Information Advice	Counselling/ Consulting	Training & Education	Finance	Other
DEPARTMENT OF TRADE & INDUSTRY	*Government department with major responsibility for Small Firms policy. Has a Small Firms Division. (H.Q. staff 47) (Field staff 130) Support for start-ups a major part of their activity.	*Variety of booklets on aspects of Business Start. Video productions on business start-ups *Small Firms Information Centres. (Regional advice centres in regions throughout country). Provides signposting to local services and information	*Counselling service using retired executives. Organised on a regional basis. Three free counsellings then small charge. 75% of counselling with start-ups. Total number of counsellors = 275. Counsellings 1983 = 18.000 of which 75% are start-ups *Enterprise Allowance Scheme. Involving payment of 40 pounds p.w. allowance for one year to unemployed persons with a business idea plus 1,000 pounds of own or borrowed capital. Operated jointly with the Manpower Services Commission (see next page). Introductory seminars/workshops arranged and available counselling from DTI counsellors (up to three free sessions). 25,000 places a year and rising	*Half day or one day conferences and seminars in regions and clinics in association with Enterprise Allowance Scheme (see below)	*Loan guarantee scheme operated through clearing banks. 80% guarantee. Almost 50% of enquiries are start-ups. (Lending guaranteed 1983 = 175.000 pounds of which 50% start-ups *Business expansion scheme offering tax write off margin to individual tax payers to invest in small companies. (So far not extensively developed) *Carry back provisions to offset new company losses against previous three years personal taxation	*Support for small workshops buildings (up to 400 sq. ft.) English Industrial Estates (National Industrial Estates Corp.)
DEVELOPMENT AGENCIES. SCOTLAND & WALES. HIGHLANDS AND ISLANDS DEVELOPMENT BOARD FOR RURAL WALES	*Autonomous state financed agencies charged with all aspects of industrial development and promotion in Scotland and Wales. Have small firm division.	*Information and Advice Booklets and offices in collaboration with D.T.I. Small Firms Service	*Counselling schemes as per the D.T.I. service but in addition with own consultants providing initially free conselling to start-ups	*Seminars, workshops and longer start-up programmes in collaboration with higher education sector	*Selective financial assistance available but to all under UK regional policy. Loans, grants and European Investment Bank loans. Wide range of assistance	*Provision of small workshop space reduced rents and occasional "managed workshop" with associated services
COUNCIL FOR SMALL INDUSTRY IN RURAL AREAS (COSIRA)	*Autonomous state organisation funded by the UK Department of Environment with responsibility for development of rural areas Operates through five regional offices. Areas of less than 15,000 population	*Information and advice	*Organised service to answer start-up enquiries and associated fee-charging consultant service of specialists (marketing, finance, etc.)	*Start-up seminars, workshops and short courses	*Operates "lender of last resort" loan scheme at commercial rates	*Provides small workshop premises for rent

231

ORGANISATION	NATURE OF ORGANISATION	SOFTWARE			HARDWARE	
		Information Advice	Counselling/ Consulting	Training & Education	Finance	Other
MANPOWER SERVICES COMMISSION	*Semi-autonomous. State owned institution charged with industrial training throughout the UK. Has small firms division (8 staff). A higher proportion of its funded programmes is for start-ups			*Supports a number of start-up programmes mainly in the higher education sector throughout the UK including: -New Enterprise Programmes. A 4 month programme for those with a new business idea which is employment generative. Run at 5 UK Business Schools (11 courses p.a.) -Start Your Own Business Programmes. Eight to ten week programme. For those with business ideas (usually of a smaller scale). Run at Polytechnics and Colleges throughout UK (151 courses p.a.) -Self-employment programmes (123 courses). Skill into Business aimed at unemployed skilled or semi-skilled who wish to explore going into business. Eight day programme run at number of higher education colleges throughout the UK. In 1984/85 will provide in total 4,000 start-up training places *Various "managed workshops" for training (retraining) unemployed particularly young people: based upon producing a marketable product. Some degree of financial subsidy in providing premises and "management". Community Enterprise Programme		

ORGANISATION	NATURE OF ORGANISATION	SOFTWARE			HARDWARE	
		Information Advice	Counselling/ Consulting	Training & Education	Finance	Other
BANKS	*The four major clearing banks in the UK dominate the banking scene with branches all over the country *All usually have separate small firms offices as part of corporate affairs departments	*Wide variety of booklets	*Offer secondees to local Enterprise Agencies	*Occasional seminars/work- shops	*Provide financial support for local Enterprise Agencies and other local initiatives	*Have links with local authorities and other agencies in small premises provision
EDUCATION SECTOR; BUSINESS SCHOOLS, POLYTECHNICS, HIGHER EDU- CATION COLLEGES	*Supported by mixture of local and national funds. They represent the main thrust of "start-up" education in the UK	*Occasional organisation of College based "Small Business Centres" to give advice and counselling		*Run the programmes described above under M.S.C. funding as well as wide range of part-time (evening and week-end courses)		
LOCAL ENTER- PRISE AGENCIES (Large company involvement)	*Agencies usually set-up as company limited by guarantee including representation of large companies and banks together with local government support *Some agencies completely funded by private or alternatively public initiative. (170 LEA's in UK Dec. '83). *Use secondees from large companies *Range of services varies substantially from one agency to another *Majority of their work at present is for start-ups	*Booklets and other literature for start-ups *Advice Centres and offices *Some agencies provide "ideas" service and organise "can you make it" exhibition with large companies	*Free counselling business start-ups	*Some agencies run start-up seminars and conferences and sponsor courses often in collaboration with local education college or Manpower Services Commission	*A few agencies have their own grants schemes. Others administer local authority grant schemes or advise	*Some agencies organise or manage workshop space for new starters on behalf of the local authority
LOCAL AUTHORI- TIES & DEVELOP- MENT OFFICES, LOCAL AUTHORITY, DEVELOPMENT AGENCIES, LOCAL ENTER- PRISE BOARDS, NEW TOWN DEVELOPMENT AGENCIES	*Varying in structure, power and area and degree to which they "specialise" in small business or start-up support. May include services independent of Local Enterprise or other agencies	*Provide free advice to small business start-ups. Wide range of information booklets often in "advice" centres	*May have free counselling service	*Occasional workshops or seminars on start-ups	*May provide range of start-up finance (grants, loans and even guarantees)	*May provide small factories and workshops

233

Technological Innovation and Research and Development

ORGANISATION	NATURE OF ORGANISATION	SOFTWARE			HARDWARE	
		Information Advice	Counselling/ Consulting	Training & Education	Finance	Other
WIFI	*Federal Institute for Economic Development, supported by the Vienna Chamber of Commerce	*Since 1980, WIFI has established a number of special services for the promotion of innovation including: -seminars on innovation, microprocessors and robotics for managers and executives -publications dealing with the topics of innovation, systematic product planning, microelectronics, robotics -permanent training of high qualified innovation consultants -new advisory campaigns from product and process innovation themselves to all other areas of management concerned with stimulating cooperation activities especially between small and medium-sized enterprises -Techniform: a special technology information centre, which is connected with important international documentation centres via a terminal, helps with "technology transfer" by relaying relevant information -the Council for the Promotion of Patents supported by the Ministry of Commerce, Trade and Industry -Promotion of research and development: through close cooperation between commercial bodies and the universities and the Austrian Research Council (special collection of documents) *In addition to the existing services of the Economic Chamber, a new "Technology and Innovation Agency" was created by the Ministry of Commerce, Trade and Industry together with other institutions in 1984				
INNOVA	*A subsidiary to the "Zentral-sparkasse und Kommerzialbank, Wien"		*Innovation consulting		*Innovation credits to finance buildings, land, machinery and installations of necessary equipment	
HERNSTEIN INSTITUTE	*Management Training Centre supported by the Vienna Chamber of Commerce			*Offers special courses on modern information technology in SMEs		

ORGANISATION	NATURE OF ORGANISATION	SOFTWARE			HARDWARE	
		Information Advice	Counselling/ Consulting	Training & Education	Finance	Other
FUND FOR PROTOTYPES	*Within the Ministry of Economic Affairs				*Provides interest free funds to finance up to 80% of research costs. These funds are refunded as soon as the programme has resulted in successful production and marketing. Criteria for application are: the originality of products, technical and financial capabilities of the applicant, technical, economic and social advantages of projects, possibilities for industrialisation	
INSTITUTE FOR SCIENTIFIC RESEARCH WITH- IN INDUSTRY & AGRICULTURE (IRSIA)	*Public body which promotes, organises and subsidises research projects in all industrial fields except nuclear engineering and mining. 70% of grants go to business and 30% to joint sectoral centres managed and administered by member firms	*Stand-by research creation within a collective research centre of a working group for limited and specific research for a company	*Technological guidance			*Grants subsidies to finance from 50 to 80% of fundamental research projects within companies or universities
SERVICE OF ECONOMIC EXPANSION OF SB OF THE WALLOON REGION	*Regional authority implementing in Wallonia the legislation on economic expansion				*Interest rate subsidy more favourable terms for innovating companies (see general matrix)	
MINISTRY OF THE BRUSSELS REGION	*Idem for Brussels Region					
MINISTRY OF THE FLEMISH REGION	*Idem for Flanders					
MINISTRY OF NEW TECHNOLO- GIES & SB	*Regional ministry within the Ministry for the Walloon Region	*Launched "Athena Operation" in 1982 to encourage companies to invest in new technologies through: information; R&D support; provision of specialist support; facilitation of communication & innovation awards				
MANAGING UNIT FOR TECHNOLOGI- CAL CONTRACTS (CGTC)	*Created by the regional executive authority of Wallonia				*Finances projects aimed at the development of new products and processes likely to lead within 5 years to a profitable economic activity in Wallonia. This aid covers 50 to 80% of research projects presented to the Minister of new technologies and SB	

ORGANISATION	NATURE OF ORGANISATION	SOFTWARE			HARDWARE	
		Information Advice	Counselling/ Consulting	Training & Education	Finance	Other
UNIT FOR THE TECHNOLOGICAL PROMOTION OF INDEPENDENT COMPANIES (CPTI)	*Created by the regional executive authority of Wallonia				*Advances interest free capital for the purchase of intangible investments or to cover up to 60% of research costs and buys ordinary bonds to finance SB working capital. To benefit from this aid, enterprises must employ less than 100 persons, be independent, innovative, performing and job creating	
FLANDERS INVESTMENT OPPORTUNITY COUNCIL (FIOC)	*Within the office of the Head of the Flander's Government	*Promotion and stimulation of industrial policy concentrating on three basic technologies: micro-electronics, biotechnology and new material and 8 applied technologies *Has established a micro-electronics centre *Research Promotion of new technologies		*Allocation and training programmes	*Investments and aids mentioned in general matrix	
FLANDERS CREATIVITY (STICHTING CREATIV)	*Created by the regional Authority of Flanders	*Promotion of creativity among Flemish companies through contest -international fairs -exhibitions -centre of ideas -context				
FLANDERS TECHNOLOGY INTERNATIONAL	*Created by the regional Authority of Flanders				*Award of 1.000.000 Bf. to the Flemish company employing less than 250 persons which has conceived, used in production or commercialized a high technology product or process	

238

ORGANISATION	NATURE OF ORGANISATION	SOFTWARE			HARDWARE	
		Information Advice	Counselling/ Consulting	Training & Education	Finance	Other
NATIONAL AGENCY OF TECHNOLOGY	*Directorate of Ministry of Industry administering: *Council of Technology *The Industrial R&D Fund *The Product Development Scheme				*Financial support includes: -teaching and training carried out by Technological Institutes (see below) -Micro-Electronics Consultancy Service (see below) -Entrepreneurs starting new science-based firms -Industrial R&D (see also general matrix)	
DANISH TECHNOLOGICAL NETWORK	*Network of approved institutes and Technological Information Centres (one per county-see general matrix)	*Technological Information Centres offer free information and contact services (see general matrix)				
TECHNOLOGICAL INSTITUTES (TI) (TAASTRUP & JUTLAND)	*Independent non-profit involved in: -comments on technological and managerial issues -courses -R&D projects -new product testing -counselling (see general matrix)	*Answer questions on technological matters	*The TIs EC & six authorized electronic consultants provide up to 40 hours free consulting on micro-electronics	*Courses provided on advanced/new technologies		
ATV INSTITUTES	*20 R&D Institutes (see general matrix)	*Involved in R&D, consulting, testing, training, & dissemination of information (see general matrix)				

ORGANISATION	NATURE OF ORGANISATION	SOFTWARE			HARDWARE	
		Information Advice	Counselling/ Consulting	Training & Education	Finance	Other
MINISTRY OF TRADE & INDUSTRY	*Government Ministry	*Information on investment and development projects *Counselling assistance (see general matrix)			*Finances (loans and grants) product research and product development	
FINNISH NATIONAL FUND FOR RESEARCH & DEVELOPMENT (SITRA)	*Operates in association with Bank of Finland *Emphasis on technological & product development	*Regular bulletin on current projects			*Provides financing for product development design funding, cooperative research (for details, see general matrix)	
THE FOUNDATION OF FINNISH INVENTIONS	*Established in 1971 to support and promote the development & commercialisation of inventions & know-how *Financed primarily by Finnish Government & SITRA (see above)				*Provides working capital for commercial exploitation of new inventions *Licenses inventions	
TECHNOLOGY DEVELOPMENT CENTRES	*Financed by Ministry of Trade & Industry *Coordinate & promote technological development	*Consulting assistance in product development & marketing through small units across Finland *Specialize in studying the technical & economic feasibility of new product ideas			*Finance product development work, particularly high technology	
FEDERATION OF FINNISH METAL & ENGINEERING INDUSTRIES (FFMEI)	*Industry Federation	*Provides general information on new technologies *Maintains comprehensive files on Finnish metal firms and their products *Provides contacts between buyers and subcontractors				
REGIONAL ASSOCIATION OF SWEDISH SPEAKING ENTREPRENEURS (OF)	*Association	*Counselling and advice on adaption to new technologies				

240

ORGANISATION	NATURE OF ORGANISATION	SOFTWARE			HARDWARE	
		Information Advice	Counselling/ Consulting	Training & Education	Finance	Other
NATIONAL AGENCY FOR APPLIED RESEARCH (ANVAR)	*Public organisation linked to Ministry of Industry and Research *Aims to facilitate transfer of fundamental research to commercial operations *Not specific SME but useful to them	*Information and advice on own and related activities *22 local agencies facilitate contact with smaller firms *Data bank on technology, patents, etc.	*e.g. for patent applications and development, help in finding partners, commercial outlets, feasibility studies	*Indirectly, through seminars, conferences, etc. (Journees Nationales de l'ANVAR)	*"Innovation Subsidies" granted from 1979-83 towards up to 50% of funds received by research institute or lab. on account of commercial contracts. These applied to the whole sequence of R&D (tests, trade marks, design, feasibility studies, etc.). In 1983, 4,500 grants were given (46 mill. FF total) mainly for SMEs *In 1984, a new procedure was introduced: ANVAR paying 50% of research expenses and lends up to 25% of additional expenses. However, this new procedure has proved more complicated than its predecessor. Estimated grants '84, 5000 mainly to SMEs *From 1984, ANVAR resources were significantly increased as it collected most of the funds resulting from the CODEVI system through which individuals may invest tax free a certain amount of money (now 10000 FF) in special bank accounts. ANVAR will also take over the activity of certain government committees such as CODIS, CIDISE (see general matrix) ANVAR may subscribe shares (under certain conditions) in small companies undertaking a research/ innovation programme. The limit is set at 20% of total equity and may range from a few thousand francs to 500000, or exceptionally more	
MINISTRY OF INDUSTRIAL REDEPLOYMENT & TRADE & REGIONAL DELEGATIONS (DRIRs)	*Established to decentralise the Ministry's activities *For details see general matrix	*Have information offices to help in the selection of appropriate assistance channels	*Assist SMEs in pre and full diagnoses on technical/ innovation/R&D matters. Counsel provided by experts selected in cooperation with Chambers of Commerce. This system now in test stage and will gradually be extended throughout France *DRIR's can also facilitate links between research centres and companies, albeit on a limited basis		*Funding is decided upon by committees. Funds are derived from Fonds d'Indus-trialisation et de Modernisation and local authorities' budgets *The DRIR's may grant subsidies up to 50% of research to research centres concluding research contracts with SMEs	*DRIR's may lend certain equipment to SME's to be tested for a period of time the purchase being concluded only if tests have been satisfactory
INNOVATION FINANCING COMPANIES e.g. SOFFINNOVA, BATINOVA & SOFINDEX; SOGINNOVE INODEV REGIONAL DEVELOPMENT COMPANIES DEVELOPMENT INSTITUTES (IDI & SOPROMEC)	*Public, semi-public or private financing institutions specialized in "venture capital" through temporary subscriptions of shares	*Beside financial assistance, may act as "advisors" regarding innovation, design, product development, etc.			*Shares subscribed (and resold after relatively short period), e.g. in 1982 SOGINNOVE (equity 150 million F) has subscribed to 19 operations to an amount of 14.5 million F	

ORGANISATION	NATURE OF ORGANISATION	SOFTWARE			HARDWARE	
		Information Advice	Counselling/ Consulting	Training & Education	Finance	Other
CEPME (BANK FOR SMALL BUSINESS)	*See general matrix	*See general matrix			*As well from activities described in the general matrix, CEPME grants "Agreement Letters", a procedure in which the Ministry of Industry and Research also intervenes, which facilitates the granting of low-interest loans	
THE BANKING SYSTEM					*All types of finance, including low interest rates (9.75 or 11.75% end 1983) and "prets participatifs"	
TECHNICAL CENTRES (see Centres Techniques - general matrix)	*See general matrix	*Provide technical & specialised information	*May enter into consultancy arrangement for technical matters	*Intervene in technical training programmes	*May grant "equipmnent" or innovation medium or long term loans without guarantees low interest rates. May be part of financing schemes involving public funds (ANVAR, MIR)	
STATE RESEARCH AGENCIES OR SPECIALISED MINISTERIAL BODIES E.G. National Research Centre, Department of Scientific Development & Department of Electronic & EDP Industries of Ministry of Industry & Research				*Organize training programmes, seminars, etc.	*May grant advances or subsidies for specialized programmes, such funds being reimbursable only in case of success	
NATIONAL AGENCY FOR THE DEVELOP- MENT OF AUTO- MATION (ADEPA) Tel: 33.1.6571270 INSTITUTE FOR DEVELOPMENT & INNOVATION (INODEV)		*For instance, has developed stimulation programmes showing impact of automation on operations of the small company asking for advice			*Grants counter- guarantees for medium term loans for innovation and for "prets participatifs- innovation" (subordinate loans for innovation)	
AGENCY FOR REGIONAL DEVELOPMENT (DATAR)					*Grants subsidies to finance operations designed to create or maintain employment in selected regions, especially if related to high technology	

242

ORGANISATION	NATURE OF ORGANISATION	SOFTWARE			HARDWARE	
		Information Advice	Counselling/ Consulting	Training & Education	Finance	Other
AGENCE FRANÇOISE POUR LA MAITRISE DE L'ENERGIE (AFME) 27 Rue Louis Vicout 75015 Paris Tel: 33.1.7652000	*Agency for Energy Savings				*Firms employing less than 100 people & consuming less than 5000 tons petrol equivalents per year may obtain no cost technical assistance to advise on systems designed to reduce energy consumption	

ORGANISATION	NATURE OF ORGANISATION	SOFTWARE			HARDWARE	
		Information Advice	Counselling/ Consulting	Training & Education	Finance	Other
FEDERAL MINISTRY OF RESEARCH & TECHNOLOGY	*Government Department with special project oriented project in the promotion of the smaller firm	*Publication of a series of information booklets, e.g. -Advisor on Research and Technology (Promotional programmes and advisory help) -Information Technics -Production Technics -BMFT Journal *In cooperation with the Ministry, on the basis of a pilot project or as a following-up measure or independently, the Chambers of Industry and Commerce, the Chambers and Assocations of the Craft Industries, the Business Associations and others provide information services and mediation of technological supply and demand	*The Chambers, several business assocations and specialized centres offer innovation consultancy, partly by providing public subsidies up to 50% of the costs of an assignment but not more than 12.500 DM annually. The scientific supervision of the publicly sponsored bodies is carried out by the Institute of System Technics and Innovation Research (141) of the Frauenhofer Society for the Advancement of Applied Research (see below)	*Financial support is provided from time to time for selected training measures	*A number of specialized agencies are commissioned to administer various R&D resp. innovation projects (see below). In order to stimulate R&D as well as innovation business actions the government has issued two tax relief laws: special depreciations on R&D investment and a tax for R&D investment extra pay. A Pilot experiment, Technological Oriented Business Establishment, (TOU) has been launched recently	*Stimulated and partly financially assisted by the BMFT about 30 recent initiatives either from municipal or universities, chambers, banks, bigger firms, etc. have based the preconditions for the establishment of "Technology Parks" (see below)
FRAUNHOFER SOCIETY FOR THE ADVANCE-MENT OF APPLIED RESEARCH (FhG) Leonrodstr. 54 D-8000 Munchen 9 Tel: 49.89.12051	*Independent Institute charged by Federal Ministry of Research & Technology (see above) to sponsor a public programme, "External Research & Development Commissions"				*Through the programme, SMEs can apply for financing if they lack their own R&D facilities. 30-40% of the R&D costs is refunded by the Confederation of Industrial Research Associations *Additional financial advantages are obtainable if FhG acts as the SME's research contract partner - a 50% grant	
ARBEITSGEMEIN-SCHAFT INDUSTRIELER FORSCHUNGS-VEREININGEN (AIF) Bayenthalgurtel 23, D-5000 Koln 51 Tel: 49.221.3720 91	*Confederation of industrial research associations *Private working committee of 92 research centres *Charged to take care of government small business technological promotion	*Administration of the BMWi R&D Manpower Grant Programme *BMWi Grants Project to assist joint research of SME's by specialised programmes AIF member institutes				

ORGANISATION	NATURE OF ORGANISATION	SOFTWARE			HARDWARE	
		Information Advice	Counselling/ Consulting	Training & Education	Finance	Other
TECHNOLOGIE- ZENTRUM DES VEREINS DEUTSCHE INGENIEURE (VDI-TZ) Budapesterstr.40 D-1000 Berlin 30 Tel: 49.30.26090	*Private organisation charged by the Federal Ministry of Research and Development to sponsor a special governmental assistance programme	*Private information and advice to interested people	*Offers consultancy referring to innovation and transfer of technology	*Organizes seminars concerning technical- technological topics	*With regard to the government programme "Application of Micro-Electronics" in order to promote micro-electronic know-how and to establish R&D capacities in which micro- electronics are an essential component, smaller firms may get grants to meet personnel expenditures, contract expenses of third parties and of product-oriented advice, and special equipment costs	
KERNFORSCHUNGS ZENTRUM KARLSRUHE (KfK)-NUCLEAR RESEARCH CENTRE D-7500 Karlsruhe 1 Tel: 49.7.21.249 71	*Nuclear research centre *State financed organisation, charged by the Federal Ministry of R&D to sponsor a special governmental assistance programme				*A government scheme called "Development of Production Techniques" offers grants for the costs of personnel, advice, training, research and equipment in the case of the development of an individual adapted CAD/CAM application. Also the development of robot-systems will be subsidized	

TECHNOLOGY PARKS
*AACHEN
*BERLIN
*BONN
*HEIDELBERG
*HILDESHEIM
*KARLSRUHE
*STUTTGART
*SYKE

*Quite a number of communities either founded technology parks in 1983 or intend to establish such a park. The main purpose of these technology parks is fostering the start-up of new-technology-based-companies because they are supposed to create new jobs due to their growth potential. Furthermore, they are supposed to secure the competitiveness of the German economy.

*These technology parks are either financed by public authorities like the federal government, the land or the community or by private orgnanisations such as banks or insurance companies. In these technology parks, the young technical entrepreneur might ask for management advice as well as for technical advice. In such a park, the technical entrepreneur must not buy expensive office equipment and he must not pay a full-time employee in order to run the office properly, the information infrastructure as well as the employees are furnished by the technology park. Furthermore, the residential rent is in general subsidized

ORGANISATION	NATURE OF ORGANISATION	SOFTWARE			HARDWARE	
		Information Advice	Counselling/ Consulting	Training & Education	Finance	Other
TECHNOLOGICAL INFORMATION & ADVISORY CENTRES -Ostbayerisches Technologie-Transfer-Institut (OTTI), D.-Martin-Luther-Strasse 10, D-8400 Regensburg 11 -Technologie-Vermittlungs-Agentur (TVA), Hardenbergstr. 15, D-1000 Berlin 12 -VDI-Technologie-zentrum (VDI-TZ), Budapester Str. 40, D-1000 Berlin 30 -Hamburger Institut fur Technologie-forderung (HIT), Harburger Schlossstr. 20, D-2000 Hamburg 90 -Kommunale Technologie-Beratung Ruhrgebiet, Havensteinstr. 50, D-4200 Oberhausen 1 -Technologie-Beratungstelle Ruhr (tbr), Ostring 30-32 D-4630 Bochum D-6600 Saarbrucken -Zentrule fur Produktivitat und Technologie Franz-Jose-Roder-Str. 9	*Independent Institutes with State support	*Special information is provided as well as mediation of business relations	*Consultancy analysis work, market survey, etc. by involving external experts will be publicly subsidized up to 50% of the costs, but not more than 12.000 DM annually			

Federal Government also suports equivalent centres of the trade unions:
-Innovations- und Technologie-Beratungsstelle der Industrie-gewerkschaft Metall, Alte-Jakob-Str. 148/155, D-1000 Berlin 61
-Innovations-und Technologie - Beratungsstelle der Industriegewerkschaft Metall, Besenbinderhof 57, D-2000 Hamburg 1
-Technologie-beratungsstelle beim DGB- Landesbezirk NRW, Havensteinstr. 50, D-4200 Oberhausen 1

Finally, a business association service is subsidized:
-Wirtschaftsverband Eisen, Blech und Metallverarbeitende Industrie und Wirtschaftsverbank Stahlverformung, Goldene Pforte 1, D-5800 Hagen-Emst

Moreover numerous and mainifold equivalent services are available from privately operating centres (i.e. the chambers of industry and commerce, of the craft industries)

ORGANISATION	NATURE OF ORGANISATION	SOFTWARE			HARDWARE	
		Information Advice	Counselling/ Consulting	Training & Education	Finance	Other
INSTITUTE FOR INDUSTRIAL RESEARCH & STANDARDS	*National technology body for Irish Industry *Statutory body funded mainly by grants and by Ministry of Industry, Commerce and Tourism *Objective is to encourage the use of science and technology in industry. Is not a specialist small business organisation but has special services. Total staff 650. Budget 12.5m	*Technical Information Desk. Industrial Liaison Service (6 officers)	*Graduate Placement Scheme to help small firms raise level of technology in linking with external technological support systems *Small Firm Development Fund. 5 days free consultancy to help company absorb technologies. 30 small firms in pilot *In-house consultancy to place member of institute for 2-3 days a week over number of weeks or months *Inventors Service provides help in patenting *Technopaks- technological services for small firms costed at appropriate fees			
YOUTH EMPLOYMENT AGENCY	*Autonomous state owned company funded by special 1% levy on all declared income. Aims to provide training and work experience for young people and to develop new approaches to job creation (120m budget 1983)			*Young Scientists and Technologists Employment Scheme to place unemployed graduates under 25 in a small company for 12 months to tackle a particular technical problem. Free to the firm. 80 graduates in 1982/83		
KILKENNY DESIGN WORKSHOPS	*Government sponsored agency with prime responsibility for advancement of good design in craft indutry. Is limited liability company. Does substantial part of its work with small industry and craft. Has retail outlets in Dublin and Kilkenny (120 employees with 2m turnover)	*Runs exhibitions and promotions	*Retail and Industrial Design services on fee and sales royalty basis -Model making -Prototype development -"Soft" model development	*Some seminars on design and Work Experience Programme		*Have model making and prototype development workshop (mainly craft)

ORGANISATION	NATURE OF ORGANISATION	SOFTWARE			HARDWARE	
		Information Advice	Counselling/ Consulting	Training & Education	Finance	Other
THE INNOVATION CENTRE LIMERICK	*Funded by Shannon Development Corporation but with National responsibility. Autonomous organisation with Board of Directors from range of relevant institutions	*Product ideas newsletter published *Sources of information on licences or collaborative possibilities *Market fact pack service or report on technical research	*Product Development Service -Assistance with development of prototype -Assistance with the buying and selling of technology -Assistance with idea evaluation, business plan development, market testing, venture capital approaches, (have 70 currently under way)	*Seminars on licencing new product development. *Group Entrepreneurship programme, aimed particularly at formation of multi-disci-plinary partner-ships to launch ambitious ideas in the U.S. venture market	*"Intern" scheme paying salaries of "innovators" for up to 18 months. (Some external to Centre, others internal). Company search, testing and other costs. 20 interns in December 1983	*Provision of workshop space for prototype development and testing and pilot production
SHANNON DEVELOPMENT CORPORATION	*Limited liability company with shares held by three ministries. Has responsibility for promoting indigenous industry (under 40 employees) in area surrounding Shannon Airport				*Research and Development Grants up to 50% of costs to maximum of 250,000. Grants for up to 33% of cost of research studies	

248

ORGANISATION	NATURE OF ORGANISATION	SOFTWARE			HARDWARE	
		Information Advice	Counselling/ Consulting	Training & Education	Finance	Other
MINISTRY OF INDUSTRY, COMMERCE AND HANDICRAFT	*National Government		*Through technical laboratories (stazioni sperimentali) in different provinces		*Law 17/2/1982 n. 46-Special Rotary Fund for Technical Innovation (20% of yearly global Fund reserved to small and medium sized firms). 15 years loans to programmes of product or process innovations (project - test - development maximum amount: 80% of the programme cost interest rate: 15% of the "reference rate" in the first five years 60% of the "reference rate" in the last 10 years	
MINISTERO PER IL COORDINAMENTO DELLE INIZIATIVE PER LA RICERA SCIENTIFICO E TECNOLOGA Langotevere Thaon de Revel 76 00100. Roma Tel: 39.6.369941	*Ministry of Scientific and technical research through imm - istituto mobiliare italiano *National Government				*Law 17/2/1982 n. 46 15% of yearly global Fund is reserved to small and medium sized firms. Grants for applied research up to 50% of the costs and not more than 200 millions lire yearly to each firm	
CONSIGLIO NAZIONALE DELLE RICERCHE (CNR - NATIONALE DELLE RICHERCHE) P. Aldo Moro 7 00185 Roma Tel: 39.6.49931	*Government funded organisation to develop the applied research in selected fields *Not specifically small firm *Acts as link between universities and industry	*Funds research and development in Italian universities' research programmes				
CESTEC CSO Plebisciti 15 Milano Tel: 39.2.73875 05 **AND OTHER SIMILAR REGIONAL TECHNOLOGICAL CENTRES**	*Independent Regional Government funded company *Specific small firm *Shares owned by Regional Government and Regional Federation of Industry		*Programmes of technological transfer in the selected fields			*Sensitizing campaigns to groups of small firms of the same industrial field (textile, shoes, etc.)

ORGANISATION	NATURE OF ORGANISATION	SOFTWARE		HARDWARE		
		Information Advice	Counselling/ Consulting	Training & Education	Finance	Other
CHAMBERS OF COMMERCE, INDUSTRY, AGRICULTURE, HANDICRAFT, THEIR REGIONAL UNIONS AND ASSEFOR	*Public organisations .who represent by law the local economys controlled by Ministry of Industry *Private association of the Chamber to coordinate the training programmes not specific but highly appropriate to small firms	*Of every type		*FORMAPER and similar ASSEFOR programmes look at micro-economic premises of innovations (firm's structure and change)	*Limited grants to the most effective innovations of small firms	*Agreements with CNR, engineering companies to let facilities to the small firms
CENTRO INFORMATIONI STUDI ESPERIENZE (CISE) Via Reggio Emilia 39 20090 Segrate Milano Tel:39.2.213.32. 41/2/3/4/5	*Centre for information studies and experiments *Not SME specific	*On lasers, electrics, robots	*Programme of transfer to handicraft			
ASSOCIAZIONE ORGANIZZAZIONI DI INGENERIA E DI CONSULENZA TECNICO ECONOMICA (OICE) Largo Messico 7 Roma Tel: 39.6.851685	*Association of techno-economic engineers & consultants *Private engin- eering company *Not SME specific		*Consulting assistance			
FEDERAZIONE DELLE ASSOCIAZIONI SCIENTIFICHE E TECNICHE (FAST) Pzza. Morandi 2 00100 Milano Tel: 39.2.783051	*Federation of scientific and technical association *Private supported by industry association	*On automation				
DATAMONT, Via Taramelli 28 20124 Milano Tel: 39.2.63331	*Branch of Montedison private *Not SME specific	*Technological data bank				

250

ORGANISATION	NATURE OF ORGANISATION	SOFTWARE			HARDWARE	
		Information Advice	Counselling/ Consulting	Training & Education	Finance	Other
MINISTRY FOR ECONOMIC AFFAIRS	*Has directorate of SMEs with staff of 200.		*Funds special intensive counselling experiment for innovation scheme with selected companies. Ten consultants - free service - a limited experiment with relatively few firms *Transfer point scheme to improve access of small companies to technical know-how. Scheme links demand (SME's) with supply side. Started with five "supply" points (TNO, Technological Institutes & Universities) and three "demand" points located in RND. Now about 20 such points. Experimental scheme - rated as successful. Subsidised by Ministry (2 1/2 man years each year in each location). Certain other schemes not subsidised			
	*INSTIR (Innovation Stimulation Scheme) from October, 1984					*Subsidy for R&D -wage costs of personnel involved in R&D - 40% up to 300000 guilders -15% for 300000 to 2.5m guilders -Subsidy applied to 50% of external consultant fees for R&D at same rates as above. Government to budget 1.1 bn guilders over years
	*New product development support (from January 1985)					*Subsidy of 60% up to 30000 guilders of costs of seeking advice on innovation and business plan for products that are new to the Netherlands. Costs must be at least 20% of total capital of the firm and firms equity involvement has to be over 30%. Government has 1 mn guilders a year for this scheme
	*With private banks					*Technical development loans for new products. 5% interest rate up to 75% of amount needed. With 100% grant guarantee for new products of national importance

In addition has range of general schemes in support of innovation - not specifically for small business

ORGANISATION	NATURE OF ORGANISATION	SOFTWARE			HARDWARE	
		Information Advice	Counselling/ Consulting	Training & Education	Finance	Other
PRIVATE PARTICIPATION COMPANIES (PPM's) (see general matrix under NPM)	*Under Central Bank *Equity capital companies with guarantee *Equity Guarantee Scheme for Private Participative Companies *Has led to a number of equity companies being started by the commercial banks and other organisations *Mainly aimed at assisting small firms *Aimed to improve capital base of small companies 1984 - about 30 venture companies operating *Is particularly aimed at high risk technology ventures				*Offers to private company (through specialist equity company) up to 4mm guilders. If the company is liquidated the state guarantees 50% of the equity loss. Operating for two years. 50 companies financed in this way to September 1983. 7000000 guilders average investment	
BUSINESS TECHNOLOGY CENTRES	*Autonomous centres funded by mix of private and public capital including local government. Liaison with Universities at Enschede, Wageningen and Rotterdam	*Provision of information and advice and common services for the companies in the building				*Managed workshop for very small companies
MICRO ELECTRONIC CENTRES	*Experimental advice centres to support small firm use of micro technology *Located in Delft, Endhoven, Twente	*Advice and counselling for small firms in micro-electronic applications				
NEDERLANDSE ORGANISATIVE VOOR TOEGOPOST NATUURWET ONDERZOEK (TNO)	*Non-profit making research organisation part-funded by government. Staff of 4900. 35 different locations around the country *Is not a small firm specialist organisation	*Information services for small firms. 5000 enquiries a year. *Research for groups of small firms or associations that can be given 100% government grant support. *Basic technical research for industries and products (fee paying)				
PROJECT INDUSTRIELE INNOVATIE (PII), Laan van Westenenk 501 Postbus 910 7301 BD Apeldoorn Tel: 31.55.3397 91	*Foundation set up as experimental initiative by Ministry of Economic Affairs, TNO and Employees Organisations (e.g. VNO) *Scheme ended December 1984 *Various spin-offs e.g. VNO launched "Become Your Own Employer Project		*Intensive Innovation Counselling for 25-30 recently started firms *Partly subsidized consulting assistance for 200 established firms, with quality control from PII			

ORGANISATION	NATURE OF ORGANISATION	SOFTWARE			HARDWARE	
		Information Advice	Counselling/ Consulting	Training & Education	Finance	Other
STI-NATIONAL INSTITUTE OF TECHNOLOGY	*A government sponsored institute designed to provide theoretical and practical backup services for Norwegian industry, with the emphasis on small and medium-sized firms	*Gives technological information and advice	*Research, testing and counselling	*Offers special courses in innovation	*Subsidized fees. Innovation-project supported by DU with approx. 1 mill. Nkr.	
THE BRANCH RESEARCH FUND	*Aims to encourage cooperation between R&D institutes and industry to the best advantage of the branch - institutes and its members	*An information project with aim of increasing technology transfer from branch institutes to its users, mostly small industries, was launched in 1979 and lasted to 1983. Information material and methods were improved and personal contact with the users increased		*Education through working groups	*The information project called "knowledge 1980" was financed as follows: -grants from the Fund 2.5 mill. Nkr. -grants from industry 1.2 mill. Nkr.	
THE FOUNDATION FOR SCIENTIFIC AND INDUSTRIAL RESEARCH AT THE NORWEGIAN INSTITUTE OF TECHNOLOGY (SINTEF)	*Stimulates research activities at the Norwegian Institute of Technology and carries out research for industry		*Project for small industry. Personal contact-programme towards small industry to improve technology transfer		*Grants for counselling	
THE REGIONAL DEVELOPMENT FUND (DU)	*A State administrative body in operation since 1961. Grants are financed in their entirety from the central government budget *Aims to promote measures which will ensure increased, permanent and profitable employment in districts with special employment problems or where under developed industrial conditions prevail		*Project to use technological inventions and know-how built up at SINTEF to transfer these possibilities to industry mainly in Northern Norway *Project to promote the use of micro- processors in products and in production in small industry in Western Norway		*Each project is supported with approx. 1/2 mill. Nkr.	

253

ORGANISATION	NATURE OF ORGANISATION	SOFTWARE			HARDWARE	
		Information Advice	Counselling/ Consulting	Training & Education	Finance	Other
INSTITUTE FOR THE SUPPORT OF SMALL AND MEDIUM INDUSTRIES (IAPMEI)	*Government Department depending on the Ministry for Industry and Energy	*Operates a Questions-and-Answer Service on technical subjects *Searches technical literature on request *Maintains comprehensive files on Portuguese manufacturers and their products *Provides a service for selective diffusion of technical information *Offers technical advice on production, organisation and technology through its own staff and of a board of private specialists ready to advise firms in different branches e.g. metallurgy, textiles, plastics, chemicals, welding, etc. *Manages selective dissemination of information for existing firms and publishes a quarterly review *Provides an after-care service to newly and already established grant-aided SMEs		*Promotes the idea of training to Industrial Professional Association assisting them in organizing seminars *Has a special programme for the training of fresh graduates to prepare them for admission in SME after a "stage" of 6 months free-of-charge in the firms	*Provides grants towards the cost of management and supervisory training in SMEs *Helps SMEs in developing new products and financing the prototypes *Financial support in the sharing of expenses by means of non-repayable loans, for specific actions, in particular: -Execution of technological research projects -Implementation, modernization and increase of productivity -Vocational training, refresher and reconversion courses	
NATIONAL LABORATORY FOR INDUSTRIAL ENGINEERING AND TECHNOLOGY (LNETI)	*Government Department depending on the Ministry for Industry and Energy	*Provides advice on processes, materials and other technological aspects of industry such as food, chemicals, metallurgy and electronics *Provides a service in the technical design and development of new products, equipment and processes *Aids programmes for innovation. Has testing and analysis services for materials, products, processes and equipment *Has a center for technical and technological information		*Offers a broad range of management and technological training, many of them suited to the needs of SMEs		
INSTITUTE FOR FOREIGN INVESTMENT (IIE)	*Public Department depending on the Ministry for Finance and Planning	*Gives informations of legal requests needed for foreign investments in Portugal *Analyses the "dossiers" concerning the investment intentions of investors, namely concerning the accuracy of technology transfers *Gives authorization to the import of foreign funds destined to Portuguese firms, as well as technologies from abroad				
GENERAL DIRECTORATE FOR QUALITY (DGQ)	*Government Department depending on the Ministry for Industry and Energy	*Promotes the appreciation and application of quality in industries and services through qualifications, standards, metrology and certification *Has a service for design promotion				
INSTITUTE FOR EMPLOYMENT AND PROFESSIONAL TRAINING	*Government Department depending on the Ministry of Labour and Social Security			*Provides at a national level, training courses in different skills at centers throughout the country *Has, with IAPMEI, a special programme for the training of fresh graduates to prepare them to admission in SME's after a stage of 6 months free-of-charge in firms	*Provides grants to firms for specific training activities	

254

ORGANISATION	NATURE OF ORGANISATION	SOFTWARE			HARDWARE	
		Information Advice	Counselling/ Consulting	Training & Education	Finance	Other
CENTER FOR INNOVATION AND R&D (CEDINTEC)	*Government Department depending on the Ministry for Industry and Energy	*Provides a service on development of new products, equipment and processes in some industrial branches and coordinates technological centers				
NATIONAL ORGANISATION FOR SCIENTIFIC AND TECHNOLOGICAL RESEARCH (JNICT)	*Government Department depending on the Ministry of State	*Coordinates R&D at the national level *Aid-programmes for innovation				
PORTUGUESE DESIGNER ASSOCIATION	*Private Association	*Promotes the adoption of new design in products and graphics				
PORTUGUESE ASSOCIATION FOR INDUSTRIAL QUALITY (APQI)	*Private Association			*Promotes the idea of quality through seminars		

255

ORGANISATION	NATURE OF ORGANISATION	SOFTWARE			HARDWARE	
		Information Advice	Counselling/ Consulting	Training & Education	Finance	Other
INSTITUTE OF SMALL & MEDIUM ENTERPRISE (IMPI)	*Self-governing state agency *Dependency of the Ministry of Industry				*Reduction of up to 3 points interest on loans destined for technological innovation *Participate in projects with technological innovation firms	
INSTITUTE FOR THE REFORM OF COMMERCIAL STRUCTURES (IRESCO)	*Self-governing state agency *Dependency of the Ministry of Economy and Treasury	*Information and advice on technological and training assistance available to small business firms			*Subsidies designed to reduce the cost of credits required to improve productivity and rationalize operations. Destined for commercial operations	
CENTRE FOR TECHNOLOGICAL AND INDUSTRIAL DEVELOPMENT (CDTI)	*Public agency, dependency of the Ministry of Industry	*Technological information			*The amount of assistance is usually between 45-60% of the cost of the project, which must be of technological and commercial interest. The assistance is repaid with a percentage of the sales of the new product. If the project is a failure, CDTI recovers only those costs spent on purchasing equipment. The remainder is then considered a non-refundable subsidy	
DELAGACION PARA EL CAR DESARROLLO Y LA APLICACION DE MICROPROCES SADORES (AMICRO) Ramirez de Arellano s/n 28027 Madrid Tel: 34.91.4133113 34.91.415.0691	*Agency of the Ministry of Industry and Energy	*Advice on possible applications of microprocessors. First consultancy free of charge. Feasibility studies: 50% ADAMICRO. 50% company involved				
INSTITUTE NATIONAL PARA EL FOMENTO A LA EXPORTA (INFE) Paseo Castellana 14 28046 Madrid Tel: 34.91.4311240	*Dependency of the Ministry of Economy and Treasury				*Assistance fund for technological suppliers: subsidies of up to 50% of the cost of preparing the project	
INDUSTRIAL CREDIT BANK (BCI)	*Public bank. Dependency of the Ministry of Industry				*Financing of up to 75% (max. 30 million m) for new investments in fixed assets designed to create, remodel and modernize company installations. 12.5% interest for up to 6 years	

256

ORGANISATION	NATURE OF ORGANISATION	SOFTWARE			HARDWARE	
		Information Advice	Counselling/ Consulting	Training & Education	Finance	Other
BRANCH OFFICES OF THE MINISTRY OF TREASURY	*Government				*Corporate tax reliefs: 15% tax deduction on investments in R&D programs, up to a limit of 25% of total investment *Subsidy of up to 30% of research investments	
THE PUBLIC CORPORATION FOUNDATION (OGEIN)	*Dependency of the National Institute of Industry			*Organizes courses to improve the operations of business research units and assist in devising and technological policy		
SPANISH EMPLOYERS ASSOCIATION (CEOE)	*Association	*Information and advice on technological and training assistance available to small business companies				
BUSINESS INFORMATION & DEVELOPMENT CENTRE (CIDEM) FOR CATALONIA	*Dependency of the Department of Industry and Energy of the Generalitat de Catalunya	*Information on existing systems and assistance in developing new ones: information on new products and processes, patents, etc. *Information and advice on technological and training assistance available to small business firms				
INTERDEPARTMENTAL COMMISSION FOR TECHNOLOGICAL INNOVATION (CIRIT)	*Catalan version of the CDTI. Dependency of the Department of Industry and Energy of the Generalitat de Catalunya				*Total and partial subsidies for technological innovation projects that increase or help increase the technological level and equipment in Catalonia	
BASQUE MINISTRY OF INDUSTRY AND ENERGY	*Government				*Subsidizes research and development *Creates R&D departments for individual companies or groups of companies. Finances up to 40% of the R&D department's annual costs, up to a maximum of 12 million ptas. per company per year	
EMPRESAS INNOVACIO TECNOLOGICA	*Private firms created to contribute towards technolocal renewal				*Public capital may account for up to one-third of the total capital of technological innovation companies	

ORGANISATION	NATURE OF ORGANISATION	SOFTWARE			HARDWARE	
		Information Advice	Counselling/ Consulting	Training & Education	Finance	Other
STYRELSEN FOR TEKNISK UTVECKLING (STU), Liljeholmsvagen 32, Box 43200, 100 72 Stockholm Tel: 46.8.744.51. 00	*Swedish Board of Technical Development *An organisation under Dept. of Industry *Provides technical inquiry service *Supports research at technical universities *Provides grants for inventors *Supports collective technical research	*Provides free technical advice and counselling (1-2 days) *Provides free telephone service *Provides technical advice and counselling through the 24 regional development agencies (see general table) *Seven collective research institutes are financed by STU and by private industry and trade (graphic, food processing, corrosion, furniture, packing)			*Grants for supporting research and development of knowledge products, methods and systems *Long-range programme for developing new technical knowledge *About 20 grants per year	*For researchers at universities (up to 100%) *To firms (up to 50%) for project support *Conditional loans *Supports programmes at technical universities (up to 100%) *Free to inventors (can also be owners to small firms)
KONTAKTSEKR	*Contact secretaries *At technical universities for supporting contacts universities - industry and trade	*Give free advice about actual research and researchers who are able to do consultancy in small firms	*Researchers at universities perform research at the request of firms	*Carry out training and education (normally 1 day - 3 weeks) in firms		
INDUSTRIFOND Regeringsgaten 30-32 1153 Stockholm Tel: 46.8.144345	*Industry fund to stimulate research within firms (mainly larger firms)				*Can finance 50% of costs of projects that can be of great interest for expansion of the Swedish industry	*Conditional loans which the firm must pay back if the project is a success
BRANCH RESEARCH INSTITUTES	*About 25 branch research inst. financed by industry and trade	*Six institutes (graphic, food processing, corrosion, furniture, packing) have obtained grants from STU to support info/counselling/training to small firms				
INDUSTRIELLT UTVECKLINGS- CENTRUM, (IUC) Bockholmsvagen 18 931 21 Skelleftea Tel: 0910.364.50	*Industrial Development Center (IUC)	*For supporting industries in a region in the north of Sweden				
NORDISK INDUSTRIFOND Birger Jarlsgatan 27 111 45 Stockholm Tel: 08.24.36.55	*Nordic Fund for Technology and Industrial Development				*Grants, conditional loans	*Cooperative projects between firms in the Nordic countries
NORRLANDFONDEN Box 831 951 28 Lulea Tel: 0920.207.80	*Fund for Northern Sweden *Has a yearly contribution from Dept. of Industry *Supports industrial development in the north of Sweden				*Grants for research	*To research institutions, firms and private companies

258

SMALL FIRM ASSISTANCE IN SWEDEN: TECHNOLOGICAL INNOVATION & R&D

ORGANISATION	NATURE OF ORGANISATION	SOFTWARE			HARDWARE	
		Information Advice	Counselling/ Consulting	Training & Education	Finance	Other
ARBETARSKYDDS-FONDEN Box 1122 111 81 Stockholm Tel: 08.14.32.00	*The Fund for working env. *Organisation financed by contributions from all firms				*Grants for research and technical development of methods and processes that reduce risk for accidents	*If the project is a success the company has to pay back the grants
SWEDISH NATIONAL INDUSTRY BOARD (SIND)	*SIND is an organisation under the Department of Industry *SIND has a special programme for: -Textile industry -Fur industry -Manual glass industry -Wood industry -Casting industry		*Free for casting industry *75% of costs for analyzing the future of the firm	*Covers costs of planning and complementary education programmes	*Guarantee loans for supporting restructuring of the branches *50% of costs for joint-venture projects	
REGIONAL DEVELOPMENT AGENCIES	*24 regional foundations financed by SIND and communities	*1-2 technical experts give free information			*Guarantee loans. Conditional loans	
TECHNICAL CENTERS (TC) OR RESEARCH CENTERS	*Normally situated near a regional university	*TCs offer services in different areas. These vary due to the competence of the people working at the different TCs				*Only possible for high technological companies to have premises at some of the bigger universities

ORGANISATION	NATURE OF ORGANISATION	SOFTWARE			HARDWARE	
		Information Advice	Counselling/ Consulting	Training & Education	Finance	Other
SWISS INSTITUTE FOR TECHNICAL INFORMATION (SITI)	*Semi-public institute affiliated to the Swiss Association for the promotion of research	*On state of affairs in the field of engineering by investigation in data banks of natural science technics and patents				
INSTITUTE OF MANAGEMENT AND INDUSTRIAL ENGINEERING OF THE FEDERAL INSTITUTE OF TECHNOLOGY	*Semi-public university institute		*Consulting for manufacturing, etc.	*Provide continuation training, especially in the field of management		
SWISS CENTRE FOR TESTING ELECTRONIC COMPONENTS (CSEE)	*Semi-public institute supported by Swiss Electrotechnical Association	*Manual of CSEE testing instructions and procedures	*Consult smaller firms for questions of quality and reliability of electronic components	*Training of testing and service personnel	*Initial Government support of 8 million SFr.	
SWISS FEDERAL LABORATORY FOR MATERIALS TESTING AND RESEARCH	*Public Institution		*Tests on order material and supplies for firms and authorities			
INDELEC HOLDING AG (INAS) (FINANCING CORPORATIONS)	*Proviate companies associated to main merchant banks				*Provide venture and development capital	
CHAMBERS OF COMMERCE/ INNOVATION CONSULTING CENTRES	*Private associations partly with public subsidies		*Several chambers of commerce established special innovations centres providing also management assistance		*Subsidies for management consulting may be obtained	
INNOVATION CENTRE OF THE ASSOCIATION OF YOUNG MANAGERS	*Private association	*Collection of data and information on new products				
PROFESSIONAL ASSOCIATIONS	*Private association: 191 associations; 134000 member firms			*Numerous associations provide technical continuation training		
SWISS WORK GROUP OF HANDICRAFT FIRMS FOR THE DEVELOPMENT OF DESIGN AND EXHIBITIONS	*Private association		*Promotes design of members through expert judging of products and exhibition			

ORGANISATION	NATURE OF ORGANISATION	SOFTWARE			HARDWARE	
		Information Advice	Counselling/ Consulting	Training & Education	Finance	Other
DEPARTMENT OF TRADE AND INDUSTRY R&D DIVISION 24 Bressenden Place, London SW1E 5DT Tel: 44.1.213.5839	*Section of government department with special responsibility for support for innovation *Financial support for technology development (introduction covering microelectronics, computer aided design, computer aided manufacture, computer aided production, robotics, flexible manufacturing systems, fibre optics) *Not special for small firms *Innovation Linked Investment Scheme (ILIS)		*Feasibility studies: first 2 days free plus 75% of costs of consultancy up to 120 days. 50% of project each for planning studies up to 150,000 maximum		*Specialist finance support *Grants for hardware, e.g. for companies with less than 500 persons for robot installation: grants up to 20% of costs *Grant of up to 20% towards cost of launching production for firms up to 500 employees. Maximum expenditure of 2 million pounds	
DEPARTMENT OF TRADE AND INDUSTRY AND SCIENCE AND ENGINEERING RESEARCH COUNCIL, Polaris House, North Sted Avenue, Swindon, Wiltshire Tel: 44.795.262 22	*The Science and Engineering Research Council is an independent government funded organisation concerned with development and research in British Higher Education. Teaching Company Scheme (Group)	*Scheme designed to link Universities and Polytechnics with companies in the field of Research and Development by establishment of Graduate Associates working on company problems and linking back into the institutes *Is being applied to groups of small firms				
INDUSTRIAL AND COMMERCIAL FINANCE CORPORATION, VENTURES DIVISION 91 Waterloo Road, London SF1 8XP Tel: 44.1.92878 72	*Investors in Industry is owned largely by the Clearing Banks (formerly Finance for Industry) *The Industrial and Commercial Finance Corporation (ICFC) is one arm specialising in small/medium company equity/lending. The Ventures Division is concerned with high technology/ innovation				*Equity Loan Finance for high risk ventures involving innovation/ technology	

261

ORGANISATION	NATURE OF ORGANISATION	SOFTWARE			HARDWARE	
		Information Advice	Counselling/ Consulting	Training & Education	Finance	Other
BRITISH TECHNOLOGY GROUP 101 Newington Causeway, London SE1 6BU Tel: 44.1.403.66 66	*Autonomous organisation funded by government. Concerned with funding research and development in British Industry *Not specific to small firms, but has special schemes e.g. Small Firms Innovation Fund, Oakwood Finance Ltd.	*Funds research and development in British Universities			*Equity and loan finance for innovation. Loans up to 5m for technological companies	
PRODUCTION AND ENGINEERING RESEARCH ASSOCIATION, Melton Mowbray Leicester LE1B OPB Tel: 44.664.641 33	*Technical enquiry service operated through Production and Engineering Research Association *Manufacturers Advisory Service *Quality Assurance Advisory Service *Quality Assurance Support Scheme	*Provision of technical advice and counselling: one free day per 25% of the cost of consultancy *Provision of production and technical advice and counselling by a scheme involving linkages with the Production Engineers Research Association (PERA): two free days per 75% subsidy of costs up to 13 man days Two free consultancy days by specialist adviser plus up to 13 days at 75% subsidy of cost to help firms in manufacturing up to 1,000 employees meet standards			*Grants for hardware and software (counselling) *25% grant of costs of implementing consultants report on quality assurance procedures. Costs up to 100,000 pounds. For companies up to 500 employees. Complements the Advisory Scheme	
DESIGN COUNCIL 28 Haymarket London SW1Y 4SU Tel: 44.1.82980 00	*Autonomous organisation with government support aimed at improving the design and quality of British goods	*Design Advisory Service. Service of Advisory Officers on design problems	*Design Advisory Service Consultancy Scheme. 15 free days of consultancy plus 15 further days at 50% of cost (60 - 1,000 employees)			

ORGANISATION	NATURE OF ORGANISATION	SOFTWARE			HARDWARE	
		Information Advice	Counselling/ Consulting	Training & Education	Finance	Other
INNOVATION CENTRES e.g. Merseyside Innovation Centre, Ltd. 131, Mount Pleasant Liverpool L3FTF Tel: 44.51.70801 23	*Organisations funded from a variety of sources depending upon local circumstances *Often involve local authorities for base funding Usually linked with University or Polytechnic. Usually small firms oriented. Perhaps half a dozen schemes in the U.K. *Aimed at assisting investors/innovators in getting idea to market	*Advice and counselling on design and market application			*Linkage possibly with local authority finance for prototype and market testing	*Provision of "workshop" facilities for prototype development
SCIENCE PARKS Further Information from: English Educational Estates, St. Georges House, Kingsway, Team Valley, Gateshead Tyne & Wear Tel: 44.91.48789 41	*Isolated but growing development in the U.K. linking Universities/ Polytechnics with local authority and occasional sources of assistance funding (e.g. banks). Takes many different forms *Not specific to small firms	*Advice and Assistance on research and development with University and Company working together				*Premises workshop usually near to University sites